W9-DEL-147

Financing American Higher Education
in the Era of Globalization

Financing American Higher Education in the Era of Globalization

William Zumeta

David W. Breneman

Patrick M. Callan

Joni E. Finney

HARVARD EDUCATION PRESS

CAMBRIDGE, MASSACHUSETTS

Second Printing, 2015

Library of Congress Control Number 2011941948

Paperback ISBN 978-1-61250-125-3
Library Edition ISBN 978-1-61250-126-0

Published by Harvard Education Press,
an imprint of the Harvard Education Publishing Group

Harvard Education Press
8 Story Street
Cambridge, MA 02138

Cover Design: Sarah Henderson
The typefaces used in this book are ITC Stone Serif and ITC Stone Sans.

Contents

Acknowledgments

Financing American Higher Education in the Era of Globalization is the product of a collaborative project sponsored by the National Center for Public Policy and Higher Education. The National Center is deeply grateful for the contributions of the coauthors and for the support of founding board chairman James B. Hunt, Jr. and members of the board of directors.

Two National Center staff members provided indispensible assistance in each phase of development and publication. Noreen Savelle skillfully coordinated the entire project and contributed significant research and editorial support. Darcie Harvey provided research, analytical, and editorial support to every draft of every chapter.

We also acknowledge with appreciation the contributions of William Doyle coauthor of chapter 5. Dennis Jones, Patrick Kelly, and John Clark of the National Center for Higher Education Management Systems shared their expertise and insights, particularly on topics addressed in chapter 2, and on technical and data issues. Debbie Frankle Cochrane, Robin LaSota, Alicia Kinne, and Shannon Matson provided research support. As he has for many National Center projects, Thad Nodine edited the manuscript with skill and thoughtfulness.

The Curry School of Education and the Frank Batten School of Leadership and Public Policy of the University of Virginia, the Daniel Evans School of Public Affairs of the University of Washington, and the Graduate School of Education of the University of Pennsylvania provided support and working environments that facilitated the participation of three of the coauthors. Students enrolled in seminars in public policy and higher education finance taught by David Breneman, Joni Finney, and William Zumeta in 2010 and 2011 read and offered helpful reactions to drafts of the chapters.

Grants to the National Center from the Bill & Melinda Gates Foundation and the Lumina Foundation for Education supported substantial portions of the research and writing.

Patrick M. Callan
President
Higher Education Policy Institute

Foreword

Higher education has never been more important to America's future. The knowledge-based global economy, international education and economic competition, demographic shifts, constrained public finances, and the emergence of digital and online technologies are converging to confront higher education and public policy with historic challenges and opportunities. Transformations of comparable magnitude have occurred in earlier eras as well. The roles of colleges and universities in American society were reshaped and reconfigured by the emergence of the land grant colleges in the nineteenth century, by the expansion of American higher education to accommodate World War II veterans and the baby boom generation, and by the responses to the moral and legal imperatives of the civil rights era. The modern research university emerged during the twentieth century as the predominant American institution for creating new knowledge. These transformations were stimulated by major shifts in American society (industrialization, war, and Cold War) and by evolving requirements for individual opportunity. Each of these transformations required departures from earlier expectations of higher education and of the public policies that stimulated and sustained it.

The remarkable success of American higher education has become an impediment to the next transformation. For five decades after World War II, American higher education led the world in college participation and attainment as well as in university-based research. But one consequence of this success is that those in higher education as well as state and federal government leaders have generally underestimated the number of necessary policy changes to meet the nation's required education beyond high school in the twenty-first century. While much of the world is surpassing the United States in college participation and attainment, our institutional and public policy has focused almost exclusively on matching past achievements, making only modest improvements to current programs, and devoting inadequate attention to the need for new and restructured strategies and policies. However, American higher education and public policy infrastructure cannot tweak or spend its way to the future.

International educational competitiveness is a prerequisite for economic competitiveness, as President Obama indicated when he articulated a national goal to restore the United States to global leadership in higher education attainment by 2020. To achieve this goal, significantly more Americans would have to enroll in and graduate from higher levels of postsecondary education with a higher level of knowledge and skills. Our higher education system, with its current configuration and funding, cannot accomplish this. Colleges would also need to enroll larger numbers of students from low-income families and ethnic minority groups, who were underserved in the twentieth-century expansions of higher education. These groups now constitute a growing proportion of Americans, particularly American youth. Because access to the middle class increasingly requires postsecondary education, fundamental American values of individual opportunity, social mobility and equity, as well as national prosperity, are at stake. The transformation of higher education is fundamental to America's success.

Given the severity of the recent recession and its continuing aftermath, it is tempting for education and public policy leaders to attribute most problems in higher education to depressed national and state economies. But the *Measuring Up* state and national report cards issued biennially by the National Center for Public Policy and Higher Education over the last decade showed only modest gains and some significant declines in critical areas of higher education performance: college preparation, access, completion, and affordability. Similarly, the international comparisons published by the Organisation for Economic Co-operation and Development (OECD) confirm that college attainment rates have plateaued for young Americans while several other nations, including many of our economic competitors, are advancing at a faster rate. Yet, according to OECD rankings, the United States remains the leader in proportion of gross domestic product devoted to higher education. This shows that American higher education has been underperforming in relation to national needs and international competition—underperformance that predates the Great Recession.

The core message I take from *Financing American Higher Education in the Era of Globalization* is the need for a fundamental reexamination of the costs of higher education, and of how we will pay for college in the future. This evaluation must encompass the roles and responsibilities of all stakeholders and participants—federal and state governments, institutions of higher education, students, families, and philanthropy. It should include all types of public and private subsidies. Public policy must, as it has in the past, play a leadership role in articulating public purposes and building and sustaining public understanding and consensus around a policy framework of strategic investment and accountability.

Such a framework must harness our national capacity for education and training beyond high school. That capacity will be found in diverse states, in public and private colleges and universities, and in the potential of electronic technologies to improve learning and cost effectiveness on and off our campuses. We must have higher education that is affordable to the students and the taxpayers, that values and rewards educational innovation, and that encourages institutional productivity gains as reflected by high performance. We must do all this because the American economy and American values require it.

The authors of this book recognize that the transformation of American higher education must be national in its dimensions. Neither federal nor state nor institutional initiatives alone will be sufficient for the task ahead; they cannot be considered in isolation or operate at cross purposes. What is called for here is a revision of the social contract that served the country well in the decades after World War II but no longer meets our society's needs in this new century. The challenges ahead are political and educational as well as financial.

As a governor and as a participant and leader in educational reforms at all levels, I have learned that good intentions are not enough. High aspirations for improvements in education must be accompanied by strategic investments of new and existing resources. The issues raised in this volume challenge America to realign college finance with core public values. This is a critical twenty-first century agenda for higher education and public policy. It must be approached with a sense of urgency, confidence, and shared responsibility.

Governor James B. Hunt, Jr.
North Carolina

CHAPTER 1

American Higher Education
Twenty-First Century Context

Three hundred and seventy years after the first college in our fledgling nation was established to train Puritan ministers in the Massachusetts Bay Colony, it is no exaggeration to declare that higher education in the United States has become one of our greatest success stories. Whether America's colleges and universities are measured by their sheer number and variety, by the increasingly open access so many citizens enjoy to their campuses, by their crucial role in advancing the frontiers of knowledge through research discoveries, or by the new forms of teaching and learning that they have pioneered to meet students' changing needs, these post-secondary institutions have accomplished much of which they and the nation can be proud.

—*A Test of Leadership*, The Secretary of Education's
Commission on the Future of Higher Education, 2006[1]

Sentiments like those quoted have long made Americans proud, particularly those who are insiders in its academic institutions, but also policy makers and ordinary citizens. The United States has a vibrant and diverse private collegiate sector in addition to many universities in both public and private sectors that are clear world leaders by any measure. The idea of the community college—widely dispersed, locally oriented, and in theory open to all—originated in the United States, and the country now boasts more than a thousand of them in addition to hundreds of other two-year colleges.[2] Between research universities and community colleges stands a vast and diverse sector of four-year and comprehensive colleges and universities whose business is primarily undergraduate education but that also—particularly in the latter case—offer master's degrees. Private colleges tend to predominate in the four-year college category and public schools in the comprehensive class, but both varieties are found under each type of control. Finally, the country has witnessed a

1

rapid growth of for-profit postsecondary institutions in recent years, including more than one thousand accredited, degree-granting schools,[3] many of which respond with near-lightning speed to shifting market opportunities.

Until recently, these various sectors of American higher education were all experiencing growing enrollments and budgets, albeit after a rough patch in the early years of the century when state support fell off, tuition rates climbed sharply, and financial aid to students did not keep up, while enrollments were capped or cut. Some students were unquestionably denied access to higher education during that period.[4] The Great Recession of 2007–2009 and its aftermath produced similar effects, although the data about these are incomplete as yet. Still, although the period between recessions was shorter than usual in the latest cycle, history shows that eventually higher education's support recovers to some degree after recessions and tuition increases moderate.[5] Why, then, should policy makers or attentive citizens be concerned about the higher education enterprise or its finance once the deep recession is clearly behind us?

As we will explain in this book, beyond the lingering effects of the worst downturn since the Depression of the 1930s, there are a number of reasons for serious concern about the capacity of American higher education to address the challenges it faces in the coming decades. By capacity, we mean *physical* capacity (buildings and technology adequate for modern research and teaching of many more students), *fiscal* capacity (the wherewithal of states, localities, the federal government, and students and their families to finance the necessary investments), and *motivational* capacity (in the sense of attitudes and incentives embedded in academic culture and current funding arrangements) to address the varied challenges ahead. Perhaps most important is *political* capacity in the best sense of ability to mobilize the opinion leaders and public understanding and support necessary to create policies and mechanisms that can enhance the other forms of capacity. We think the United States can meet the challenges however, and indeed, it must. Our major purpose here is to explain how, with a primary focus on the finance-related policies and mechanisms and the incentives embedded therein that must now be altered and reshaped.

After this introduction, in this chapter we begin by laying out what the modern economy and society and global competition demand of higher education, both in quantitative and qualitative terms. Then, we turn to the supply side of the equation, describing some troubling trends in U.S. production of graduates relative to our global competition and some emerging concerns regarding the quality of graduates' preparation. We also summarize the dramatic demographic changes taking hold in the labor force as the well-educated, largely Caucasian, baby-boom cohort moves toward retirement, while the younger cohort is made up increasingly of ethnic groups who have historically had much lower college-attainment rates.

Then we turn to finance questions explicitly, tracking the trends over recent decades in the level and mix of higher education funding coming from states versus students. State support has been quite volatile with the ups and downs of the economy and, in aggregate, inflation-adjusted terms, is slightly lower per student (in the current trough) than the level of the mid-1980s. Meanwhile, tuition's share of total funding has moved inexorably upward, a trend that does not bode well for improving student access and persistence. We also examine student aid trends and take an initial look at the cost patterns in higher education that underlie price (tuition) trends. In short, does higher education have to cost so much?

Finally, we describe some shortcomings in state policy capacity that impede the ability of many state higher education systems to respond effectively to the contemporary challenges. The chapter concludes with a summary of the book's major arguments and a brief description of the contents of each of the succeeding chapters through which we make our case.

CHALLENGES FACING AMERICAN HIGHER EDUCATION

In this section, we consider the implications for higher education of the dramatic changes in the economy and society in recent decades. Prominent among these are the emergence of very serious competition from abroad in both education and economics, the rapidly changing demographics of the U.S. population, the brutal competition for funds that higher education faces at both state and federal levels, and, finally, the limitations of extant policy-making arrangements, policies, structures, and leadership at these key nodes in our federal system in the face of a clear need for a decisive shift in direction.

The New Economy and Society and the Education It Requires

The rapid pace of technological change is expected to continue to propel demand for highly skilled workers who can develop the new technologies and bring them to market and who can exploit the new technologies in the production of goods and services. Moreover, the transition to a knowledge-based economy continues to fuel demand for well-educated workers. Maintaining a high-skilled workforce is also a key component of U.S. comparative advantage in the world economy.[6]

Technological change is the most fundamental force shaping the new economy, and higher education plays a key role in generating the ideas that lead to new products and process improvements that drive the economy forward. Research plays a major role here, of course, and is also key to devising technology-based and other methods to control the undesirable side effects of new technologies. Even more basic than the new ideas themselves is higher education's role in the education and inculcation of breadth of perspective in the people who think of them as well as in those who can envision new markets and create appropriate new products and production processes for them. Whether in the same minds or different ones, higher education also plays a key role in shaping those who must take into account the human and societal implications of new technologies. Modern information technology (IT) is both a prime example of these processes at work and a facilitator of their workings in a huge variety of other domains. Research and the creation and diffusion of knowledge in this once instrumental but now fundamental field of IT have had enormous economic and societal implications and by most accounts will continue to do so.[7]

From the standpoint of education, what is most different from the past is the extent to which the need for relatively sophisticated thinking skills has permeated a large slice of the labor force. Beyond the scientists, engineers, and entrepreneurs are the many more workers who now need to be prepared to learn and use new technologies more or less continuously and to handle the organizational changes that often accompany them. Flattening of organizational hierarchies and cost-cutting pressures to be competitive have pushed more demanding work to frontline workers in many types of organizations (governmental and nonprofit included), which means more workers need more knowledge, problem-solving, and general thinking skills.[8]

Flexible response to changing markets in a cost-conscious world also means that even in relatively prosperous periods, more workers are laid off or find it desirable to seek new employment periodically. Sometimes they work as limited contract employees for one or more employers or become self-employed, in some cases as entrepreneurs in their own right. In this context, they need to be able to understand their skill sets, their training needs, and the potential markets for their services. While practical job experience certainly remains important in the modern workplace, formal education plays an increasing role not only because of the knowledge, skills, and credentials it imparts but also because it enables people to learn more efficiently, whether in formal training or, increasingly, on their own. Most analysts agree that the trend of recent decades for the labor market to reward increased levels of worker education will continue for the foreseeable future.[9]

A second powerful force defining the contours of the new economy is globalization. The growth in trade and global competition in recent decades was driven largely by advances in transportation and communications technology (including of course IT), but creates its own dynamics as well. Globalized competition means more rapid change and more pressure to improve products, streamline processes, and identify and respond quickly to new market opportunities wherever they may be. It also highlights skills in working with people from different cultures, with different customs and monetary and legal systems, and who speak different languages. Clearly, higher education has an important role to play here and a broadly defined one not confined to business and technical subjects.

In short, rapid technological change, associated environmental and social effects, and increased interactions across countries make the world that all citizens live in more complex. For example, the Boeing Company performs many of the final steps in assembly of its airplanes in the Seattle, Washington, area but in recent years has outsourced the lion's share of production of components to contract suppliers, many of which are based in its customers' countries (seen as a practical necessity if it is to win orders from national airlines). Yet, the company must actively manage this complex system of foreign suppliers to ensure quality, interoperability, timely delivery, and cost control. As this giant, high-technology firm has learned at some pain, the new model is a far more complex system to negotiate and manage than that of the "old days" (the early 1990s and before) when most production work was done in Seattle and environs. The social effects of the rather sudden shift and associated changes in the company's labor force needs also required complex and sensitive negotiations with unions and training organizations—because the jobs remaining in the Seattle area are more demanding—and local political decision-making bodies, as well as sophisticated media relations. Not surprisingly, the company became much more interested in the state of Washington's public education systems at both the K–12 and higher education levels roughly coincident with these changes.

A basic understanding of science and technology—processes, benefits, and drawbacks, and mechanisms for social control—in the populace seems essential for a modern democratic society to function well. Indeed, to be effectively exercised, citizenship itself now calls for higher levels of critical thinking, problem solving, and social and political interaction skills in a multicultural context that higher education, at its best, can cultivate and hone.

This is not intended to be a full catalog of higher education's benefits in modern society and work.[10] Rather, it is merely indicative of some of the key ways in which relatively recent changes and the ongoing processes they have set in motion require more of higher education, including educating a broader swath of the population as well as doing the job better for all.

The United States and Global Competition

The United States has long been a leader in science and technology and in higher education generally, but ominous signs are beginning to show themselves. After remarkable gains in American educational attainment for the baby-boom generation, more recent performance in higher education indicators has been considerably less impressive. Whereas the United States had long been the world leader in higher education participation and attainment rates, other nations have now caught up and even exceeded the U.S. rates for young adults. High school credentials are nearly essential for college entry. The proportion of the American labor force with a high school credential (89 percent including General Educational Development or GEDs (according to the ACE site) is third-highest among the countries that are members of the

Organisation for Economic Co-operation and Development (OECD), next only to the Czech and Slovak republics (91 percent and 90 percent, respectively), but the U.S. proportion (88 percent) of younger adults (25–34) with such a credential is now surpassed by Korea, the Slovak and Czech republics, Poland, and four other countries.[11] Also, a relatively large proportion of U.S. holders of high school credentials earn these belatedly, usually the GED, and this pattern has been shown to be associated with low rates of postsecondary attainment and limited labor market benefits.[12] On-time high school graduation rates in the United States are around 75 percent and essentially stagnant.[13]

International comparisons imply that increases in higher education enrollments in several competitor countries reflect increased participation rates rather than primarily population increases, as is the case in the United States.[14] While an all-time high percentage (68.6 percent) of high school graduates continued immediately to college enrollment in 2008 (tied with the earlier high point in 2005) out of a near-record class of 3,151,000 2007–2008 graduates, the *four-year* college continuation rate has declined since 2005 from 44.6 to 40.9 percent, and the 2008 four-year college continuation rate was the lowest since 1995.[15] The percentage of 18- to 24-year-olds in the United States who enroll in college is much smaller (34 percent), compared with Korea (highest at 53 percent), Greece, Poland, Ireland, Belgium, and Hungary.[16] U.S. college enrollments have increased with the population, and the likelihood of a ninth-grader attending college by the time he or she is age nineteen has increased a bit over the past decade, but enrollment of working-age adults in college-level education or training has declined since the 1990s.[17]

College completion rates are also sobering: only 59 percent of white students complete a bachelor's degree within six years of enrolling in college compared to 47 percent of Hispanic students, 40 percent of African Americans, and 39 percent of Native American students.[18] The rates for part-time students and those beginning at two-year colleges are much lower. Another, more comprehensive indicator of degree productivity is the ratio of degrees and certificates awarded per student enrolled.[19] Eighteen degrees and certificates are awarded for every one hundred students enrolled in the United States, compared with twenty-six completions per one hundred students in Australia, Japan, and Switzerland (the world's highest completion rates).[20] Eleven other OECD nations lead the United States on this measure.[21]

Turning to trends in rates of degree attainment in the population, 39 percent of U.S. adults aged 35–64 hold associate's degrees or higher (second only to Canada's 44 percent), but this percentage has not improved among U.S. adults aged 25–34, such that nine countries now best the United States in postsecondary attainment at the associate's degree level or higher.[22] With higher postsecondary graduation rates than the United States, countries such as Finland, the Slovak Republic, Iceland, and Poland now have higher ratios of graduates to the population at typical graduation ages.[23] This is truly an ominous trend.

In sum, the comparative strength of the U.S. work force in terms of education—the baby-boom generation—is about to retire, and their younger counterparts are not well positioned to either replace them or to compete in a knowledge-based global economy.

The United States must not be too sanguine about the quality of education in its colleges and universities either. Consider the following:

- The most recent National Assessment of Adult Literacy (NAAL), a nationally representative sample survey, found that the percentage of college graduates deemed proficient in prose literacy had actually declined from 40 percent a decade earlier to 31 percent in 2003. The average document literacy score for college graduates dropped by 14 points and fell by 17 points for those with some graduate education (on a 500-point scale). The survey authors found no difference between the quantitative literacy of today's college graduates compared with the earlier group.[24]
- Another study, by American Institutes for Research (AIR), found that more than 50 percent of students in their last year of a degree-seeking program at four-year colleges and more than 75 percent at two-year colleges lacked the skills to perform complex literacy tasks. They could not interpret a table about exercise and blood pressure, understand the arguments of newspaper editorials, compare credit card offers with different interest rates and annual fees, or summarize results of a survey about parental involvement in schools.[25]
- Mathematics was a particular problem for these same students, according to the AIR study. Almost 20 percent of students pursuing four-year degrees had only basic quantitative skills, for example, being able to estimate if their car had enough gas to get to the next service station. About 30 percent of two-year college students had only basic math skills. (This study used the same test as NAAL, but administered it to a larger sample of two- and four-year college students).[26]
- Literacy gaps between ethnic groups persist even among college students. Much like the general population, white college students scored higher in 2003 on prose, document, and quantitative literacy tests than African American, Hispanic, and Asian students. The differences were particularly pronounced for African American college students, only 5 percent of whom were proficient in quantitative literacy compared to 40 percent of white students.[27]

It is hard to know exactly what to make of these limited results. Do college graduates responding to such surveys take the tasks they pose seriously? How closely do the surveys reflect skills needed in the contemporary workplaces and other important social roles these graduates inhabit? A study published in early 2011 gives further cause for concern.[28] Sociologists Richard Arum and Josipa Roksa studied more than twenty-three hundred traditional-age college students across twenty-four U.S. colleges and universities of varying selectivity from 2005 to 2009 to see what they learned in college, as measured by the Collegiate Learning Assessment.[29] Arum and Roksa found that a disturbing 36 percent of the students showed no significant gains in "critical thinking, reasoning or writing skills over four years in college." Based on survey responses, they also found that students spent relatively little time each week in class or studying, compared to time spent socializing or in extracurricular activities.[30]

While these studies are far from definitive as to what college graduates know and can do, their results should be seen as a signal that there may be considerable room for improvement in graduates' learning in college and preparation for adult life.

Another concern for U.S. competitiveness in the global, knowledge-based industries is the growing prowess of enormous China and India in producing large numbers of educated workers. While good direct comparisons are difficult, given the differences in educational systems and degrees, Gary Gereffi and Viveck Wadhwa estimated that China produces about 350,000 baccalaureate-level engineers (from accredited four year degree programs) per year and India 112,000 compared to 137,000 by the United States.[31] While they argue that graduate quality is generally better in the United States, there are certainly many strong programs in these emerging countries, and the size of their populations makes it possible for their degree numbers to grow at much faster rates. Recent evidence of the export of significant numbers of lower-end technology jobs to India and China to take advantage of these nations' growing capabilities and lower costs shows that it is essential for the United States to work to retain its quality edge while also increasing degree output. To do so, we will need to make much better use of the population groups that are growing fastest in this country.

Rapid Demographic Change and Its Implications

The U.S. work force is in the midst of a sweeping demographic transformation. According to the U.S. Census Bureau, the proportion of the working-age population (defined here as ages 25–64) that is white decreased from 82 percent in 1980 to 72 percent in 2000 and is projected to fall to 63 percent by 2020 (see figure 1.1).

Correspondingly, the aggregate share of workers from other population groups is expected to more than double over this period, to 38 percent, by 2020.[32] In states with especially large minority populations, the work-force change is particularly remarkable—California's nonwhite work-force share will jump from 29 percent to 61 percent from 1980 to 2020. New Mexico and Texas are also projected to shift to a majority nonwhite work force by 2020.

Nationally, the Hispanic and Asian American shares of the work force will grow most dramatically. The shares of both groups will approximately triple

FIGURE 1.1   U.S. working-age (25–64) population by ethnicity, 1980–2020

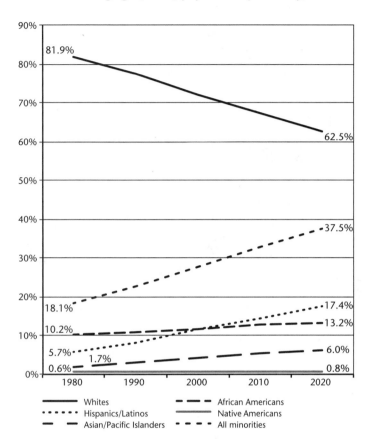

Notes: Population projections are based on historical rates of change for immigration, birth, and death. The Census category "other races" is not included.

Sources: U.S. Census Bureau, 5% Public Use Microdata Samples (based on 1980, 1990, and 2000 Census), and U.S. Population Projections (based on 2000 Census).

over this forty-year period, with the Hispanic share reaching 17 percent and the Asian American share (including Pacific Islanders) about 6 percent by 2020. The work-force representation of African Americans and Native Americans (including Alaskan natives) will also grow but at much smaller rates, as whites decline. Whites at or near retirement age will increase in numbers substantially, but at working age and below they will decrease in absolute numbers, while the other groups, especially Hispanics, will increase rapidly (see figure 1.2).

FIGURE 1.2   Projected change in U.S. population by age and race/ethnicity, 2000–2020

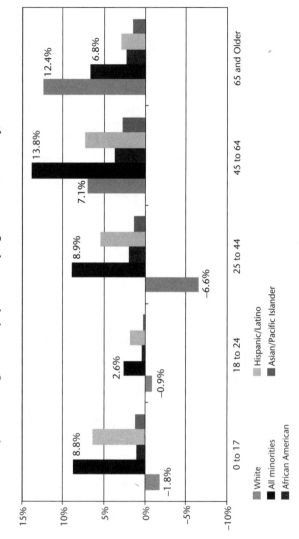

Notes: Population projections are based on historical rates of change for immigration, birth, and death.
Projections based on 2000 Census are not available for Native Americans.

Source: U.S. Census Bureau, 5% Public Use Microdata Samples (based on 2000 Census).

Ethnic diversity in the population is increasing in nearly all states, but the largest minority groups, Hispanics and African Americans, are concentrated in about half the states (see figure 1.3).

Now, compare the performance to date of the U.S. education system with these various population groups. One growing population group, Asian Americans, has the highest bachelor's degree attainment rate of any ethnic group—a stunning 57.1 percent of those 25 and older in 2007.[33] This is nearly twice the baccalaureate attainment rate among Caucasians (31.8 percent), more than three times that of African Americans (18.5 percent), and 4.5 times that of Hispanics (12.7 percent) who are the largest and fastest-growing minority group.[34] The National Center for Education Statistics reports trends in educational attainment by ethnic background over the past few decades: "Between 1975 and 2010, the percentage of 25–29 year olds who had completed a bachelor's degree or higher increased from 22 to 32 percent; however, most of the increases occurred prior to the last decade. Between 1975 and 2010, the percentage who had attained a bachelor's degree increases from 24 to 39 percent for Whites, from 10 to 19 percent for Blacks, and from 9 to 13 percent for Hispanics. Thus, ethnic differences in attainment actually increased during this period."[35]

Figure 1.4 summarizes the large differences in bachelor's degree attainment by ethnicity, as well as the trends, for the entire postcollegiate working-age (25–64) population. Attainment rates for Hispanics, African Americans, and Native Americans are increasing, but they remain far below those of whites and Asian Americans and they are growing less steeply.

Ominously, figure 1.5 shows that, for the three underrepresented ethnic groups, younger workers (25–34) are no better educated than the entire work force of the same ethnicity, while for whites and Asian Americans, the younger workers are better educated than the older.

Of course, college degree attainment rates are not the first place in the educational pipeline where ethnic gaps in educational attainment are evident. In fact, the educational playing field is far from level long before this point. High school graduation rates of African Americans and Hispanics also lag those of whites and, as the basic entry qualification for higher education, are critical to improving higher education participation and completion.[36] While there is disagreement as to the best way to measure graduation rates, it is clear that significant gaps among ethnic groups exist.[37] Longitudinal studies have shown that high school graduation rates for Hispanics have risen from 48 percent to 68 percent from 1971–2008, helping to close the white-Hispanic gap, but this large and fast-growing group continues to lag behind whites by a huge 25 percentage points.[38] In short, much remains to be done before all ethnic groups have equal access to even the most basic level of qualification for higher education—a high school diploma—and the opportunities provided by it.

FIGURE 1.3   Ninety percent of the Hispanic/Latino work force (ages 25–64) live in these states.

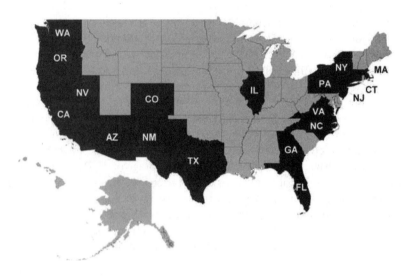

Ninety percent of the African American work force (ages 25–64) live in these states.

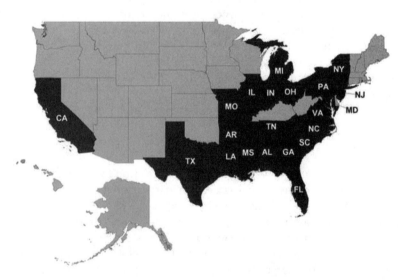

Note: Estimates as of July 1 of specified year, which is 2008. Run date: 12-02-09.

Source: U.S. Census Bureau State Resident Population Estimates by Age, Sex, Race, and Hispanic Origin: 2008, http://www.census.gov/popest/states/asrh/. Data aggregated by the National Center for Higher Education Management Systems (John Clark, Data Analyst, 303-497-0308).

FIGURE 1.4   Share of working age (25–64) population with a bachelor's degree or higher by ethnicity

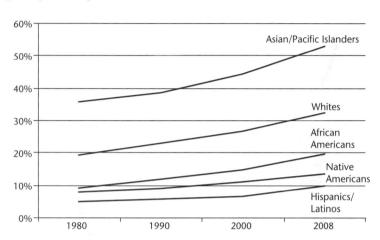

Source: Steven Ruggles, Matthew Sobek, Trent Alexander, Catherine A. Fitch, Ronald Goeken, Patricia Kelly Hall, Miriam King, and Chad Ronnander, Integrated Public Use Microdata Series: Version 4.0 [Machine-readable database] (Minneapolis, MN: Minnesota Population Center [producer and distributor], 2008).

Given the educational gaps discussed and in light of the dramatic demographic changes that have already begun across the United States, surprising shifts are set to occur in the educational level of the American work force. The widely varying degree attainment rates by age and ethnicity point to the root of the problem: groups with high rates of educational attainment are shrinking as a proportion of the U.S. population, while the proportions of those groups with low and relatively stagnant attainment are increasing.[39] While these gaps in attainment have long been an issue of moral concern for many in a nation presumably dedicated to social equity, they are rapidly becoming an urgent matter for economic competitiveness in the knowledge-based economy as well. As increases in work-force quality have consistently led to economic growth throughout the last century, declines in quality relative to the global competition could correspondingly reduce productivity growth and weaken competitiveness, understandably worrying business and other leaders.[40]

The National Center for Public Policy and Higher Education projected the impact of simply maintaining the 2000 working-age population attainment rates by ethnicity on the educational attainment of the work force in 2020, given the shifts in the ethnic mix that are underway.[41] The results, shown in figure 1.6, are sobering.

The 2020 work force would be less educated than the 2000 work force and would contain substantially more people with less than a high school diploma. Given

FIGURE 1.5   Share of population with a bachelor's degree or higher, by ethnicity and age, 2008

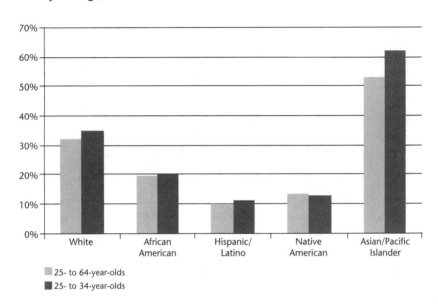

Source: Steven Ruggles, Matthew Sobek, Trent Alexander, Catherine A. Fitch, Ronald Goeken, Patricia Kelly Hall, Miriam King, and Chad Ronnander, Integrated Public Use Microdata Series: Version 4.0 [Machine-readable database] (Minneapolis, MN: Minnesota Population Center [producer and distributor], 2008).

the recent evidence on high school completion and college participation and completion rates by ethnicity just cited, this projection may not be unreasonably pessimistic if current educational success rates of the growing groups cannot be improved.

Academic Research Policies in the Knowledge-Based Economy

The importance of research in the modern knowledge-based economy is clear. As described earlier, it is at the root of innovation in products and processes and thus of economic growth. It is also relevant in many cases to how society can cope effectively with the environmental, social, and human consequences of the changes growth brings. Academic research plays a special role in that universities are the main provider in American society of the basic knowledge development underlying all of the purposes that private actors are unwilling to pay for, usually because the benefits are too broad to be captured by the sponsor and turned into profits. The federal government pays for much of this basic research, but states also contribute importantly by recognizing the research function in their funding policies, which underlie higher faculty salaries, lower teaching assignments, support for graduate education, and the

FIGURE 1.6   Share of working population (25–64) at various attainment levels, actual and projected if current gaps remain

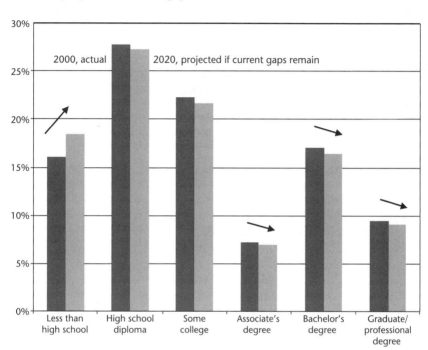

Note: These categories represent highest level of education attained.

Sources: U.S. Census Bureau, 5% Public Use Microdata ,Samples (based on 1980, 1990, and 2000 Census), and U.S. Population Projections (based on 2000 Census).

nature of capital support in research universities. Thus, these institutions are quite costly in comparison to teaching-focused colleges and universities.

In recent years, it has been increasingly recognized that quality research universities can be important linchpins for economic development in a region, attracting (and even creating) technology-based firms and the high-paying jobs and economic spinoffs that go with them. Silicon Valley in Northern California, the Route 128 corridor around Boston, and the Research Triangle including the University of North Carolina–Chapel Hill, North Carolina State University, and Duke University are well-known examples of this. Firms in technology-based industries with a high research and development (R&D) component place a premium on proximity to quality research institutions and the people within them.[42] Although it is very expensive and time consuming to build research universities to the point that they materially have an impact on a region's development, local boosters and state policy makers have strong incentives to seek to build up their institutions, and of course, the schools themselves are willing partners. States are increasingly trying to reinforce and even seed this economic development process with research grants of their own to universities, often tied to university-industry partnerships that bring in corporate funding as well.[43]

This pursuit of competitive, state-level science policies, with strong political backing from competing local interests within states, presents a variety of issues.[44] The main one of concern here is that this pursuit may push states in the direction of seeking to create more research universities than they can (or should) afford. This type of competition could easily drain precious resources and attention from what should be the states' primary business in higher education at this time, which is—in addition to adequately supporting the research universities they already have—increasing college participation and completion rates. Most of this crucial latter activity, in terms of sheer numbers, will necessarily be at the levels of the community college and regional or comprehensive institution (as well as in the for-profit sector).[45]

It will surely take visionary and tough-minded state policy leadership to tame the competitive pressures to expand the research sector just described and keep—or bring—the states' focus squarely on the most urgent problems they face in higher education. We believe that the federal government, and particularly Congress, can help here by resisting pressures to allocate its R&D funding by methods other than rigorous peer review. Politically driven earmarking of federal research and research facilities funding, which has skyrocketed in recent years, exacerbates incentives toward "mission creep" by institutions and their supporters who seek to build new research universities and weakens the resolve of state policy makers to resist.

WORRISOME TRENDS IN FINANCE

In light of the emerging demands on the nation's system of postsecondary education, in what shape is its capacity and system of finance? Alas, there are some reasons for serious concern. We introduce these concerns next to set the stage for the analysis that follows in later chapters.

State Funding Ups and Downs

State and local appropriations, at $88.5 billion in fiscal year 2010, remain the largest source of educational revenue for public colleges and universities, which enroll nearly three-fourths of all U.S. students.[46] States also provide several billion dollars annually in support to private colleges and their students. These appropriations are subject to large cyclical fluctuations that are closely linked to states' economic fortunes. State and local appropriations per full-time, equivalent (FTE) student tend to fall sharply with states' tax revenues during and after recessions, as occurred in the early 1980s, early 1990s, early 2000s, and late 2000s downturns (see figure 1.7).[47]

FIGURE 1.7 Public FTE enrollment and educational appropriations per FTE, U.S., fiscal 1985–2010

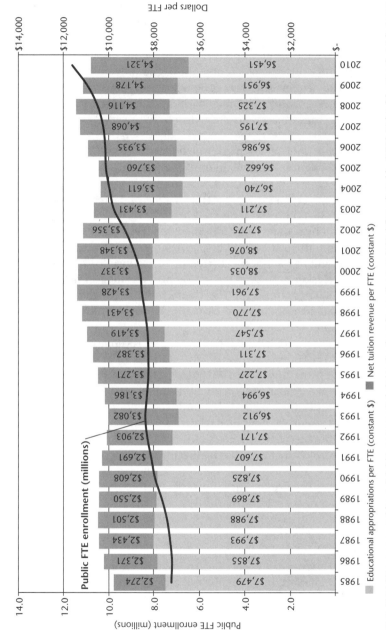

Year	Educational appropriations per FTE (constant $)	Net tuition revenue per FTE (constant $)
2010	$6,451	$4,321
2009	$6,951	$4,178
2008	$7,325	$4,116
2007	$7,195	$4,068
2006	$6,986	$3,935
2005	$6,662	$3,760
2004	$6,740	$3,611
2003	$7,211	$3,431
2002	$7,775	$3,356
2001	$8,076	$3,348
2000	$8,035	$3,337
1999	$7,961	$3,428
1998	$7,770	$3,431
1997	$7,547	$3,419
1996	$7,311	$3,387
1995	$7,227	$3,271
1994	$6,994	$3,186
1993	$6,912	$3,082
1992	$7,171	$2,903
1991	$7,607	$2,691
1990	$7,825	$2,608
1989	$7,869	$2,550
1988	$7,988	$2,501
1987	$7,993	$2,434
1986	$7,855	$2,371
1985	$7,479	$2,274

Note: Net tuition revenue used for capital debt service are included in the above figures. Constant 2010 dollars adjusted by SHEEO Higher Education Cost Adjustment (HECA).

Source: SHEEO, State Higher Education Finance, 2010, Figure 3, http://www.sheeo.org/finance/shef/SHEF_FY10.pdf.

In the earlier cases, these key funds subsequently turned sharply upward once policy makers were sure that prosperity had been restored, but that pattern has been weaker after the recent downturns.

As Figure 1.7 shows, appropriations per student peaked in fiscal 2001 at $8,076 (in 2010 dollars) just slightly above the previous peak in fiscal year (FY) 1987. The decline after the 2000–2001 recession was steeper than the previous two recessionary declines, with appropriations per FTE falling by 17.09 percent from FY 2000 to 2005 (to $6,662), a level below the two previous troughs. By FY 2008, per-student educational appropriations to public colleges and universities had climbed back to $7,325, still 9.3 percent below the 2001 figure. There were simply not enough "good years" before the 2008–2009 recession hit to permit what in previous times might have been called a full recovery in state support for public higher education. The initial impact of the Great Recession was seen in FY 2009, when state appropriations per student fell by 5.10 percent from the 2008 level, to $6,951, with a further 7.2 percent drop to $6,451 in FY 2010.[48] Almost certainly, further declines in state support will be seen over subsequent years, once the data are in.

The deep recession of 2008 and 2009 and its sluggish aftermath took a heavy toll on states' finances. The Center on Budget and Policy Priorities (CBPP) estimated that states had closed budget shortfalls totaling a staggering $430 billion over fiscal years 2009–2011.[49] CBPP estimated in early 2011 that gaps between projected expenditures and revenues for FY 2012 would total another $140 billion across the fifty states, with at least another $70 billion shortfall on the horizon for FY 2013.[50] These are staggering (and cumulative) budget gaps, much of which have been or will be covered by spending reductions. This is never a good sign for higher education, which is typically the largest discretionary item in state general fund budgets and tends to suffer disproportionate cuts in state funding during downturns compared to recession-sensitive functions like Medicaid, public assistance, and criminal justice, and basic state commitments to K–12 education funding.[51]

Even if state finances eventually recover from the effects of the latest painful recession, their longer-term future does not look bright. Inevitable declines in federal recession-related subventions, the effects of permanent state tax cuts made during the 1990s, and erosion of state tax bases as a result of shifts in the economy from goods subject to sales tax toward lightly taxed services and Internet sales, plus health cost inflation and the aging of the dependent population, mean that states are projected to face structural deficits in their budgets for a long time.[52] Absent significant changes in how some of higher education's services are delivered, this cannot be good news for meeting labor market and societal needs, especially if enrollments and degrees are to increase.

The figures on higher education funding reported earlier include only state and local support for operating expenditures by public colleges and universities, not their spending from tuition revenue or state support for capital purposes or expansion. Unfortunately, the data currently available on college and university capital needs are seriously incomplete, but it is widely agreed by experts that spending on major maintenance and renewal of higher education's capital plant appears to be well below desirable levels.[53] Many of the existing buildings were built during the 1960s and 1970s and are in need of significantly more upkeep than they are getting, not to mention upgrading to keep pace with the needs of modern technology.[54]

According to available data, colleges and universities in the United States spend "about $20 billion annually on facilities operations (including maintenance, energy, and utilities) and $14 billion annually for construction of new facilities and renovations of existing buildings. Colleges and university campuses provide more than 5 billion square feet of floor space in 240,000 buildings, with a current replacement value of $700 billion, excluding the costs required for utilities, infrastructure, roads, and landscaping. The backlog of deferred maintenance projects is estimated to cost more than $36 billion, or about 7 percent of current replacement value (CRV)."[55] Over two decades, from 1980 to 2000, U.S. public college and university spending on operations and maintenance of physical plants decreased by more than 26 percent—from 8.7 percent to 6.4 percent of annual educational and general (E&G) expenditures.[56]

Only a few states have developed facilities master plans that would help them identify, prioritize, and develop support for needed capital support programs, probably in good part because they are not committed to consistent funding for this purpose, so careful planning seems futile. While it is clear that state funding for capital purposes needs to be increased, we suggest that here, as in other aspects of higher education finance, considerable efficiencies in use of existing facilities are possible that have not been sufficiently explored, much less exploited.

Increasing Tuition

With more or less acquiescence from state policy makers, public colleges and universities have partially mitigated the effects of state revenue downswings on their budgets by raising tuition rates sharply during these periods. For example, between fiscal years 2000 and 2005, a period of state economic and fiscal stress instigated by the dot.com recession, per-student state appropriations to higher education fell by 17.09 percent, or $1,373 (in constant 2010 dollars), while net tuition revenue per student received by public institutions jumped by 12.7 percent, or $423 (see figure 1.8).[57]

When state support began to rebound after 2005, tuition growth eventually moderated somewhat but, as in past cycles of recession and recovery, tuition never returned to previous levels. An important effect of this pattern is reflected in the long-term trend in the increase of net tuition revenue as

FIGURE 1.8 Public higher education appropriations per FTE and tuition as a share of total educational revenue, fiscal years 1985 to 2010

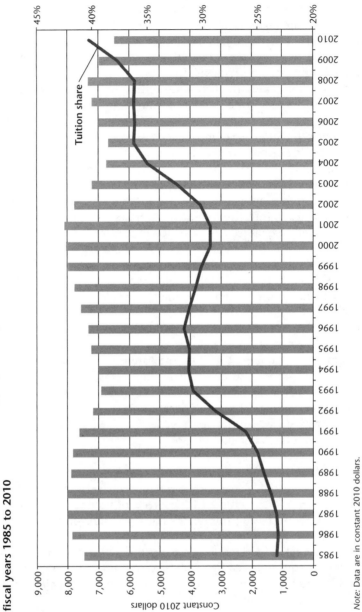

Note: Data are in constant 2010 dollars.

Source: SHEEO, State Higher Education Finance Report, 2010, http://www.sheeo.org/finance/shef/SHEF_FY10.pdf.

a percentage of public higher education's "total educational revenue" (figure 1.8).[58] The long-term trend in tuition as a source of institutional finance is distinctly and strongly upward. Net tuition represented just 23.3 percent of public higher education revenues in FY 1985 but was up to 36.2 percent by 2000 and, after two recessions in the ensuing decade, climbed to over 40 percent in FY 2010.[59]

Another key effect is a long-term trend of increased tuition rates as a proportion of median family annual incomes, especially in relation to incomes of families in the lowest two quintiles of the national income distribution, where the decision to enroll is most price sensitive. Clearly, as college costs continue to climb at rates far above growth in most people's incomes, affording higher education becomes an increasing challenge for lower- and middle-income families. Table 1.1 shows the dramatic increase in just eight years in the share of income represented by "net college costs" (defined here by the National Center for Public Policy and Higher Education as tuition, room, and board minus grant aid). The shares of incomes needed to meet college costs have undoubtedly grown further in the most recent years of economic difficulty for states, colleges, and individuals.

Political responses to the long-term real growth in tuition at a time when more citizens want to access higher education have now materialized—including pressure on elected officials to seek to moderate increases—but have not generally resulted in clear, robust state policies on tuition and affordability.[60] The recent Great Recession and its expected aftermath of years of sluggish economic growth and strained state budgets are certain to put more upward pressure on tuition as institutions seek to mitigate the effects of limited state support.[61] Indeed, in academic year 2010–2011, the average increase in tuition and fees at public four-year colleges and universities was 7.9 percent for state residents and 6.0 percent for nonresidents. Public two-year schools raised tuition and fees by an average of 6.0 percent.[62]

Student Aid Is Not Keeping Up

In the aggregate, it might be said that states have made significant efforts to respond to the affordability problem by increasing their support for student aid, although this varies widely from state to state. Total state aid to college students exceeded $10 billion in 2008–2009, an increase of 2.7 percent from the previous year.[63] According to the National Association of State Student Grant and Aid Programs, total state-funded financial aid to undergraduate students grew by an impressive 71 percent, after adjustment for inflation, between 1998–1999 and 2008–2009.[64] But student grants based on financial need grew much more slowly during this same time period (more than 51 percent) than grants based on "academic merit" or other criteria (more than 158 percent), though the latter are less likely to make a difference in whether or not a student attends college. Most importantly, nearly two-thirds

TABLE 1.1
Net college costs* as a percent of median family income

The burden of paying for college has increased for all families, but has increased more for middle- and low-income families.

At public four-year colleges and universities	1999–2000	2007–2008	% points increased
Lowest income quintile	39%	55%	16%
Lower-middle income quintile	23%	33%	10%
Middle income quintile	18%	25%	7%
Upper-middle income quintile	12%	16%	4%
Highest income quintile	7%	9%	3%
At public two-year colleges	1999–2000	2007–2008	% points increased
Lowest income quintile	40%	49%	9%
Lower-middle income quintile	22%	29%	7%
Middle income quintile	15%	20%	5%
Upper-middle income quintile	10%	13%	3%
Highest income quintile	6%	7%	2%

Source: National Center for Public Policy and Higher Education, Measuring Up 2008 (San Jose, CA: 2008), www.highereducation.org.

*Net college costs equal tuition, room, and board minus financial aid. The numbers may not exactly add due to rounding.

of need-based aid is concentrated in just ten states (California, Illinois, Indiana, New Jersey, New York, North Carolina, Ohio, Pennsylvania, Texas, and Washington), while five states provided less than $2 million in need-based aid and six more provided less than $10 million.[65]

The federal government is by far the largest provider of student aid, giving more than $146 billion to undergraduate and graduate students in 2009–2010 in the form of grants, work-study aid, direct and guaranteed loans, and tax credits and deductions.[66] Federal education tax benefits, first introduced in 1998–1999, constituted 4 percent of federal aid to postsecondary students in 2009–2010.[67] Pell Grants, the major federal grant program targeted at low-income students, benefited approximately 7.7million students in 2009–2010, compared with 6.2 million the previous year and just 3.8 million ten years earlier.[68] Congress enacted legislation to raise the maximum Pell Grant to $5,350 in 2009–2010 with further annual increases scheduled so as to reach $8,000 by 2014–2015.[69] Federal spending on Pell Grants increased by a remarkable 58 percent in 2009–2010, and federal grants to veterans enrolled in college also grew sharply under newly enacted legislation.[70] Only one-quarter of students qualified for the maximum grant, however. The average grant in 2009–2010 was $3,646.[71] The average grant is sufficient to cover tuition at most community colleges but with little left over for books and living costs. Even the maximum Pell Grant currently covers just over a third of average total costs at public four-year colleges and universities and only 15 percent of average total charges at private four-year colleges.[72]

Although federal grant aid grew by an unprecedented amount in 2009–2010, still nearly two-thirds of the federal aid total was in the form of loans.[73] Federal loan aid more than doubled in inflation-adjusted terms over the ten years ending in 2009–2010, reaching $96.8 billion.[74] Among the federal loans, the largest category is now "unsubsidized" Stafford loans (meaning that the government does not forgo interest payments while the student is in school), a big change from ten years earlier.[75] About 55 percent of 2008–2009 bachelor's degree recipients from public four-year institutions had loan debt at graduation, averaging just under $20,000. The comparable figures for graduates of private nonprofit colleges were 65 percent who borrowed and an average debt of $26,100. In the fast-growing for-profit sector, nearly all graduates had borrowed, and average debt levels at graduation were substantially higher.[76]

Notably, after years of large annual increases, the financial crisis and federal policy actions led to a sharp shift in the sources of students' educational borrowing in 2008–2009 and 2009–2010. Nonfederal loans—mostly private loans by banks and other lenders outside the federal programs and their protections for borrowers—had grown dramatically during a number of years when individual borrower ceilings in the government programs were unchanged. These nonfederal loans peaked at 25 percent of all (known) student borrowing in 2007–2008 but then fell off sharply over the next two years, dropping to just 8 percent of the total in 2009–2010, with the federal government stepping in to pick up the slack.[77] The Obama administration moved to replace much of the historic financial institution-based lending to students that occurred through the federally subsidized loan guarantee program, as well as the college lending through purely private loans outside the federal programs, with direct lending by the government.[78] Also, in the Higher Education Opportunity Act of 2008, the government sharply reduced interest rates on federal loans to students, in theory reducing the net cost of college to students. According to the U.S. Department of Education's summary of the act's provisions, interest rates on undergraduate subsidized Stafford loans will be reduced in stages from 6.8 percent in 2008 to 3.4 percent for loans disbursed on or after July 1, 2011.However, rates are scheduled to revert to 6.8 percent for loans disbursed after July 1, 2012. Interest rates for unsubsidized Stafford loans for undergraduates and all Stafford loans for graduate students remain at a fixed 6.8 percent.[79]

While students with sizable debts may make some different career and life choices as a result, the biggest policy concern may be the effects of limited need-based grant aid and dependence upon loans on the decisions of students who are on the margin of college attendance or continuation. We know that students from minority ethnic groups, first-generation students, and lower-income students are reluctant to borrow for college.[80] Federal survey data show that, among those who are enrolled, unmet financial need (after aid is awarded) is on average largest among low-income students, which cannot bode well for their capacity to persist.[81] Yet, it is among these very groups that the nation most needs additional college students and graduates.

Cost Control Efforts in Higher Education

Economist Howard Bowen propounded several decades ago a "revenue theory of costs" in higher education and other values-driven nonprofit enterprises.[82] According to this perspective, these institutions will find ways to spend whatever revenues they can acquire in the pursuit of such value-driven goals as educational quality (or reputation for it), so their expenditures will be primarily a function of the revenues they obtain. Stronger competition only heightens this tendency to the extent that students choose schools more on the basis of quality or reputation than price, at least within broad categories.[83] More intense competition has emerged in the years since Bowen wrote, first during the "birth dearth" years of the 1980s and early 1990s when schools had to compete aggressively to keep their classrooms filled and, more recently, as the rise of widely available college rankings has fueled the competitive struggle.

There are also "cost push" factors that tend to drive up college and university costs per student more rapidly than costs in the general economy as measured conventionally by the Consumer Price Index. The basic reason for this is the labor intensity of higher education, which is like other service industries in that cost growth is generally also higher than in the rest of the economy.[84] Exacerbating this general tendency is the fact that much of the labor used in higher education is highly skilled and wage premiums for skills have been growing rapidly in recent years, as suggested earlier.[85]

Organizational structures in academe also play a significant role in that norms of disciplinary equality, decentralization of authority to departments, a strong faculty role in governance, and faculty tenure make it difficult to reduce resources devoted to less current or low-demand fields even as initiatives in newly emerging fields are undertaken. Institutions and their faculties, especially four-year colleges and universities, have also generally been unenthusiastic about exploring ways in which new instructional technologies might be used to make instruction more efficient as opposed to simply adding on the technology to existing instructional costs.

State policies often make their own contribution to higher than necessary higher education costs. State policy makers (with some exceptions) have had a notoriously difficult time controlling natural tendencies, in a political structure where local interests have strong representation, that push toward the authorization of arguably too many public institutions and particularly too many doing essentially the same thing. Thus, institutions, often supported by influential boosters and politicians from their local area, tend to push for comprehensiveness of programs or sometimes focus on particular, often high-cost, specialty fields (e.g., a medical school or program in a technology-oriented field thought likely to spur economic development) as a matter of regional equity.

These tendencies are complemented by pressures that originate among the academics themselves but are quickly picked up by local supporters of "status drift" (sometimes called mission creep), a process whereby schools seek to move up a notch in the conventional academic status hierarchy. Community colleges may want to offer bachelor's programs when the opportunity arises, state colleges seek to become universities, and universities seek to become research universities and then ever more selective and highly regarded ones. Since communities perceive real local benefits from much of this and local pressures and interinstitutional equity norms are quite potent in state legislatures, it is not surprising that statewide policies designed to limit duplication, control system costs, and generally rationalize expansion are difficult to enforce consistently.

State fiscal policies relating to higher education overall have been quite unstable, with appropriations varying sharply with the fortunes of the economy, as previously documented. This does not help institutions, to the extent they are so disposed, to be highly efficient, as they feel they must spend money when they have it and have little flexibility under most states' fiscal management policies to save money internally for rainy days. When a downturn occurs and state funding is cut or is stagnant, public colleges and universities tend to turn to tuition increases to mitigate the effects as well as to temporary cost-saving and deferral measures, such as restricting travel, deferring purchases and maintenance, leaving vacant positions open longer than usual, and the like. In some cases, this leads to enrollment restrictions, even though demand for enrollment tends to increase in recession periods. Given the past cycles in state funding already described, this tendency to take temporary measures and wait for better times is not surprising or irrational from the institution's standpoint. The funding has historically come back after a few years and typically even grows at a fairly strong rate for a time. After the Great Recession of 2007–2009, though, all indications are that the recovery in higher education's support will take substantially longer than usual and will likely be less than complete.[86]

The longer-term pattern of stagnancy in state support per student, which might have suggested that some more basic restructuring was in order, has not produced much in the way of serious efforts to alter internal arrangements and incentives so as to better moderate costs. Rather, the major efforts of institutions to improve their financial position have focused on the revenue side— higher tuition, more private fund-raising efforts, efforts to increase research grants, and entrepreneurial programmatic initiatives of various kinds—rather than on the more difficult work of restructuring internal organization and incentives.[87] The most prominent cost-control strategies utilized have been replacing full-time with part-time faculty paid only to teach and deferring major maintenance and rebuilding projects. Both these approaches, when carried out over a long time, erode capacity and educational quality.[88]

Clearly, colleges and universities and the states that support and depend upon them need to come up with fiscal, allocation, and financial management policies better suited to today's realities. We will explain how this might be done in this book.

Implications of Finance Trends

The trends in finance sketched here have serious implications for key public policy goals for higher education. First, the long-term growth in the price charged to students, even when student aid is accounted for, is making access to higher education and success in completing degrees more difficult for the population groups the nation most needs to reach—in particular Latinos, African Americans, Native Americans, some Asian groups, low- and moderate-income students of all ethnic groups, and adult working students. High prices for higher education also produce concerns about affordability among more affluent population groups—concerns that might be tapped to increase political support for more state funding—but generally these groups have survived the long run-up in prices without serious increases in the proportion of family income needed to pay tuition.[89] According to data from the 2007–2008 National Postsecondary Student Aid Study, the net price of attending four-year, private colleges and universities for students from the top income quartile grew from 14.3 percent to 18.3 percent of family income between 1990–2008, whereas the net price as a percent of family income for students in the bottom quartile rose from 64.8 percent to 82.3 percent.[90] Similarly, the net price of attending four-year, public colleges and universities for students from the top income quartile grew from 8.1 percent to 11.2 percent of income between 1990–2008, whereas the net price as a percent of family income for students in the bottom quartile rose from 38.4 to 48.2 percent.[91]

Yet, the concerns of the more affluent about college affordability have also succeeded in shifting some of the focus of both government and institutional student aid programs away from strictly need-based aid toward distribution criteria like high school grades and test scores, usually termed "academic merit," which tend to benefit students from more affluent circumstances disproportionately. Indeed, enrollment and degree-attainment rates of the children of the affluent, never much in doubt, have actually been increasing.[92] Thus, the way the political economy of the affordability issue has so far played out is unfortunate insofar as equity in educational opportunity is concerned. Even more importantly, it threatens the competitiveness of the nation's future work force, which depends increasingly on the groups now poorly served.

The long-term shift in higher education finance away from state support and toward more dependence on students and families and entrepreneurially generated revenues leads to several problems for the capacity of the system to respond to public needs. It not only makes access and persistence more difficult for the lower-income and minority populations that higher education most needs to reach, but also works to the disadvantage of the institutions that serve most of them. Research universities have by far the greatest ability to take advantage of increased leeway to raise tuition and to pursue external funds from wealthy alumni, corporations, and federal research agencies than do the broad-access institutions with primarily teaching missions—comprehensive state colleges and universities and community colleges—that mainly serve these population groups.

Even the research universities are finding their capacity to serve their public purposes, such as uncompensated public service, the nurturing of fields that do not bring in large amounts of external support, and generally providing opportunities for advanced education to a reasonably broad range of students, circumscribed by the types of steps they feel the new, more market-driven fiscal environment obliges them to take.[93] In short, given current finance patterns, the capacity of all these types of institutions to respond effectively to the needs in many states to educate growing numbers of young people,[94] and in nearly all states to enroll and retain more lower-income and minority students, is in question.

Of critical importance also is the fact that neither higher education leadership (much less faculty) nor state policy makers have fully accepted the likely reality of a future with no greater, and perhaps fewer, resources per student than they have been accustomed to. There is as yet no strong inclination to look hard at ways to educate students more efficiently from start to finish as long as it appears more attractive to blame state leaders (or taxpayers) for not providing more financial support. Perhaps the lingering aftermath of the Great Recession will change this, at least in some quarters. Indeed, the lengthy economic stagnation provides a valuable opportunity to revisit premises and mind-sets. In any case, once reasonable prosperity is restored, we think there is potential for eliciting greater public investment in higher education as, increasingly, business leaders, policy makers, and the public recognize its crucial role in modern society and economic competition. But the evidence is also clear that this will not happen absent a serious and transparent effort to show these groups how the education system—including here importantly higher education's links to the elementary and secondary education enterprise—can and will operate in a more systemically efficient and publicly accountable way. In short, the citizenry and their elected representatives will want to know what they are getting for any increased investment of precious tax funds.

STATE CAPACITY AND POLICY LEADERSHIP

In the post-World War II era, public policy for higher education has concentrated primarily on building, developing, maintaining, and overseeing our institutions of higher education. The primary state role has been to oversee the institutions on behalf of the state, ensure efficient allocation of resources, avoid duplication of effort, and manage expansion to ensure an orderly disposition of funds. Approximately half of the states did this through statewide governing boards, with responsibility for governance of public institutions, as well as for statewide planning; the others relied on coordinating boards, which focused on mission and program allocation, planning, student aid, and coordination of public and private institutions and higher education sectors.[95] Economic access was maintained largely through low-tuition policies and state-funded student aid programs that—when they existed and were funded at a significant level— were also designed to enable students to choose independent institutions.

In the last decade, there has been a substantial change in the role of the state in higher education. In almost every state, legislatures and governors have responded to the changed policy climate for higher education by refocusing the state role away from institutional oversight and regulation in favor of greater campus autonomy and market adaptability. Many states have loosened or abandoned traditional attention to mission differentiation, and are encouraging institutions to be entrepreneurial to best compete in the markets they deem most appropriate.

Higher education institutions have benefited unevenly from the deregulation movement. Many public flagships and well-positioned regional universities have probably come out ahead, some at the expense of serving the students and employers in their states. For many public flagship institutions, this loosening of regulatory restraints has resulted in increased recruitment of out-of-state and academically meritorious students, attractive both for the hefty tuition checks they pay and for their impact on college ratings. Whether the majority of public and private, two- and four-year colleges have been similarly advantaged is debatable.

Still, few would argue that the movement away from state regulatory control has been anything but good for individual institutions of higher education. But evidence over the past decade argues that it has not been equally beneficial for the state itself and for the public interest, which is more than the sum total of institutional interests. This evidence shows that some key functions that serve the public do not flourish in a market-defined climate: creating affordable college access, particularly for low-income students; addressing achievement gaps between racial and economic subgroups; retaining students to a degree or other objective; assuring learning results across multiple institutions; assuring adequate programs and student places in areas of public need and high costs, such as nursing and engineering; and responding to high-priority needs of employers and communities. These issues, particularly concerns about escalating tuition and mission creep, are now leading some states to consider reinstating tighter regulatory controls.

As old models for state policy development and oversight, which relied substantially on regulation, have eroded, there has been little progress toward development of new forms of policy capacity capable of using state policy tools to address public needs—provided through public, private nonprofit, or even for-profit institutions. Addressing this problem will require new forms of state policy for higher education and different kinds of organizations and strategies, not a rebuilding of traditional structures that focus primarily on regulatory aspects of institutional oversight. Instead of zigzagging between regulatory and market-based approaches, states must find ways to blend policy and market solutions in pursuit of the broader public interest. This will require greater capacity to identify broad societal and economic trends, to articulate and build consensus around broad goals for higher education, to leverage change using a variety of strategies and incentives, to devise approaches to accountability that assess progress toward goals, and to identify performance gaps.

States must develop the tools to look at the broad intersections between higher education and public needs in order to make judgments about how to leverage performance improvements through strategic investment of resources. For most states, this means development of organizations or bodies that have the intellectual capacity and the political sophistication to provide and sustain policy leadership and engage key government, higher education, public school, business, and public constituencies. Lacking this, it is unlikely that entrenched finance and incentive patterns will change.

CONCLUSION

The United States faces many competitive challenges as well as challenges at home and abroad in this complex world. As we have explained, higher education is crucial to successfully meeting them. But the country needs new strategic direction in this field, new structures for policy leadership at the state level, and new approaches to show and convince opinion leaders and the public that the enterprise is both efficient and socially accountable and thus worthy of new investment. Most importantly, it needs to find ways to improve college access and completion even though competition for resources is extremely vigorous and the student mix is in many ways becoming more challenging to serve. Neither government nor higher education can do the job alone; the elementary and secondary education sector and the broader community, especially the business sector, will need to play important supporting roles.

In this book, we elucidate these issues and provide the latest available pertinent data and policy analysis based upon it. We offer policy ideas drawn from this analysis that take account of the American federal system and the respective roles of the states and the federal government in higher education policy, as well as the wide diversity in higher education structures and systems among the fifty states. Our primary purposes are: (1) to assert the urgency of the issues, and (2) to suggest a path to closing the gap between the nation's growing needs in higher education and the resources readily available. Clearly, more resources need to be invested in higher education, but this is not likely to happen if business continues to be conducted entirely in the accustomed ways in this vital sector. Thus, we also indicate how long-held assumptions need to be rethought and new policies, incentives and institutional arrangements designed.

In the next chapter, we seek to answer the basic question: how much higher education does the nation need? We review the literature related to this key issue and consider various recent, empirically grounded assessments. We come to the conclusion that, while no simple, fixed-point estimate of need can be valid in a flexible market economy and open society, there is strong evidence that the nation will benefit greatly from having substantially more educated graduates than our institutions are now producing or are on track to produce. We also show that increasing degree output substantially will be a considerable challenge since most of the growth in the young population will be among groups whose past educational attainment has been far below the U.S. norm. To reach necessary goals, our education system simply must serve these—and all—groups better.

Chapters 3 and 4 document and explain the pertinent history of U.S. higher education finance. Chapter 3 focuses on the pre-World War II history of higher education through the 1970s, emphasizing the manifestation of American federalism in this field and considering the legacy of those early choices. Chapter 4 emphasizes the major patterns and changes in the financing of American higher education over the past three decades; analyzes the forces behind the general growth in both enrollments and real resource costs per student over that period; and tracks the sharp ups and downs in state financing and related growth in tuition charges in both public and private sectors that have consistently exceeded general inflation as well as gains in typical family incomes. We also note the inconsistent patterns in governmental aid to students at both federal and state levels and the explosive growth in student debt in recent decades. We show that the factors mentioned have combined to produce results that, absent significant policy changes, do not bode well for the goal of substantially increasing system output of well-qualified graduates, especially in light of projected structural deficits in both federal and state budgets. Yet, produce more high-quality graduates we must if the nation is to prosper and meet its basic social equity commitments.

After setting the stage in these first four chapters, we turn to exploring how we can get where we need to be in terms of higher education system output and quality in light of the resource challenges the states and the nation face. In chapter 5, we confront the great diversity across the fifty states' higher education systems, in resources and policy cultures as well as in their key challenges. We categorize states along these lines and identify the policy levers available to the various types of states and specific to particular major challenges they face in increasing system productivity and equity in outcomes. We suggest ways in which performance, efficiency, and public confidence in state higher education systems might be improved so that both resources are used most efficiently and necessary new resources can be mobilized and tapped. In the end, we recognize that different specific steps will need to be prioritized in different state contexts, and we use our state categorization to frame thinking about this.

In chapter 6, we take up the issue of the American higher education system's capacity to educate many more students at a high level of quality, considering the incentives built into current policies and funding arrangements. We weigh the capacity and behavioral incentives of the various types of public institutions, from community colleges to research universities, as well as those of private colleges and universities, both nonprofit and for-profit. In brief, we find that the main burden will inevitably fall to broad-access, less selective institutions—the comprehensive institutions in both sectors but especially the public; public community and technical colleges; and private, for-profit institutions. We suggest that new policies and approaches will be necessary to harness these resources more effectively to serve the new goals. We also conclude that traditional approaches to delivery of instruction will not be adequate by themselves to meet ambitious goals for increased degree production. We assert that instructional technology will need to be utilized much more strategically, not only to reach new student audiences via distance learning but also to help restructure large course instruction to be both more efficient and more effective in terms of student learning. Finally, we find that higher education need not teach all students who "walk in the door" of postsecondary education all that they need to know to earn meaningful certificates and degrees. Rather, the capacity for credible assessment of students' prior learning has improved and can (indeed must) play a role in bringing more people to the point of earning educational credentials.

Finally, chapter 7 concludes the volume with a summary and synthesis of our analysis and thinking about how the urgent need to improve performance and cost effectiveness in U.S. higher education so as to produce substantially more degreed graduates at internationally competitive quality levels can be accomplished. We offer specific recommendations that are national in their reach but embedded in the American model of federalism, realistic in fiscal and political terms, and, where necessary, tailored to different types of states. They are also ambitious in their aspiration to meet the nation's large needs with limited new resources, and they place major emphasis on using finance-based incentives strategically while also ensuring accountability. These elements are critical, we believe, to coaxing additional investment from those who could provide it—that is, individual and business taxpayers and those who represent them—if convinced that it would produce the results they seek.

We see this broad approach as a good fit for a nation and a sector as diverse and important as is higher education in the United States today. Such new thinking is essential if America is to meet the global challenges to continued prosperity that it faces.

CHAPTER 2

How Much Higher Education Does the Nation Need?

Given the challenges of a global, knowledge-based economy, the United States appears to need substantially more college graduates than it is on track to produce. But to what extent is this demand the case? As we examine in this chapter, there are differences between society's need for educated people and labor market demand for them, and we suggest that market demand is a lower-bound estimate of societal needs. For example, society may need more medical researchers for newly discovered diseases, environmental technologists to respond to unforeseen crises, or math teachers in urban schools than predictions of future market demand would suggest. Such shifts, while not strictly predictable by standard forecasting techniques, may be quite important to societal well-being and thereby significant for policy making. In our view, society's need for educated people is more likely to exceed standard, largely trend-based, projections than to undershoot them.

We next explore in this chapter the trends regarding return on investments to higher education, wage premiums related to college degree attainment, and growing income inequality linked to educational attainment. In the last half of the chapter, we examine some of the key evidence and analytic issues concerning recent and projected labor-market demand for graduates of higher education and address the arguments of those who see an overeducated work force rather than too few college graduates as the chief concern. We conclude that the evidence points toward the need for and benefits of strong, steady gains in the numbers of college graduates, though we recognize the risks of projecting labor market trends in a global, knowledge-based economy with considerable unknowns, including the susceptibility of some occupations to outsourcing overseas. However, we think that official labor-market projections underestimate the growing need for well-educated workers who not only fill existing positions but can create new demand for their skills and services. Yet, the nation will be challenged to maintain historical patterns of moderate growth in degree output, much less increase production substantially, given the changing nature of the young population and its educational preparation and the severe budget restraints facing states and the nation. Thus, this chapter sets the stage for our analysis later in the book, which calls for altering current priorities via both direct persuasion by political leaders and by changing incentives tied to public funding of higher education.

LABOR MARKET DEMAND AND SOCIETAL NEED

Labor market demands, as reflected in job openings and earnings trends, provide important benchmark indicators of the nation's needs for individuals who have specific credentials and skills at a given time. For example, if job openings for those with a bachelor's degree in electrical engineering are plentiful, unemployment is low, job-search times are short, and salaries are rising compared with job openings for those with other credentials, then demand for those with a degree in electrical engineering is strong relative to the current supply. The general implication is that these indicators of labor market demand—that is, job openings, unemployment levels, search times, and salaries—can serve as a measure of society's need for more degree holders in a particular field.[1]

If the indicators suggest that demand is weak in specific fields, then the general implication from economic theory is that society has sufficient numbers of graduates in these areas—or even that fewer new graduates might be appropriate. For example, this might apply to some social service professions or to PhDs in the humanities, where salaries are relatively low and some degree recipients are unable to find relevant employment. It is important to note that many degree holders in such fields may find productive and well-rewarded work in other fields, suggesting that "relevant" employment might be too narrowly conceived. In addition, the impetus to equate societal need with market demand may be overly simplistic in some areas, particularly in those fields that are supported substantially by tax dollars, such as social work and teaching. For example, it could be that Americans, through their political and policy choices, might in the future judge it socially desirable to fill chronic vacancies in math and science teaching in the public schools by providing the necessary financial or other incentives to draw more talented people into these occupations. Then societal need and market demand would come into harmony. Short of that, however, reasonable people could say that societal needs exceed labor market demand in a number of fields though, of course, not all would agree.

In a fast-moving, technology-driven, knowledge economy, however, another important dynamic is at work. In circumstances where the supply of well-educated people exceeds market demand for them in traditional types of employment, the evidence suggests that the educated find creative ways to employ themselves and that these new jobs often turn out to be productive for society and the economy in the long run. This pattern is sometimes referred to as "supply creates its own demand." For example, in a recession or after an episode of corporate downsizing, some of those with undergraduate or graduate degrees may become self-employed as consultants or entrepreneurs.[2] In general, the educated have advantages in finding decent-paying piecework and tend to be more successful as entrepreneurs.[3] Although the shift to self-employment may cause people to experience dislocation, discomfort, or reduced earnings, it offers a viable way for well-educated people to wait out slack periods in the economy. These self-employment opportunities will likely grow for those who are prepared to take advantage of them, given the increased pattern of white-collar layoffs related to corporate restructuring and the multitude of niche markets being created by technological changes, marketing efforts, and the global reach of information and communications technology.[4] Those who are better educated are, in general, better prepared to take advantage.

Moreover, the educated are more likely to seek additional education and to benefit readily from it.[5] That is, those with higher levels of educational attainment are more likely to seek additional training or education and thereby qualify for employment in fields that are in greater demand. In addition, workers with higher levels of educational attainment tend to be more willing to move geographically for better job opportunities. Finally, were excess supply to last for a lengthy period, there is good evidence that incoming students adjust their enrollment patterns over time to reduce production of unwanted degrees.[6] Economic theory and evidence show that labor market imbalances—both surpluses and shortages of workers in relation to jobs that call for their qualifications—are short-lived as long as market forces are allowed to clear them over time.

There is a theoretical downside, however, to having plentiful supplies of degree holders relative to traditional sources of demand. For example, with plentiful supplies of college degree holders available for jobs that formerly employed high school graduates, some employers may decide to hire those with college degrees even though such degrees were not previously a requirement for employment, thereby displacing those whose educational credentials are no longer competitive. Some analysts call this "credential inflation," and its occurrence has been documented in conditions of a slack economy.[7] If the higher level of education were genuinely superfluous, this would represent a waste of society's resources. Yet, if employers found the additional credentials to be of no value in the workplace, then why would they make such choices, particularly when retaining better-educated workers leads to higher wages in the long run? Most studies show that the earnings trajectories of college graduates are steeper over time than those with less education working in the same job.[8] Unless employers are profligate or unobservant enough to reward employees without regard to their productivity, it is likely that they are willing to pay more at the outset for the signals that advanced educational credentials provide about applicants' motivations or abilities, including the ability to learn more when necessary. These positive attributes are then further rewarded over the employee's job tenure. This pattern is another example of the apparent excess supply of the well educated creating new sources of demand for them.[9] The displaced workers with lower, noncompetitive credentials may need assistance, but it is likely that more education is part of the solution for them, too.

RETURNS TO INVESTMENTS IN HIGHER EDUCATION

The private rate of return to investment in higher education can be defined as that which accrues to individuals, through their labor market earnings and other benefits, as a result of their investment in higher education. For decades, this rate of return has been growing substantially in the United States. From 1980 to 2007, the annual earnings advantage for 25- to 34-year-olds who have a bachelor's degree, compared with those with only a high school diploma, climbed from 34 percent to 67 percent for women and from 19 percent to 61 percent for men.[10] Currently, those with a master's degree earn about 24 percent more than graduates with only a bachelor's degree, and those with a graduate-level professional degree earn 85 percent more than those with a bachelor's degree. According to standard economic theory, earnings from work generally represent a good approximation of the relative value to the economy of the skills, or human capital, associated with different levels of education.[11] Of course, students and parents are also well aware of the association between college degree attainment and other aspects of desirable careers, such as job-related benefits, satisfaction, social status, longer life, better health, better child-rearing outcomes, and lower rates of social dysfunction.[12] Public opinion research suggests that a substantial majority of the population now believe that higher education is a necessary investment for most young people today.[13]

Econometric studies indicate that as much as 90 percent of the difference in earnings between those with more education compared with less is likely accounted for by education alone rather than other variables.[14] Economists have also found that investments by individuals and governments in the development of human capital are generally good economic investments, with a rate of return at least comparable to that for physical capital investments such as in industrial machines and public infrastructure.[15] George Psacharopoulos and Henry Patrinos, in their review of international research spanning ninety-eight countries, estimate individual ("private") returns to higher education investment to average about 19 percent annually across these countries. They also estimate the "social" returns, which take into account public costs in addition to tuition and other costs paid by students but generally do not consider societal benefits other than earnings and taxes paid, to be about 11 percent annually.[16] Their estimates for member countries of the Organisation for Economic Co-operation and Development (OECD) are lower but still strong: 11.6 percent for private returns and 8.5 percent for social returns. The latest available study for the United States estimated social returns to investment in higher education at 12 percent annually.[17]

Also for the United States, Psacharopoulos and Patrinos cite a number of studies using identical twins to identify the unique effect of education on earnings, independent of family background and genetic factors. These consistently find annual earnings advantages of about 10 percent for an additional year of schooling.[18] By comparing several studies in the United States that used similar methodologies, the authors also report a positive trend over time in the effect on earnings from an additional year of schooling: from 7.5 percent in 1976 to 10.0 percent for the period from 1991 to 1995.[19]

The knowledge economy can be characterized as depending increasingly on pervasive information and communications technologies that change rapidly and allow companies to respond promptly to market developments. It is also an economy in which globalization makes environmental challenges more ominous and intercultural understanding more important. In this context of increasing complexity, it is likely that advanced education will continue to bring increased economic and social returns.[20]

GROWING "WAGE PREMIUMS" FOR EDUCATION AND GROWING INEQUALITY

As the U.S. economy has restructured in response to new technology and global competition, college graduates—particularly women—have been doing considerably better in the labor market than those with less education, in spite of general increases in numbers of the better educated in the labor force (see figures 2.1 and 2.2). Most striking are the relative gains in the real incomes of those with graduate and professional degrees to which the bachelor's degree provides the gateway. The stronger link between education and income evident in recent decades is closely related to the growing inequality of incomes in the United States (and elsewhere).[21] Thus, the gaps are increasing between those in the upper parts of the income distribution and those in the lower parts (see figure 2.3). In addition, all income groups below the top quintile are experiencing rather sluggish gains in real incomes compared to the earlier postwar period up to 1973, the date usually associated with the onset in earnest of economic restructuring.[22] Of course, the upper-income groups contain far more college graduates than the lower-income quintiles.

FIGURE 2.1   Median income for men 25 years or older, in constant 2008 dollars, 1963 to 2008

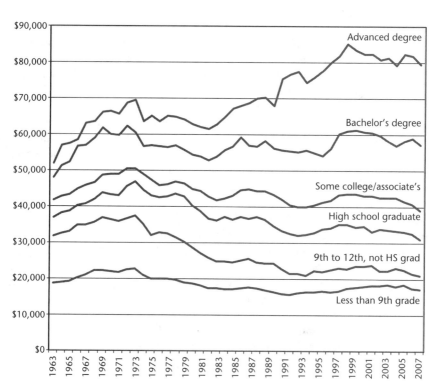

Source: Calculated from the U.S. Census Bureau (2010), tables P-16 and P-18.

Moreover, educational attainment has been increasing much more rapidly at the upper end of the income distribution than at the middle and lower ends (see figure 2.4). According to estimates by Thomas Mortenson, the percentage of people with a bachelor's degree by age 24 increased by 41 percentage points from 1978 to 2006 for the top income quartile but just 3.5 points for the bottom quartile, with the second and third quartiles gaining 8.3 points and 13.1 points, respectively.[23] Also, there are large and growing differences by ethnic group in the percentage of 25- to 29-year-olds with at least a bachelor's degree, according to data from the U.S. Census (see figure 2.5). As of 2008, 31.1 percent of non-Hispanic whites ages 25 to 29 had a bachelor's degree or more, as compared with 20.6 percent of blacks and 12.4 percent of Hispanics. Bachelor's degree attainment rates for young blacks have been increasing since about 1990, although they remain well below those of whites, while rates for young Hispanics have changed little for twenty-five years.

FIGURE 2.2   Median income for women 25 years or older, in constant 2008 dollars, 1963 to 2008

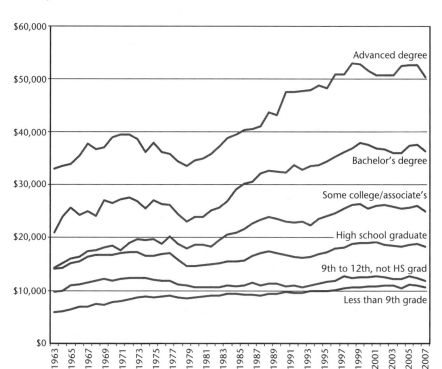

Source: Calculated from the U.S. Census Bureau (2010), tables P-16 and P-18.

A recent study by the Brookings Institution found that education is strongly related to economic mobility, as measured by comparing income data for adults at about age forty during the period 1995 to 2002 with family income data for their parents at about the same age during 1967 to 1971.[24] For children whose parents were in any of the five income quintiles during the period 1967 to 1971, the chances of moving into a higher quintile (or staying in the top quintile) were much greater for those who attained a baccalaureate degree than for those who did not. Of particular note, for individuals without a degree, 45 percent of those starting in the bottom quintile of (parental) family income remained there at age forty, but only 16 percent of those with a college degree were so mired. In fact, 41 percent of those starting in the lowest income quintile who attained a bachelor's degree had made it into one of the top two quintiles at age forty, but only 14 percent of their cohorts without a degree had done so. For those from the second-lowest (parental) family

FIGURE 2.3   Mean family income for each fifth of the population of families earning income, and for the top 5% of families, in 2008 CPI-U-RS adjusted dollars, 1966 to 2008

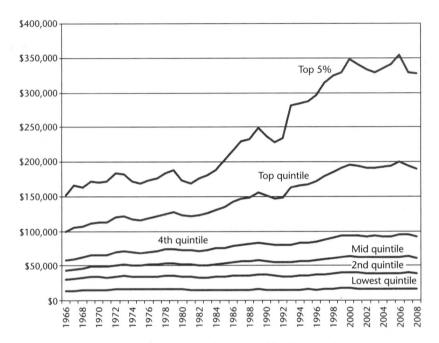

Note: Each quintile represents a fifth (20%) of the total population of families earning income.

Source: U.S. Census Bureau (2010), table F-1.

income cohort, almost half (47 percent) of those with a bachelor's degree had reached one of the top two income quintiles at age forty compared to just 23 percent of those without a degree.[25]

It is not surprising that higher education has been found to be a key factor in achieving the American dream, as represented by intergenerational social and economic mobility. Whereas figure 2.5 displays the gaps in college attainment by race and ethnicity, figure 2.6 shows the differences by parents' income. According to Haskins, 53 percent of children whose parents were in the top income quintile had earned a bachelor's degree at age forty, compared with 20 percent for those from the second-lowest quintile and just 11 percent for those in the bottom fifth of the population by income.[26] In our view, a society with aspirations to social equity should seek to develop policies to decrease these gaps substantially. In addition, if the United States is to produce more college-educated people in an era when a growing share of young people will come from minority ethnic groups and families of modest

FIGURE 2.4   Estimated bachelor's degree attainment by age 24 by family income quartile, 1970 to 2007

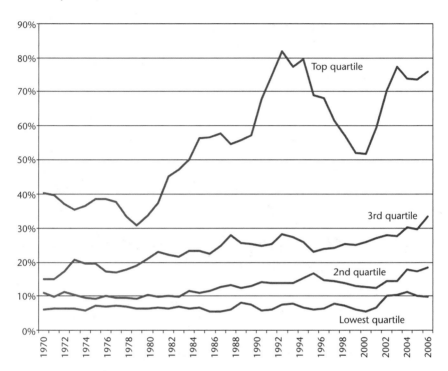

Note: Each quartile represents 25% of the total population of families earning income. Attainment rates for each year represent three-year moving averages.

Source: Calculated from Tom Mortenson, *Postsecondary Education Opportunities*, 2009, http://www.postsecondary.org/spreadslist.asp.

means, then the nation's public policies must be designed to improve performance in preparing these students for college and helping them succeed in earning a degree.

INCREASES IN JOBS CALLING FOR HIGH LEVELS OF EDUCATION

Recent decades have seen steady increases in the proportions of jobs held by individuals with college degrees.[27] Based on the most recent comparative data from the Department of Labor's Bureau of Labor Statistics (BLS), professional and related occupations had the largest increase in the number of jobs (4.1 million) and growth rate (17.8 percent) from 1999 to 2008 (see table 2.1). Compared with other employment categories, this grouping of professional jobs contains the largest proportion of baccalaureate and advanced degree

FIGURE 2.5   Percentage of 25- to 29-year-olds with at least a bachelor's degree, by race and Hispanic origin, selected years, 1940 to 2008

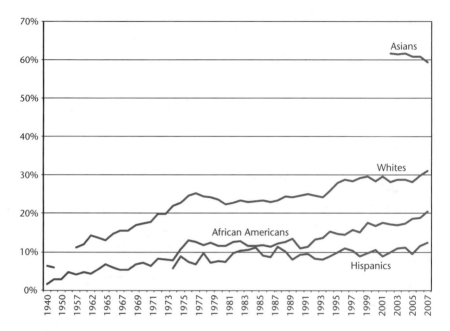

Note: White category does not include Hispanics.

Source: U.S. Census Bureau (2010), table A-2. Data are not available for all years.

holders. Management, business, and financial occupations, the other category that contains large numbers of college graduates, lost jobs overall during the ten-year period, but all of the losses were from 1999 to 2004, during the economic downturn that affected business hiring at the start of this century. From 2004 to 2008, management, business, and financial occupations recovered, gaining jobs steadily. Note that service occupations, which employ a relatively low proportion of college graduates, grew almost as much (3.8 million jobs) and almost as fast (16.8 percent) as professional occupations. Both sales and construction occupations, with modest but growing proportions of college-educated workers, also grew faster than overall employment, but their numerical gains in jobs were far lower than those for the professional and service categories. Meanwhile, production occupations—that is, manufacturing—lost a staggering 21.4 percent of their employment over the decade and saw only moderate and short-lived gains after the economic downturn of 2000 to 2003. There was below-average growth in the other major job categories that generally require modest levels of education: office and administrative support services and installation and maintenance occupations each gained

FIGURE 2.6   Percentage of children with a bachelor's degree, by parents' family income quintile, 2005

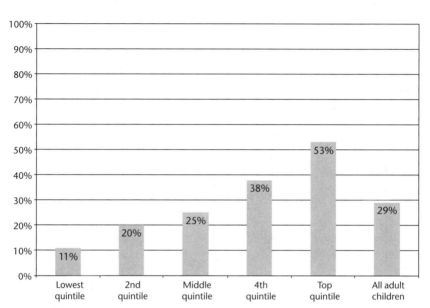

Source: Haskins, "Education and Social Mobility," 96.

less than 5 percent in number of jobs. Farming, fishing, and forestry jobs declined by more than 5 percent. These numbers reflect the disparate trends in a labor market that tends to favor the well educated but also employed many people in low-paid service occupations that require little education.

The BLS also projects future trends in the U.S. labor market. Its estimates are derived from underlying projections of growth in aggregate economic output and of particular industries and sectors (on which estimates of the demand for labor in more than 750 occupational categories are based).[28] Consistent with the trends over the past decade, the rapid growth in professional and related occupations is projected to continue from 2008 to 2018.[29] The BLS estimates that this grouping of occupations will add more than 5.2 million jobs (or 16.8 percent) over the decade, which is more than a third (34 percent) of the 15.3 million total net jobs the economy is expected to gain (see table 2.2). This category includes a large share of jobs typically occupied by workers with higher education credentials, such as health-care practitioners and technical occupations, a subcategory expected to gain about 1.6 million jobs, or 21.4 percent (see table 2.3).[30] Professional and related occupations in education, training, and library services are expected to gain 1.3 million jobs, or 14.4 percent, and the grouping of computer and mathematical

TABLE 2.1
Employment by major occupational group from 1999 to 2008 (numbers in thousands)

National employment matrix code and title	1999	2000	2001	2002	2003	2004	2005	2006	2007	2008	Change, 1999 to 2008	
											Number	Percent
00-0000 Total, all occupations	127,273	129,739	127,980	127,526	127,567	129,145	130,305	132,604	134,352	135,185	7,912	6.2
15-2900 Professional and related occupations[1]	23,197	23,913	24,102	24,236	24,427	25,203	25,510	26,111	26,680	27,325	4,128	17.8
31-3900 Service occupations[2]	22,449	23,022	23,076	23,416	23,674	24,481	24,749	25,183	25,730	26,215	3,766	16.8
41-0000 Sales and related occupations	12,938	13,507	13,418	13,340	13,534	13,714	13,930	14,115	14,332	14,336	1,398	10.8
47-0000 Construction and extraction occupations	5,939	6,187	6,239	6,125	6,085	6,303	6,370	6,681	6,708	6,549	610	10.3
49-0000 Installation, maintenance, and repair occupations	5,140	5,318	5,323	5,216	5,226	5,247	5,305	5,352	5,390	5,374	234	4.6
43-0000 Office and administrative support occupations	22,562	22,936	22,799	22,755	22,678	22,622	22,784	23,077	23,270	23,232	670	3.0
53-0000 Transportation and material moving occupations	9,539	9,593	9,411	9,395	9,415	9,597	9,594	9,648	9,629	9,509	-30	-0.3
11-1300 Management, business, and financial occupations[3]	12,425	12,402	11,889	11,865	11,578	11,339	11,371	11,719	12,019	12,289	-136	-1.1
45-0000 Farming, fishing, and forestry occupations	463	461	453	451	462	445	443	450	448	438	-25	-5.4
51-0000 Production occupations	12,621	12,400	11,270	10,727	10,488	10,194	10,249	10,268	10,146	9,919	-2,702	-21.4

Source: Adapted from U.S. Bureau of Labor Statistic (2008), Historical Occupational Data.

[1]Major occupational groups 15-0000 through 29-0000 in the 2000 *Standard Occupational Classification*.
[2]Major occupational groups 31-0000 through 39-0000 in the 2000 *Standard Occupational Classification*.
[3]Major occupational groups 11-0000 through 13-0000 in the 2000 *Standard Occupational Classification*.

TABLE 2.2

Employment by major occupational group in 2008 and projected for 2018 (numbers in thousands)

2008 national employment matrix code and title	Employment (number)		Percent distribution		Change, 2008 to 2018	
	2008	2018	2008	2018	Number	Percent
00-0000 Total, all occupations	150,932	166,206	100.0	100.0	15,274	10.1
15-2900 Professional and related occupations[1]	31,054	36,280	20.6	21.8	5,227	16.8
31-3900 Service occupations[2]	29,576	33,645	19.6	20.2	4,069	13.8
47-0000 Construction and extraction occupations	7,810	8,829	5.2	5.3	1,019	13.0
11-1300 Management, business, and financial occupations[3]	15,747	17,411	10.4	10.5	1,664	10.6
43-0000 Office and administrative support occupations	24,101	25,943	16.0	15.6	1,842	7.6
49-0000 Installations, maintenance, and repair occupations	5,798	6,238	3.8	3.8	440	7.6
41-0000 Sales and related occupations	15,903	16,883	10.5	10.2	980	6.2
53-0000 Transportation and material moving occupations	9,826	10,217	6.5	6.1	391	4.0
45-0000 Farming, fishing, and forestry occupations	1,035	1,026	0.7	0.6	–9	–0.9
51-0000 Production occupations	10,083	9,734	6.7	5.9	–349	–3.5

Source: Bartsch, "The Employment Projections for 2008–18," table 3, 9.

[1]Major occupational groups 15-0000 through 29-0000 in the 2000 *Standard Occupational Classification*.

[2]Major occupational groups 31-0000 through 39-0000 in the 2000 *Standard Occupational Classification*.

[3]Major occupational groups 11-0000 through 13-0000 in the 2000 *Standard Occupational Classification*.

science occupations is projected to have the largest percentage gain, at 22.2 percent, with an increase in job numbers of 786,000.

Management, business, and financial occupations, a second broad category with a large share of jobs calling for college and advanced degrees, are projected to add nearly 1.7 million jobs from 2008 to 2018 (see table 2.2). The projected growth rate for this grouping of jobs, at 10.6 percent, is slightly higher than that expected for employment overall. Service occupations are projected to grow at a rate of 13.8 percent and are projected to add about 4.1 million new jobs, in part to serve the needs of aging baby boomers. Among the other broad categories, those with projected job losses (that is, production occupations and farming, fishing, and forestry) and those with smaller numerical gains (that is, installations, maintenance, and repair occupations and transportation and material moving) tend to have low densities of college graduates. Projected for somewhat larger numerical gains over the decade are office and administrative support jobs and sales and related occupations, both of which tend to require moderate levels of education.

Based on the projected shifts in employment and the current levels of education needed in each occupation, the BLS projects the numbers of employed individuals at each level of education in 2018 (see table 2.4). The largest percentage growth rates in employment are expected to be for those holding associate's degrees (19.1 percent), master's degrees (18.3 percent), first professional degrees (17.6 percent), bachelor's degrees and doctoral degrees (both at 16.6 percent), and postsecondary vocational awards (13.2 percent). The less education-intensive categories have projected growth rates below the 10.1 percent gain expected for employment as a whole. In aggregate, the number

TABLE 2.3

Employment within professional and related occupations for 2008 and projected for 2018

	Numeric change (thousands)	Percent change
Total, professional and related occupations	5,227	16.8
Computer and mathematical science	786	22.2
Health-care practitioners and technical	1,560	21.4
Life, physical, and social science	277	19.0
Community and social services	448	16.5
Legal	188	15.1
Education, training, and library services	1,324	14.4
Arts, design, entertainment, sports, and media	333	12.1
Architecture and engineering	271	10.3

Source: Lacey and Wright, "Occupational Employment Projections to 2018," table 2, 85.

of employed postsecondary degree holders (that is, associate's degree and up) is expected to increase by 15.7 percent, compared with about half that (7.8 percent) for those with only work experience or on-the-job training and no postsecondary credential. The growth in employment for those holding postsecondary vocational awards is projected to be in between at 13.2 percent. Thus, the BLS projects that the U.S. labor market will become appreciably more education intensive over the 2008–2018 decade.

It is important to note, however, that these growth rates do not imply that "college for all" is on the near horizon in terms of the demands of the labor market. The total number of jobs in 2018 that will be held by people without any postsecondary credential is still expected to be far larger, at about 104.3 million, than the number where a college degree (associate's or higher) is the predominant credential, at 37.8 million, and the absolute gain in the former classes of jobs will outstrip the latter by 8.1 million to 6.0 million.[31] This bifurcated pattern in labor market demand by level of education reflects the same underlying forces in the economy that have led to growing inequality in earnings by level of education.

In terms of public policy, we believe that the implication of these disparate patterns is not to try to engineer the education system to meet or follow the market, but rather to have educational output lead the market modestly. As long as the rate of growth in the well educated is not too great, this approach will likely attract and help create more high-quality jobs within the economy. Such a growth pattern is a fairly ambitious goal, but the evident prospects of continued stronger growth in jobs for and earnings returns to the more educated suggest that facilitating more individual investment in college or graduate education is warranted, at least until the returns show signs of diminishing.[32] Further, college attendance and degree attainment rates in relation to the size of the U.S. population have been sluggish in recent years.[33] The number of Americans in the traditional college-age group is leveling off. And increasing numbers of these young people are from racial and ethnic groups that have lower historic enrollment and completion rates in college. Under these conditions, there appears to be little danger of overshooting the mark—that is, of producing too many graduates—any time soon.[34]

Moreover, many labor market analysts have suggested that the BLS projections concerning the gains in educational credentials sought by employers (observed as workers' credentials) are too conservative. Alpert and Auyer and Stekler and Thomas have assessed the accuracy of the projections, focusing mostly on BLS forecasts from 1988 to 2000.[35] The major conclusions from these and earlier such evaluations are that, while the BLS is generally accurate about the direction of employment changes, there are substantial projection errors in many job categories, averaging in the 20 percent to 25 percent range. The projections tend to be conservative, underestimating job growth in more occupations than are overestimated and underestimating large

TABLE 2.4

Employment and total job openings, by education and training category, in 2008 and projected for 2018 (numbers in thousands)

Most significant source of education and training	Employment				Change, 2008 to 2018		Total job openings due to growth and net replacement needs, 2008 to 2018[1]		May 2008 median annual wages[2]
	Number		Percent distribution						
	2008	2018	2008	2018	Number	Percent	Number	Percent distribution	
Total, all occupations	150,932	166,206	100.0	100.0	15,274	10.1	50,928	100.0	$32,390
Associate degree	6,129	7,297	4.1	4.4	1,168	19.1	2,372	4.7	$54,320
Master's degree	2,531	2,995	1.7	1.8	464	18.3	1,008	2.0	$55,170
First professional degree	2,001	2,354	1.3	1.4	353	17.6	746	1.5	$122,550
Bachelor's degree	18,584	21,669	12.3	13.0	3,085	16.6	7,072	13.9	$57,770
Doctoral degree	2,085	2,430	1.4	1.5	345	16.6	743	1.5	$61,200
Postsecondary vocational award	8,787	9,952	5.8	6.0	1,164	13.2	2,927	5.7	$32,380
Bachelor's or higher degree, plus work experience	6,519	7,068	4.3	4.3	550	8.4	2,106	4.1	$89,720
Work experience in a related occupation	14,517	15,697	9.6	9.4	1,180	8.1	4,196	8.2	$45,650
Moderate-term on-the-job training	24,568	26,531	16.3	16.0	1,963	8.0	7,059	13.9	$30,640
Long-term on-the-job training	10,815	11,621	7.2	7.0	806	7.5	3,081	6.1	$39,630
Short-term on-the-job training	54,396	58,593	36.0	35.3	4,197	7.7	19,619	38.5	$21,320

Source: Lacey and Wright, "Occupational Employment Projections to 2018," table 3, 88.

[1]Total job openings represent the sum of employment increases and net replacements.

[2]For wage and salary workers, from the Occupational Employment Statistics survey.

changes on both the growth and decline sides. (This is not surprising, since impacts of dramatic technological and structural changes are inherently difficult to predict.) In fact, the BLS projections from 1988 to 2000 of growth in what was then called the "professional specialty" category (similar to what is now called "professional and related occupations") were underestimated by the largest absolute amount among the major occupational categories—by 2.29 million jobs, or 11.2 percent of the actual 2000 employment level.[36]

Economist Anthony Carnevale, director of the Center on Education and the Workforce at Georgetown University and former vice president at the Educational Testing Service, has also argued that the BLS projections are too conservative. His main analytic point is that the bureau's methodology for estimating the future distribution of educational credentials among workers ignores long-standing upward trends in these credentials *within* job categories, since the bureau considers only the effects of shifts *among* occupational categories. He estimates that only one-third of increases in educational requirements can be attributed to changes in occupational mix, while the remaining two-thirds are more appropriately credited to "upskilling" within job categories, which BLS ignores.[37] Table 2.5, from Carnevale, compares BLS projections for the period 2002 to 2012 with projections he and Jeffrey Strohl derived from a "projection of postsecondary upskilling [based] on a relatively simple and conservative regression model produced by an analysis of actual changes in postsecondary attainment by occupation and industry between 1992 and 2004."[38] In short, these analysts have extrapolated recent past trends in the proportion of college graduates in jobs into the future.

On this basis, Carnevale projects relatively large additional employment for bachelor's degree holders (2.9 million, or 42 percent more shown in column 6 than in column 3) and graduate degree holders (7.75 million, or 221 percent more) compared to the gains BLS projected for 2012. At the same time, the upskilling trend leads to reduced need for associate degree holders and those with some college relative to the BLS projections, though Carnevale's projected numbers for 2012 are still higher than the actual numbers of jobs held by people with these credentials in 2002.

In 2010, Carnevale and associates published an update of their projections of demand for and supply of workers with various education levels in the U.S. economy.[39] These latest projections cover the decade from 2008 to 2018. Figure 2.7 shows how these analysts see the inexorable growth in demand for postsecondary credentials and also provides historical context. In 2007, about 59 percent of the work force had some postsecondary education or training and 32 percent held a bachelor's degree or more, compared to just 28 percent and 16 percent, respectively, in 1973. By 2018, they project that the percentage with any postsecondary education or training will climb to 62 percent, while the fraction with a bachelor's or more will reach 33 percent. Carnevale et al. express concern, though, that the supply side of the system

TABLE 2.5

Differences between official projections of jobs in 2012 and projections assuming historical rates of upskilling in educational credentials

	1. Actual jobs and education levels in 2002	2. Official projection of jobs in 2012 holding educational attainment constant by occupation	3. Difference between 2002 actual jobs and 2012 official projection	4. Projections of job increases or decreases to 2012 based on historical increases in postsecondary education requirements	5. Difference in number of jobs between 2002 and projected 2012	6. Difference between corrected and official projections
Less-than-high-school jobs	16,482,666	18,069,367	1,586,701	12,068,287	(4,414,379)	(6,001,080)
Jobs that require high school	44,698,388	51,612,592	6,914,204	50,256,976	5,558,579	(1,355,616)
Jobs that require some college	27,559,941	30,187,249	2,627,308	28,930,825	1,370,884	(1,256,424)
Associate's degree	12,327,598	16,912,134	4,584,536	15,044,029	2,716,431	(1,868,105)
Bachelor's degree	26,406,079	33,295,247	6,889,168	36,204,861	9,798,782	2,909,614
Graduate degree	12,809,023	15,225,880	2,416,857	22,979,341	10,170,318	7,753,461
Total civilian jobs	140,286,000	165,302,000	25,018,774	165,483,000	25,200,615	7,753,461

© 2008 from Anthony P. Carnevale, "College for All," *The Magazine for Higher Learning* 40, no. 1 (2008), 27. Reproduced by permission of Taylor & Francis Group, LLC., http://www.taylorandfrancis.com.

will fall seriously short of meeting this projected demand, estimating a short-fall of about 3 million college degree holders (associate's degrees and higher) by 2018 if degree production rates follow existing patterns and trends.[40] They estimate that an annual increase of about 10 percent would be required to eliminate the shortfall.

FIGURE 2.7   Carnevale et al.'s 2018 projection of postsecondary demand, by degree level

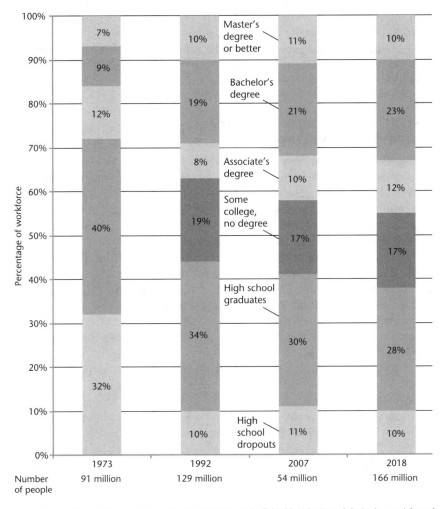

Source: Adapted from Anthony P. Carnevale, Nicole Smith, and Jeff Strohl, *Help Wanted: Projections on Jobs and Education Requirements Through 2018* (Washington, DC; Georgetown University Center on Education and the Workforce, 2010), Figure 2, 14, http://cew.georgetown.edu.

While these analysts' extrapolations from past upskilling trends may be too general, in part because they make no attempt to assess how much education is needed for particular jobs, Carnevale et al.'s underlying point seems hard to refute based on recent trends and what we know about contemporary economic change. Employment of the more educated will almost certainly reflect some upskilling within job categories over time as well as shifts in the mix of job categories that trend in the same direction. Although some might say that a part of this upskilling represents unnecessary credential inflation, we have argued earlier that, as long as earnings growth rates for the more educated remain strong over time (and especially over individuals' careers), the argument that increases in the credentials of job holders are unproductive is hard to sustain, especially in an increasingly knowledge-based economy. As we have argued, wage premiums for the more educated are the key market signal to track regarding the need for them. In spite of the Great Recession's impact on nearly all workers, these premiums remain near historic highs.

UNCERTAINTIES ABOUT THESE FORECASTS: THE POTENTIAL OF "OFFSHORING"

Forecasts are always subject to error, especially those that are dependent upon assumptions about the nature and pace of technological change. Today, economic and technological change is more than ever a globalized phenomenon; as a result, projections are now complicated by the growing interdependencies among national and regional economies across the globe and by the rapid diffusion of technological innovations. Of particular interest here is the impact of "offshoring": the international outsourcing from the United States of jobs historically performed by college-educated workers here. This phenomenon has been felt for several decades, as reduced transportation costs facilitated the movement of manufacturing overseas several decades ago and of routine services for about a decade (for example, call centers and check processing). Thus far, offshoring has had relatively little impact among highly educated workers.[41] Due to steady improvements in information and communication technologies that permit low-cost electronic transfers of work products, however, many moderately skilled and highly skilled categories of jobs may be vulnerable to such outsourcing.[42]

In its projections of the job market, the BLS seeks to account for the susceptibility of occupations to offshoring, though this process relies on judgment.[43] This is not surprising, since the emergence of offshoring for highly skilled jobs is quite recent, so that pertinent research lacks historical data.[44] Early studies estimated that the United States would lose about 3.4 million white-collar jobs overseas by 2015, a rate of about 300,000 jobs a year from their baseline.[45] Ashok Deo Bardhan and Cynthia Kroll estimated that many more jobs, about 11 percent of the total in the U.S. economy, might be at risk of being offshored, and a more recent McKinsey & Co. study produced a similar figure.[46] Alan Blinder offered a rough estimate "that the total number of current U.S. service-sector jobs that will be susceptible to offshoring in the electronic future is two to three times the total number of current manufacturing jobs (which is about 14 million)."[47]

Ray Uhalde and Jeff Strohl used the U.S. Department of Labor's O*NET database, which identifies the characteristics of occupations, to refine estimates based on offshoring patterns in relation to a range of job characteristics (such as the use of physical strength, the need for proximity to the client, and the ability to perform the work electronically and transport it instantaneously).[48] They estimate that about 8 million jobs are at high risk to be offshored eventually, and another 16 million are at medium risk. Yet another 16 million jobs are considered to be at low risk but still have potential for being offshored. Their selected list of jobs in each of these categories includes:

High Risk for Offshoring
- Computer programmers
- Software engineers
- Accountants and auditors
- Financial credit analysts

Medium Risk for Offshoring
- Management analysts
- Tax preparers
- Architects
- Civil engineers

Low Risk for Offshoring
- Physicians, surgeons, and health-care support
- Marketing and sales managers
- Real estate brokers and agents[49]

BLS analysts Roger Moncarz, Michael Wolf, and Benjamin Wright analyzed the offshoring potential of service occupations, finding that 160 of a total of 515 service occupations in the BLS inventory had some potential for offshoring.[50] As a group, these 160 occupations contained a higher proportion of those with bachelor's and advanced degrees (54 percent) in 2007 than all service occupations (37 percent). But the occupations considered most susceptible to offshoring had only about 30 percent of such degree holders and relatively low wages.[51] The analysts also found that among the offshorable occupations within the service sector, those with a larger proportion of bachelor's and advanced degree holders saw the fastest domestic employment and wage growth over the 2001 to 2007 period, while those occupations requiring lower levels of education gained the fewest jobs and had significantly slower wage growth. In its labor force forecasts at that time (for 2006 to 2016), the BLS projected the continuation of these growth rate trends.[52]

Determining that an occupational category is at risk of offshoring does not imply that all or even most pertinent jobs will move. Moreover, forecasting the pace at which they may move is difficult. In examining current job-migration patterns, studies show that the level and pace of increase is modest and that firms consider many factors other than labor cost advantages when they decide whether to move jobs or functions abroad. According to McKinsey & Co., these factors "include the location's risk profile, the quality of its infrastructure, the size of the domestic market, non-labor costs, its business and living environment, and the availability of vendors."[53] McKinsey's research shows that small companies, which make up a large portion of the U.S. economy, are much less likely to send work offshore. This is primarily because management tends to be less comfortable with the idea and does not want to bear the start-up and ongoing oversight costs that seem large relative to any potential cost savings for a small employer. Overall, McKinsey reports, "Our research finds that management resistance is the biggest factor holding back offshoring today, not government regulations."[54]

In sum, McKinsey estimates that "U.S. companies will create 200,000 to 300,000 offshore jobs per year over the next 30 years" and that "the impact of offshoring on U.S. wages is imperceptible and its effects on employment are very small compared with normal job turnover in the economy"—conditions that the authors expect to persist for the foreseeable future.[55] The report also makes the important point that, by helping U.S. companies to remain competitive, offshoring of some suitable jobs and production likely leads to net gains in U.S. employment as firms invest a portion of cost savings in new technology and market development. Many of these new jobs are in the higher-skill categories, such as systems analysts and software engineers rather than programmers.[56]

Finally, the McKinsey authors recognize the concerns and political contention that surround trade policies, and they call for better policies to help displaced workers in the United States to obtain more education and training so as to qualify for more promising employment.[57] Such policies could make it politically more palatable to pursue efficient trade policies. Their recommendation underscores the key role of higher education in preparing people to respond to the job shifts associated with the transition toward a global, knowledge-based economy.[58] As Blinder and others assure, flexible labor markets will adjust to shifting global competitive pressures and opportunities.[59] To help people respond to these market adjustments, the United States can do more to facilitate their education and training, and thereby help them take advantage of the opportunities created in a global economy.

SKEPTICAL VIEWS ON GROWING DEMAND FOR HIGHER EDUCATION

Some analysts question the more expansive forecasts of growth in labor market demand for higher education. Prominent among these are: former Labor Department official Paul Barton; analysts based at the Economic Policy Institute, especially Michael Handel and Lawrence Mishel and Richard Rothstein; and academic scholars Norton Grubb and Marvin Lazerson.[60] While all agree that there will be some growth in labor market demand for higher education, they question the forecasts of Carnevale and associates and the New Commission on the Skills of the American Workforce.[61] They also tend to see the BLS projections (see table 2.4), which we and others have suggested are somewhat conservative, as close to the true mark. Using primarily BLS data for past periods, they indicate that recent trends suggest, at most, a modest rate of upskilling of jobs and that the data on employment by education mask some overqualification for the jobs that exist. Mishel and Rothstein note the dip in real earnings of college degree holders from about 1999 to 2003 (see figures 2.1 and 2.2) and conclude that this portends a possible glut.[62] They believe that any newly available public resources would be better spent on human capital investments outside the college realm (with the exception of measures to improve equity in financial aid to students) on worker protections, subsidized health insurance, better social services for the needy, and greater macroeconomic stimulus.

Norton Grubb and Marvin Lazerson echo some of these ideas in their recommendations in *The Education Gospel*.[63] They focus on the need to improve the links between schooling and work at an earlier point in the educational system, to enhance the quality and equity of K–12 schooling, and to find appropriate pathways to attractive careers for students who are not much interested in college. They seek to improve the clarity of career ladders and "crosswalks" so that youths who choose vocational pathways at the outset have well-understood and subsidized opportunities to enhance their human capital once in the labor market—even to attain a college degree—and to be rewarded for doing so. They are skeptical about the need for any more college-educated individuals than a continuation of recent, modest, upward degree-output trends would produce.

A more theoretically based skeptical view holds that the generally strong average labor market returns to higher education may not fully, or even mostly, represent returns to skills expensively developed in schools and colleges. Rather, these returns include a substantial element of mere *signaling* to employers as to who likely has the attitudes and intellect to succeed in work because they showed they could succeed in school.[64] Moreover, it is well known that, when labor is plentiful, employers tend to ramp up the requirements for jobs in a phenomenon described earlier as credential inflation, arguably beyond that which is strictly required for jobs.[65] Even when labor market conditions shift, the higher credentialing requirements tend to persist. The implication is that society may be paying for more higher education than it truly needs.

Skeptics raise another line of argument about the priority of expanding higher education that points to the failings of the nation's elementary and secondary schools and to pervasive social conditions that relate to these failings. High school dropout rates have long been in the 25 percent range, and, even among those who make it to college, the proportions that must take remedial (precollege) classes are strikingly high: 50 percent and more for community college students and those attending nonselective baccalaureate institutions.[66] Students who begin in precollege classes are relatively unlikely to complete a college degree.[67] Given such inputs to the higher education system, this argument goes, how is a program to increase the number of graduates as a proportion of all youth realistically possible, at least until school performance can be greatly improved?

On the left politically, skeptics of the need to focus on college graduate numbers emphasize addressing poverty and inequality as more fundamental policy priorities. They argue that chronic urban and rural poverty and associated unfavorable neighborhood conditions, together with low and stagnant worker earnings in the lower end of the labor market and unequal public school resources disfavoring the less well-off, are the fundamental culprits in poor school—and eventually college—performance. For them, attacking these chronic social problems while also creating incentives for effective teachers to work and stay in the highest-need schools are the most logical routes to improving the nation's human capital over the long haul.

Interestingly, conservative skeptics build on many of the same "facts" and come to similar negative conclusions about the need to expand college output, but, of course, their priorities are ultimately different. While they generally agree that the modern economy places a higher premium than in the past on worker skills, like the skeptics on the left, they are dubious that the demand is as strong as higher education advocates claim. They emphasize the signs of overeducation for some current jobs already mentioned as well as the same chronic problems with secondary school preparation. But their favored solutions lie in efforts to improve school and social conditions by emphasizing local control, school choice, and stricter discipline, rather than by means of large-scale social or redistributive programs.[68] They tend to focus on the demands for workers with technical skills of the types created by some community college and for-profit sector vocational programs and on-the-job training.[69] At the extreme, one prominent pair of skeptics goes so far as to question how broadly distributed in the population are the basic intellectual talents and inclinations that would permit a person to benefit from a college education.[70] Students, employers, and society would be better served, they argue, by radically reducing the size and scope of the baccalaureate collegiate enterprise in favor of more explicitly vocationally oriented secondary and postsecondary schools and a much better developed system of nonschool-based testing for entry into occupations and professions.

CONCLUSION

We are well aware of the imprecise nature of forecasting the labor market's future demand for people of varying levels of education. We are also sympathetic to the notion that the future prosperity of the nation and equitable distribution of its benefits depend upon more than higher education policies. In particular, broad-ranging steps that begin early to improve students' preparation for college are crucial, and Grubb and Lazerson's ideas for creating a more seamless system spanning K–12 education, postsecondary education (including but not limited to traditional college education), and work in a knowledge-intensive society are on the right track. Our primary focus here, however, is on assessing the amount of college education capacity and output the United States needs so that the nation and the states can develop policies to meet those demands.

The predominant labor market evidence, barring large unforeseen future shifts, indicates that the economy could and would profitably absorb substantially more college graduates than the BLS forecasts call for. The BLS projections are conservative primarily because they do not take account of the long-standing—and we believe largely productive—pattern whereby educational credentials tend to increase over time within job categories. Moreover, even if growth in the number of college degrees awarded were to outpace conventionally defined labor-market demand modestly, historical patterns suggest that the excess not only would be profitably absorbed but also would likely stimulate further "endogenous growth" through innovation and entrepreneurship.

The greater challenge, however, will likely be to maintain historical patterns of growth in degree output, which stands as a minimal target if the nation is to remain competitive internationally. Overshooting the mark significantly relative to labor market demand is unlikely, given that the young U.S. population is increasingly made up of people of color and of lower-income status. With the exception of some Asian American subgroups, these populations have not fared well, relative to higher-income and white students, in preparing for college, enrolling in college, and completing college degrees. To serve these populations successfully, colleges and universities will likely need either more resources per student or, more feasibly, a great deal more ingenuity and efficiency to improve upon the gradual gains in numbers of graduates that we have taken for granted. In light of the severe difficulties facing public finances generally and the pattern of stagnation in state support for higher education that the last several decades have witnessed, this challenge is great indeed. The remainder of this book considers how the challenge can be met in practical and politically feasible ways. The next two chapters begin this task by describing historical patterns and recent trends in the finance structure of American higher education.

CHAPTER 3

Finance and Policy

A Historical Perspective

In order to understand the opportunities and constraints that the nation and states face in financing higher education over the next decades, it is essential to examine key historical factors—political, economic, demographic, social, and cultural—that have been most influential in getting us here. This chapter describes the evolution of higher education finance from the late nineteenth century through the 1970s, with an emphasis on public policy as it has shaped public and private higher education. We provide a more detailed analysis of public than private higher education, because public two-year and four-year colleges and universities have been the central vehicles for expanding access and opportunity since the mid-twentieth century. Our purpose here and in the next chapter is to paint a broad picture historically, highlighting major themes in finance policy, both at the state and federal levels. Chapter 5 offers a more detailed and contemporary analysis of state finance policy.

Under the U.S. Constitution, the individual states are responsible for higher education, and their role was well established by the end of the nineteenth century. The modern federal role in supporting student financial aid and research took shape only after World War II. Prior to that, the most significant federal initiative was the 1862 Morrill Act—the Land Grant Act—which offered federal land to the states for the support of higher education. The proceeds derived by states from land sales were to be dedicated to the support of colleges offering instruction in such applied fields as agriculture, mining, mechanics, and the military. Some states created new institutions and gave them the land-grant designation; other states provided the proceeds and the designation to existing colleges.

The gift of federal land for educational purposes had precedents, most notably in the Northwest Ordinance of 1787, which awarded land grants to states based on formulas determined by Congress. The Land Grant Act, however, can be seen as the first national initiative in higher education on the part of the federal government. Its primary influence on higher education was to support, initially, the establishment of state universities and land-grant colleges and, eventually, university-sponsored agricultural research. It was also significant in recognizing, as a key aspect of an American federal system, the states as the primary authority in higher education. The Land Grant Act deferred to the states and the institutions themselves concerning the major decisions on whether and how to respond to the federal incentive.

Two additional characteristics of the Land Grant Act—implied rather than explicit—carried over to later federal initiatives. First, the legislation responded to perceived national needs, however vaguely defined, to provide greater educational opportunity and to do so by focusing on applied disciplines. Second, much of the act's support derived from interest in resolving practical questions raised in the disposal of federal lands, as well as interest in higher education. Whatever the motivations, the impetus for the legislation was utilitarian, with higher education as an instrument of two broad national purposes: economic development and college opportunity.

World War II is the next landmark in federal financing of higher education. Prior to the war, the United States experienced the Great Depression of the 1930s, which saw falling production, prices, and employment. Indeed, unemployment rates in the United States were in double digits throughout that decade, peaking at 24.9 percent in 1933.[1] Higher education in the pre–World War II era was still a relatively limited activity. In 1929–1930, 1.1 million students were enrolled in higher education, out of a population of 15.28 million 18- to 24-year-olds, an enrollment rate of only 7.2 percent.[2] During the war, the federal government recruited and relied extensively on university research expertise to further wartime objectives, of which the invention of the atomic bomb is the prime example. Because of this collaboration, federal agencies, as well as the public, became increasingly aware of the value of higher education as a vehicle for achieving public purposes.

POST–WORLD WAR II YEARS: 1945 TO 1960

Since the Second World War, federal financing of colleges and universities has been used to meet a variety of public purposes, but generally without coherent, coordinated, or overarching federal policy. Rather, the size and shape of today's federal support can be best understood as the result of sixty-plus years of relatively distinct, ad hoc initiatives, each of which was in response to perceived public needs that have, in turn, evolved over time.

As World War II was drawing to a close, many economists, politicians, and citizens feared that the economy would slide back into depression. One measure designed to absorb veterans returning from the war, the Servicemen's Readjustment Act of 1944 (popularly known as the GI Bill), was enacted by Congress to provide financial support for veterans as an incentive to enroll in higher education.[3] This was the first federal venture into large-scale, direct support of individual students, in contrast to funding for states or colleges. Many higher education leaders initially opposed this landmark legislation, for fear that most veterans would be unprepared for the rigors of college and would, as a result, become a disruptive force on campus. In fact, the opposite was the case: veterans succeeded in college. Most observers now point to this legislation as one of the most successful social interventions in modern times. By 1949–1950, 2.66 million students were enrolled, out of a population of 16.12 million 18- to 24-year-olds, an enrollment rate of 16.5 percent, more than double the rate of 1929–1930.[4] The success of the GI Bill launched the United States toward unprecedented rates of college enrollment and attainment, an advantage that the country held over other developed nations for the next half-century.

To an even greater extent than with the Land Grant Act, the educational provisions in the GI Bill reflected national priorities that were not primarily educational. Specifically, the legislation was not enacted as part of a national policy to broaden higher education access, nor to inaugurate a new era of mass higher education, as, in fact, it did. The bill was, rather, a well-deserved expression of national gratitude to the returning veterans. Even more importantly, however, its practical purposes were to facilitate conversion to a peacetime economy and to avert massive postwar unemployment by keeping a substantial number of veterans out of the labor market.

Intellectual support for the postwar movement to mass higher education came in the form of the Truman Commission Report of 1947, officially titled *Higher Education for American Democracy*.[5] President Truman charged this twenty-eight-member commission chaired by George F. Zook with outlining the changes that would have to occur in higher education if the sharp increase in enrollments funded by the GI Bill were to be met. The commission did not limit itself, however, to the immediate challenge posed by returning veterans, but presented a larger vision for significant and permanent increases in enrollments, in financial support for institutions and students, preparation of faculty, construction of new facilities, and expansion of two-year colleges. The commission's multivolume report called for doubling college and university enrollment over the next decade. It estimated that at least 49 percent of Americans could benefit from two years of college, and at least 32 percent could achieve a baccalaureate degree. The commission cited racial discrimination and economic barriers as impediments to the goal that Americans should have encouragement and broad opportunity to pursue education to the extent of their abilities. To that end, the commission recommended expansion of community colleges, of federal graduate and undergraduate scholarships and fellowships, and of federal support to states (both for operating expenses of public colleges and universities, and for facility costs for public institutions). The commission asserted that the nation was underinvested in higher education, and it recommended that federal legislation prohibit discrimination on the basis of race or religion in college admissions. Although the short-term impact of *Higher Education for American Democracy* on federal policy was limited, the commission's analyses and findings framed the higher education policy agendas of state government, the federal government, and philanthropy over the next quarter-century, with many of its recommendations gaining political traction.[6]

By the early to mid-1950s, the enrollment surge prompted by the GI Bill had run its course. From 1949–1950 to 1955, total numbers in higher education declined slightly, from 2.659 million to 2.597 million.[7] During the Depression years, birth rates remained low in the United States; as a result, the population of 18- to 24-year-olds declined by 1.2 million from 1939–1940 to 1953–1954, and by a million from 1949–1950 to 1953–1954.[8] During this period, many colleges were experiencing enrollment declines, and they were not eager to slip back to smaller numbers permanently, after having expanded to accommodate the GIs.

After the launching of the Soviet satellite Sputnik in 1957, Congress passed the National Defense Education Act (NDEA) of 1958, which inaugurated the modern era of federal support for undergraduate education. This was not, however, the impetus for the bill's support by President Eisenhower or its legislative sponsors. Rather the NDEA was intended primarily as a short-term program to boost the nation's scientific manpower in the wake of the successful launching of the Russian satellite. The act established federal loans for college students, as well as new federal programs in elementary and secondary education, advanced scientific research, doctoral fellowships, foreign languages, and area studies. The NDEA explicitly articulated a national interest in education: "The Congress hereby finds and declares that the nation requires the fullest development of the mental resources and technical skills of its young men and women."[9]

With regard to the financing of higher education, current fund revenues of institutions totaled $554.5 million in 1929–1930 and $715.2 million in 1939–1940.[10] By the end of the next decade, in 1949–1950, current fund revenues had jumped to $2.375 billion (all in current dollars).[11] The latter figure reflects the GI Bill enrollments and the expansion of higher education generally. By 1959–1960, just a few years before the first baby boomers arrived on college doorsteps, current fund revenues totaled $5.786 billion dollars, a tenfold increase from 1929–1930. The growth era was underway.

As for tuition levels during this period, the dominant pattern in public higher education was to charge low or no tuition. That policy had been a strong recommendation of the Truman Commission, which emphasized what economists call the externalities, or social benefits, that are produced by having an educated populace, including a more informed citizenry, increased support for democracy, improved health, reduced crime, greater self-sufficiency, higher incomes, and hence higher tax payments. Low tuition was a default policy for student support, since direct aid to students based on income or academic merit had not been developed substantially in either public or private sectors.

The three key federal developments of this period—the GI Bill, the Truman Commission Report, and the National Defense Education Act—resulted in the United States having a much larger share of its young population (ages 18 to 24) attaining higher levels of education, compared with other developed nations. Today, that onetime lead has been lost. This edge provided the United States with an economic advantage for several decades but, as noted earlier, that advantage has recently evaporated.

By the end of the 1950s, higher education leaders, having lived through the doldrums of smaller enrollments mid-decade, were well aware that a tidal wave was approaching, as the so-called baby boom generation was nearing college age. What they did not know, however, was that little would be the same in higher education again.

A DECADE OF RAPID GROWTH: 1960 TO 1970

The baby boom generation is generally linked to the birth years of 1946 through 1964; the first wave of baby boomers to hit the colleges was in 1964, with large enrollments continuing through the 1970s. In 1959–1960, the U.S. population of 18- to 24-year-olds numbered 16.13 million; by 1969–1970, it jumped to 24.71 million, an increase of 53 percent.[12] From 1960 to 1970, higher education enrollments rose from 3.58 million to 7.92 million, an increase of 121 percent.[13] These numbers reveal that the growth in enrollments was caused not only by the larger age cohort, but also by gains in participation rates as the decade progressed. Thus, there were substantially more people of college age, and a much higher percentage of that larger group was enrolling in college. As another measure of this change, 2 percent of the U.S. population was enrolled in college in 1959–1960, increasing to 3.9 percent in 1969–1970, a very substantial increase.[14]

These larger numbers could hardly have been achieved if higher education had continued to be limited primarily to white males. The number thus reflects the growing percentages of women and minority students enrolling in college. The War on Poverty and the Civil Rights Movement of the mid-1960s gave great impetus to these trends, as did the movement toward women's liberation, which helped to open doors to professions heretofore closed to females. Higher education was becoming a mass movement, increasingly open to people of all incomes, races, sexes, creeds, ethnicities, and nationalities.

This increase in student numbers could not have been accommodated in existing colleges and universities, although most did expand their enrollments during this decade. New institutions were built, with their numbers increasing from 2,004 in 1959–1960 to 2,525 in 1969–1970.[15] The number of public community colleges nearly doubled over the decade, rising from 328 in 1959–1960 to 634 in 1969–1970, giving rise to the comment that a new community college opened its doors on average every twelve days during the 1960s.[16] It was during this decade that the famous California Master Plan for Higher Education was adopted, with its three tiers made up of the University of California campuses, California State Colleges, and the community college system. Similarly, under the leadership of Governor Nelson Rockefeller, the multicampus State University of New York system of two-year and four-year campuses was created.

This was also an era of staggering growth in graduate education and research, for the production of PhDs to staff the new and expanding colleges and universities was a top state and national priority. The postwar decision to concentrate federal research funds in universities also meant that laboratories and research centers of all types were developing rapidly, and their staffing required yet more new PhDs. If ever there were a Golden Age of higher education, it would be during this decade of extraordinary institutional growth and expansion, funded lushly by both state and federal governments.

On the financial front, current fund revenues of institutions nearly quadrupled in current dollars during the decade, rising from $5.786 billion in 1959–1960 to $21.515 billion in 1969–1970.[17] State support increased by a factor of five during the decade, from $1.4 billion in fiscal year 1961 to $7.0 billion in fiscal year 1971.[18] Charging low tuition continued to be the dominant policy in most states for their public systems. Private fund-raising, so prevalent today, was pursued by most private colleges and universities, but less commonly by public colleges and universities. The general unspoken agreement at this time was that private colleges would seek support from private donors, whom the public institutions would not pursue, while public institutions would receive support from state government, which the private colleges would not pursue. A neat division of labor by funding source thus maintained a modicum of decorum in the political relationships between the two sectors.

Several intellectual developments during the 1960s influenced public attitudes and policies toward higher education in a favorable way. In 1964, economist Gary Becker of the University of Chicago published a path-breaking book, entitled *Human Capital*, which documented empirically the private and social rates of return to investment in higher education.[19] His model treated expenditures on higher education in the same way one might calculate the return on an investment in physical capital. Depending on various assumptions, he estimated private returns to the individual in the 12 percent to 13 percent range, a rate that is higher generally than that found on investments in physical capital, such as plant and equipment. This finding gave rise to the argument that the United States was systematically underinvesting in higher education, and that on purely economic grounds, more people should be enrolling in college. Becker also calculated an equally impressive social rate of return, indicating that society would also benefit from additional investment in the education of its citizens.

Edward F. Denison for the Committee on Economic Development and the Brookings Institution undertook a second set of studies supporting the view that education was a sound economic investment was undertaken.[20] His painstaking studies sought to measure the sources of economic growth in various economies, including the United States, over extended periods of time. He focused on the three traditional inputs to production—land, labor, and capital—and refined the labor input by educational level. In a 1974 update to his earlier work, he examined economic growth in the United States between 1950 and 1962, and calculated that, of the average annual growth of 3.39 percent during this period, about 0.42 percentage points could be attributed to education and a further 1.15 percentage points could be attributed to advances in knowledge.[21] That is, almost half of the economic growth was related to education and research, activities largely housed in the nation's colleges and universities. Denison's conclusions dovetailed with those of Becker, although the two economists came at their estimates from entirely different approaches. The result was a considerable rise in interest in the economics of education within the profession, and a steady supply of information to the press and other media regarding the economic value of education. College presidents quickly picked up this message, and spread it in their speeches to alumni, students, and parents. Popular financial columns began touting the economic value of higher education, and legislators and other public figures responded accordingly.

A further force in the 1960s and 1970s was the work of the Carnegie Commission on Higher Education, chaired by Clark Kerr, who was president of the University of California until 1967. The commission published numerous policy reports of its own and sponsored even more books written by others.[22] This vast research and publishing effort on virtually every aspect of the enterprise placed higher education in the news constantly, so that issues related to higher education were at the forefront of national priorities; nothing since has been able to replicate this effort.

The sustained national focus on the economic and social values of higher education translated into federal legislation during this period, through the Economic Opportunity Act of 1964 and the Higher Education Act (HEA) of 1965. The Economic Opportunity Act was a central component of President

Lyndon Johnson's Great Society initiative and the administration's War on Poverty. Among the remaining vestiges of this program, which sought to remedy the educational, health, and employment issues of the poor, are the Head Start and Job Corps programs. This act was followed by the Higher Education Act, the first federal legislation centered explicitly on higher education. This groundbreaking legislation created the educational opportunity grants program (the original version of the Supplemental Educational Opportunity Grant [SEOG] program of today), the guaranteed student loan program (GSL), and several other smaller programs such as community service, college library assistance, aid to "developing" institutions, and the National Teacher Corps. The grant and loan programs established the central federal role in providing student support, a role that has continued, with modifications, to this day.

Two events, one cultural and one intellectual, caused this remarkable decade to close on a sour note for higher education. The first was the student revolt against the war in Vietnam, and the associated flowering of the counterculture of recreational drugs, sexual activity, Black Power, and a general flouting of the values held near and dear by many in the older generation. Universities were the locus of much of this dissident activity, and several university leaders were discharged for failing to crack down on the students and street people who led these campus uprisings.[23] The reverberations of this era split the country into warring camps and gave rise to ongoing culture wars, which are with us in various social and political forms to this day.

The intellectual event that challenged decades of thinking about the way to finance higher education was the 1969 publication of a modest volume by two economists, W. Lee Hansen and Burton A. Weisbrod, entitled *Benefits, Costs, and Finance of Public Higher Education*.[24] They examined the much-touted California system of public higher education under the 1960 Master Plan, which had created the highly selective university system, the less selective state college system, and the nonselective community college system. They argued that the financing was highly regressive, in that the children of the wealthy received most of the benefits of the highly resourced UC system, while the children of the poor either did not enroll or were generally consigned to the less well-financed state and community colleges. Meanwhile, they argued that taxes paid by California citizens to support public services, including the higher education system, were largely regressive, meaning that lower-income families were paying a higher share of income than the wealthy, while receiving fewer benefits from attendance in the public colleges and universities.[25]

Their thesis was easily simplified to the assertion that the poor were subsidizing the education of the rich, an inflammatory assertion during a time of increased focus on the plight of the poor and the need for greater social equity. The result was a long and hotly contested debate about the wisdom and justice of low-tuition public higher education, particularly when the best-financed institutions are academically selective, which tends to benefit children from wealthier families. The Hansen-Weisbrod book was the opening volley in what became a campaign to shift the financing of public higher education from low tuition and high state appropriations to institutions, toward higher tuition coupled with aid directed to students on the basis of their financial need, a policy known as high tuition, high aid. Thus, the golden age of higher education, roughly coincidental with the 1960s, witnessed the early signs of its own demise as that decade came to an end.

A TROUBLED DECADE: 1970 TO 1980

No sooner had the 1970s begun than a Carnegie Commission report entitled *The New Depression in Higher Education*, by Earl F. Cheit, shocked the country and the education establishment with its findings. Based on visits and interviews at forty-one colleges and universities, Cheit's report found that 71 percent of the institutions were either "headed for financial trouble, or were in financial difficulty."[26] The basic problem was that the cost of educational production was rising faster than institutional revenue, as the sharp funding increases of the 1960s began to slow, while the growth and expansion of faculty, staff, and programs continued apace. At about this time, the labor market for PhDs, which had witnessed high demand relative to supply in the 1960s, suddenly had an excess supply in many fields.[27] Apocryphal news accounts spoke of newly minted PhDs forced to drive taxicabs. Labor market troubles for recent college graduates began to show up as well, as the growing numbers completed college in the midst of a slowing economy.[28] Meanwhile, the oil shock of 1973 and the sudden quadrupling of oil prices helped to trigger an economic recession, the first officially noted since 1957. Productivity growth dropped sharply after 1973 and continued far below trends well into the next decade, for reasons that continue to puzzle economists.[29] Meanwhile, inflation took off, with the Consumer Price Index (CPI) increasing by double-digit rates in 1974 (11 percent), 1979 (11.3 percent), and 1980 (13.5 percent), and by 5 percent to 9 percent annually in the years between.[30] The combination of slow growth and high inflation was labeled *stagflation*, in recognition of the puzzling question of how such trends could coexist. Higher education did not escape the turmoil caused by these difficult economic conditions.

The population of 18- to 24-year-olds continued to grow, increasing from 24.712 million in 1970 to 30.337 million in 1980, an increase of nearly 23 percent.[31] Total enrollments climbed from 8.6 million in 1970 to 12.1 million in 1980, a gain of 41 percent, indicating that participation rates were still increasing beyond cohort growth.[32] More ominously for colleges and universities, however, the end of the baby boom generation was now in sight. The number of 18-year-olds in the population was projected to peak in 1979 at 4.3 million, beginning a plunge to 3.3 million in 1995, the so-called "birth dearth" generation.[33]

Current fund revenues of colleges and universities continued to grow, rising from $21.515 billion in 1969–1970 to $58.520 billion by 1979–1980 (in current dollars). During this period, state appropriations increased from $5.9 to $18.4 billion, while tuition and fee revenues climbed from $4.4 to $11.9 billion.[34] As noted earlier, criticism of universal low tuition in public higher education had begun to mount in the late 1960s, and that issue grew increasingly controversial. In 1973, two national reports were released that advocated a sharp increase in the share of educational costs borne by students and parents. The first, a Carnegie Commission report, *Higher Education: Who Pays? Who Benefits? Who Should Pay?*, recommended a gradual increase—from the existing 17 percent to 33 percent over ten years—in the share of educational costs covered by tuition in four-year public institutions.[35] A few months later, the Committee for Economic Development upped the ante by proposing that tuition be increased to 50 percent of costs over five years.[36] The ensuing uproar prompted the Carnegie Commission to issue a small follow-up report in April 1974, entitled *Tuition*. In this supplement to the earlier publication, the commission did not change its position, but sought to explain it more fully, updating the information on which the analyses were based, and distinguishing its proposals from those of the Committee for Economic Development, with which it had become entangled in the public mind.[37] The principal adjustment the commission made was to note that tuition in public four-year institutions in 1973–1974 had already reached 24 percent of costs, a significant change from the earlier estimate of 17 percent.[38] As a consequence, the commission argued that the gradual move over ten years from 24 percent to 33 percent would be relatively painless, a gain of roughly 1 percent per year.

In its first report, the commission had also found that students and parents were actually bearing close to two-thirds of the economic costs of higher education when one added forgone earnings to direct educational expenditures. Thus, their proposal to set tuition at one-third of educational costs, with the balance to be covered by government and philanthropic sources, meant, in true economic terms, that the student and family would bear two-thirds of the economic costs, while government and philanthropy covered one-third. These rules of thumb continue to guide a great deal of the conventional thinking in this country regarding how costs should be shared, even though many do not know where these ideas originated. As Keynes noted, "Practical men, who believe themselves to be quite exempt from any intellectual influences, are usually the slaves of some defunct economist."[39]

In 1978, David Breneman, one of the authors of this book, Chester E. Finn Jr. and Susan Nelson edited *Public Policy and Private Higher Education*, which recommended a high-tuition, high-aid policy for higher education.[40] The volume suggested that federal dollars be used as an incentive to encourage state governments to shift appropriations away from public institutional support and toward need-based student aid, leaving public universities with no option but to raise tuition. This recommendation, which came five years after the recommendations of the Carnegie Commission and the Committee for Economic Development, was opposed strongly by the national associations representing public colleges and universities, which were still solidly in support of low tuition. The American Association of State Colleges and Universities described the recommendation as "a blueprint for the destruction of low-tuition public higher education in America, and a serious blow to opportunity for the approximately nine million students who attend these colleges."[41] An equally harsh review by the former executive director of the National Association of State Universities and Land-Grant Colleges suggests that the publisher of the book, the Brookings Institution, "begin listening to other viewpoints than those of the economists who have largely dominated its studies and policy proposals in the past."[42] It wasn't until years later that these organizations and the presidents of public universities began to pursue large increases in public tuition.

In the early 1970s, equality of opportunity, a major impetus for the 1965 Higher Education Act, became the dominant purpose of federal financing of higher education. The Education Amendments (to the Higher Education Act) of 1972 expanded the federal role through grants made directly to needy students. Basic Educational Opportunity Grants (BEOG), later renamed Pell Grants, were established as portable, voucher-type, need-based grants of up to $1,400. Other student aid provisions of the amendments of 1972 included the creation of a government-sponsored enterprise, the Student Loan Marketing Corporation (Sallie May), to purchase student loans from banks, freeing capital for additional loans.[43] Another new program, the State Student Incentive Grants (SSIG), currently the LEAP program, offered incentives for states to establish or expand need-based scholarship programs. The legislation also reauthorized college work-study, guaranteed student loans, and national direct student loans. The expansion of loan volume and state scholarship programs was designed to support student choice among institutions. Finally, the legislation broadened the scope beyond traditional colleges and universities by opening participation in federal student aid programs to students attending vocational-technical and proprietary institutions.[44]

The key political debate at this time focused on the administration of the new BEOG program. The national higher education associations wanted the funds to be provided directly to colleges and universities, to be distributed among their students, as had been the case with the earlier educational opportunity grant (EOG) program. Others, including the Carnegie Commission, the analytical staff at the Department of Health, Education, and Welfare (HEW), and several key legislators, wanted the funds to go directly to students, as a form of need-based voucher. The latter group prevailed, and thus the federal government's largest student grant program was created.

The federal government was now firmly established in the student grant and loan business, with aid focused clearly on low-income students. The Education Amendments of 1972 brought both sweeping changes and, for a brief moment, greater clarity of purpose to the federal role in financing college. Of equal consequence, it laid the foundation for future dramatic expansion of federal financial support and for the predominant federal role as provider of student financial assistance. From the adoption of the 1972 amendments to the mid-1970s, federal support under the new programs increased at an unprecedented level, by over 50 percent.

But clarity of federal purpose was not sustained even through the end of the decade. As inflation gained traction during the 1970s, colleges responded by raising tuition accordingly, which often meant double-digit price increases. In the sluggish economy, many families were experiencing a loss of real income, which set the stage for a political outcry in favor of helping struggling middle-income families finance the rising price of college.[45] The conventional wisdom was that low-income students had financial aid and the wealthy could afford rising tuition, but middle-income families neither could afford the rising price of college nor were their children eligible for need-based financial aid. The Ninety-fifth Congress (spanning 1977 and 1978) saw the introduction of over a hundred bills for tuition tax credits, deductions, or deferrals, which were actively opposed by the Treasury Department and the HEW.[46] Others proposed extending basic educational opportunity grants to higher-income families. In a compromise reached in 1978, the tax credit proposals were defeated, but the Middle Income Student Assistance Act (MISAA) was enacted, which broadened eligibility for Pell Grants to more middle-income students, and lifted the income ceiling for eligibility for guaranteed student loans (which were heavily subsidized at the time). Technical amendments in 1979 and the 1980 reauthorizations increased allowances to lenders in the guaranteed loan program, established a new guaranteed loan program for parents, and increased the authorized Pell Grant award to $2,600.[47]

The almost immediate consequence of MISAA and the legislation that flowed from it was another dramatic increase in federal student aid. From 1977–1978 to 1980–1981, loan volume increased from $2.2 billion to $6.2 billion. Inflation-adjusted federal expenditures for grants and loans increased by 15 percent.[48] The primary focus on low- and lower-middle-class access that had been central to the 1972 legislation was diffused, and the stage was set for the predominance of loans in federal aid to students.

Questions about eligibility for financial aid—Who should receive it? In what form, grants or loans? On what basis, need or merit?—continued to be among the toughest issues confronting legislators, college officials, and taxpayers. The title of the 1973 Carnegie Commission report, *Higher Education: Who Pays? Who Benefits? Who Should Pay?*, had captured the central and enduring issues of educational finance.

CHAPTER 4

Finance and Policy

A Contemporary Perspective

Since the 1970s, the balance between federal and state roles in funding higher education in the United States and the responsibilities of students and families in paying for rising tuition and fees has continued to shift. This chapter describes the evolution of higher education finance from the 1980s to the first decade of the twenty-first century. As in the previous chapter, our purpose is to note the historical trends by highlighting major themes in finance policy, both at the state and federal levels.

THE 1980s: HIGHER EDUCATION IN THE MARKETPLACE

Ronald Reagan's election as president in November 1980 marked the end of a philosophical approach to government activity that some would argue extended back to Franklin Delano Roosevelt's New Deal. Reagan gained office in part by arguing that government was the problem, not the solution, for most social and economic concerns. The political activism that inspired the Great Society programs, including the Economic Opportunity Act and the Higher Education Act (HEA), was eclipsed. In place of government action, the market (it was argued) was the best vehicle for resource allocation, and private interest should supersede public interest in driving the economy. The Keynesian era of government activism in economics was declared dead, and a new upstart, supply-side economics, took center stage in political thought and action. The free-market gospel of Milton Friedman had found its great political advocate and communicator in President Reagan.[1]

The 1980s began, however, with a deep recession triggered by strong monetary medicine administered by Chairman Paul Volcker of the Federal

Reserve Board. In order to curtail high rates of inflation, Volcker raised short-term interest rates sufficiently to choke off enough economic activity to put an end to sharply rising prices. The percentage increase in inflation was 13.5 percent in 1980 and 10.3 percent in 1981. By 1983, however, the annual percentage increase had dropped to 3.2 percent. Until the late 1980s, inflation continued to inch upward minimally.[2] Labor market opportunities for new college graduates remained slim in the slowing economy, as the last of the baby boom cohorts graduated and entered the work force. Higher education leaders braced themselves for the prospect of declining enrollments, as the population of eighteen-year-olds began its fifteen-year descent.[3]

As the philosophical shift toward private interest gained ascendency, one of the central rationales for the provision of government subsidies to higher education was undermined. Human capital theory emphasized the private financial benefits of education. As that emphasis gained popularity, questions arose as to why the beneficiary of higher education (that is, the student) should not pay more, or most, of the cost. Furthermore, the pressure of growing enrollments was subsiding, and therefore the pressures to finance new institutions were diminishing. State support for public higher education continued to grow through the 1980s, but at a slower rate; outlays of $19.1 billion in fiscal year 1980 increased to $39.2 billion in 1990, doubling over the decade (in current dollars).[4] Viewed in other ways, however, the states' share of support for higher education was beginning its long-term decline.[5] State appropriations for higher education per $1,000 of personal income peaked in 1974, and that figure has dropped irregularly but sharply since then.[6] State appropriations for higher education as a share of state expenditures have also declined steadily since 1981, reflecting, in part, expanding state government responsibilities in areas such as health care (in particular, Medicaid) and public school finance, as well as pressures on state governments to reduce taxes (particularly since the adoption of Proposition 13 by the California electorate in 1978).[7] State support as a share of public university revenue has also dropped—from 46 percent in 1980 to 30 percent in 2008.[8] State appropriations per full-time equivalent (FTE) student has ebbed and flowed with economic cycles since the early 1980s, even as net tuition revenue per FTE student has increased during this period (see figure 1.7 in chapter 1 of this volume). Since 1985, net tuition has grown from under a quarter (23.3 percent) to over 40 percent (40.3 percent) of educational revenue at public colleges and universities (see figure 1.8 in chapter 1 of this volume).

The promise of rising federal support in the form of student financial aid ran into obstacles in the 1980s, as the Reagan administration tried to end the federal role in education, arguing that education was the responsibility of state government and the private sector. Symbolic of this view, repeated efforts were made to close the newly created U.S. Department of Education, but Congress would not support that action. The administration also sought to curtail or eliminate funding for most student aid programs, but Congress blocked those efforts, too. These annual budget battles did result, however, in sharply slower growth for federal grant programs to students, which were not entitlement programs and were therefore subject to annual appropriations. The Pell Grant program grew modestly from $4.1 billion in 1980–1981 to $5.4 billion in 1990–1991 (in constant 1994 dollars), a much smaller gain over the decade than its supporters had originally anticipated and less than would have been needed to keep pace with enrollments and the rising costs of college attendance.[9] The other campus-based federal grant and loan programs subject to appropriations (Supplemental Education Opportunity Grant, State Student Incentive Grants, College Work Study, and Perkins Loans) all lost ground in real terms over the decade, as a result of the relentless opposition they faced from the Reagan administration.[10]

The Social Security Administration and the Veterans Administration, while not part of the Higher Education Act programs, provided aid to college students who were children of Social Security recipients or who were veterans. The two programs, combined, supplied over $6 billion in financial support in 1970–1971.[11] Primarily due to the creation of the Pell Grant program, Social Security payments to dependents were phased out in 1982. By 1990–1991, college benefits to veterans were also sharply reduced. If these two programs were included the total federal student aid picture, the result would be an absolute decline in total federal student support (including loan programs) during the decade, from $24.6 billion in 1980–1981 to $23.5 billion in 1990–1991 (in constant 1994 dollars).[12] Yet, both enrollments and tuition rates (after inflation) increased during this decade.

Private college and university leaders had hoped that the new federal student aid programs would provide students of more modest means with the opportunity to pay for a higher-priced private education. Many had argued during the debates that accompanied the 1972 HEA amendments that the federal aid programs had two goals, *access* and *choice*, the latter being a code word for facilitating enrollment in private higher education. The failure of these programs to develop as fully as hoped was thus a disappointment for higher education leaders in both public and private sectors. One result was that private colleges and universities expanded their own institutional aid to students, often in the form of tuition discounts.[13] During this decade, institutional financial aid became a key resource for recruitment by private institutions, driven by the needs to fill classes and to enhance institutional selectivity. What began as a matter of necessity in a time of increased competition for students continues today as a significant source of student financial aid.[14]

The 1980s also witnessed a growing shift in undergraduate major fields of study from the liberal arts to professional programs. In the difficult labor market of this decade, more students sought enhanced credentials, and employers demanded more professional skills from new graduates. In addition, colleges and universities discovered the adult student during this decade, as the declining numbers of high school graduates gave rise to a search for replacements in the classroom. These adjustments helped to stave off an absolute drop in enrollments during the 1980s; higher education enrollments increased from 12.1 million in 1980 to 13.8 million in 1990.[15] The actions of colleges and universities during this period revealed the adaptability and flexibility of these institutions, which have often been described as unable to change. The institutions were helped, however, by an improved labor market for college graduates in the latter part of the decade, which was caused in part by economic changes that made it difficult for those with only a high school education to find a good job. The private rate of return for a college degree relative to a high school diploma began to rise, which helped colleges and universities maintain enrollments.[16]

On the intellectual front, the decade was devoid of substantive new thinking or research findings about higher education, other than the ideological embrace of the market as the final arbiter of social resource allocation. The Carnegie Commission had passed into history, and there seemed little demand for a replacement. Disaffection with higher education had grown in many quarters, primarily due to: rising tuition; cultural animosity during the Reagan era toward left-leaning professors thought to populate most classrooms; a growing belief that students were not learning as much as they should; and the belief that colleges and universities were wasteful and inefficient. A new era of public accountability for higher education began to emerge, and it remains to this day.

Funding difficulties began pushing presidents, deans, and other leaders of higher education toward more entrepreneurial behavior. Institutional leaders increasingly saw themselves as being forced into a competitive market, in which resources and prestige were the coins of the realm. The advent in 1983 of the annual ranking of best colleges by *U.S. News & World Report* exacerbated this trend by putting a public scorecard for every college on the newsstands. The shifting of higher education from the public sphere to the marketplace was well underway.

THE 1990s: GLOBALIZATION, PRIVATIZATION, STRATIFICATION, AND TECHNOLOGY

The 1990s began, as did the previous decade, with a sharp, yearlong recession. Whereas most of the job losses in previous recessions were confined to blue-collar, manufacturing workers, companies in this recession began laying off white-collar middle managers, as "downsizing" or "rightsizing" became the new mantra. The following statement, reprinted from a 1993 article, conveys a sense of how the economy and higher education appeared to one observer at this time:

Americans of all ages are upset, perplexed, and disquieted by an economy that has become increasingly sluggish and unpredictable. The old verities—progress, growth, rising living standards, full employment, good jobs—seem threatened at every turn. Corporate giants, such as IBM, Boeing, General Motors, and Sears Roebuck, lose billions of dollars and lay off thousands of employees; foreign competition looms as a threat to people's livelihoods, and job-security declines for virtually everyone; high school graduates entering the labor market face little but dead-end jobs; growing numbers of impoverished, inner-city youngsters lack hope and turn to crime. Federal and state governments seem unable to cope with these and other challenges facing the nation. The list of economic problems and related social ills seems endless.

Higher education could hardly be immune to this general distress and uncertainty. Families see tuitions rise more rapidly than incomes, and worry about meeting the cost; students see enrollments capped, class sections eliminated, and time-to-degree stretching to five or six years; faculty see salaries lag, research support diminish, and class sizes increase; young Ph.D.s see positions left vacant, dashing their hopes for academic careers; college administrators wrestle with sharp cuts in state support, unbalanced budgets, and frightening projections of future deficits. Critics of higher education, sensing the increased vulnerability of the enterprise, intensify their efforts and the shrillness of their attacks.[17]

As James Carville famously emphasized throughout the presidential campaign at that time, "It's the economy, stupid."

Not surprisingly, college affordability became a powerful political issue in this setting, and all parties—colleges, universities, governors, state legislators, federal executive personnel, and federal legislators—tumbled over each other in a rush to help the middle class. In the late 1970s, Congress had broadened eligibility for Pell Grants to include more middle-income students and lifted the income ceiling for eligibility for guaranteed student loans. But it was during the 1990s that the political meaning of *college affordability* shifted away from a focus on access to higher education for low-income students and toward the financing problems facing middle- and upper-income families. One of the earliest actions (and one that received much public attention) was the creation in 1993 of the Georgia HOPE scholarship, the brainchild of Governor Zell Miller.[18] Funded by the state lottery, this program was the first broad-based merit aid program launched by any state. Eligible recipients were state residents who achieved a B grade point average (GPA) in high school and maintained a comparable GPA in any four-year, public or accredited private college or university in the state. For students attending public institutions, the award was for full tuition and fees plus a book allowance, paid for by the state program. A family income cap of $66,000 for eligibility was imposed the first year, raised to $100,000 in the second year, and eliminated entirely thereafter.[19]

Miller's objectives for the new program were at least twofold: to increase college-going rates in Georgia and to keep the "best and the brightest" high school graduates. at home, on the assumption that if students attended college in Georgia, they would be more likely to remain and work in the state after graduation. A side benefit for the governor and legislators was (and is) that the program has proven wildly popular with the voting public, far more so than the targeted, need-based programs driven by concerns of efficiency and equity. Not surprisingly, many other state leaders recognized the political bonanza that Miller had uncovered, and now as many as fifteen states have established similar programs.[20]

At the federal level, the 1992 Amendments to the Higher Education Act created the Parent Loan for Undergraduate Students (PLUS) program and an unsubsidized Stafford or guaranteed student loan (GSL) program, both without income caps for eligibility. These programs marked a further shift away from need-based grants as a way to finance college for students and their families, and toward increased borrowing through loans. In particular, student loans became a way to help middle- and higher-income families finance college, much as the mortgage market helps families buy homes. This legislation responded to the growing sense of crisis in college affordability. As we described in the previous chapter, in the late 1970s, the balance of loans versus grants began to shift dramatically, and after 1982, federal student financial assistance was predominantly loans (see figure 4.1). In 1992–1993, the availability of direct and guaranteed, subsidized and unsubsidized loans for students and parents again enabled borrowing on an unprecedented scale. When all sources (federal, state, institutional, and private) are taken into account, loans eclipsed grants after 1993–1994 (see figure 4.2). This represented a fundamental shift in the ways students and families finance college attendance, with loans accounting for 66 percent of federal student aid in 2009–2010 (see figure 4.3). In 2009–2010, there were 10.2 million recipients of Stafford and PLUS loans. The average amount borrowed was $8,008.[21]

This period also witnessed the early but steady growth of private student loans not guaranteed by the federal government. In 1996–1997, private student loans totaled $2.2 billion (in 2009 dollars); by 2007–2008, private loans increased to $21.8 billion, or 12.6 percent of the total $172.5 billion for all forms of student aid.[22] Commercial banks flocked to this new market, using intermediary organizations such as Sallie Mae and First Marblehead to securitize the loans into bonds sold to investors through Wall Street.[23]

Colleges and universities also increased their own institutional aid. In 1990–1991, institutional grants amounted to $9.1 billion (in 2005 dollars), which grew to $24.4 billion by 2005–2006.[24] As in the 1980s, the institutions continued to shift toward academic "merit" rather than relying primarily on financial need as a criterion for aid, and this shift was caused by the combination of enhanced competitiveness amon g institutions for enrollments

FIGURE 4.1 Shift from grants to loans in federal funding (federal grant and loans only)

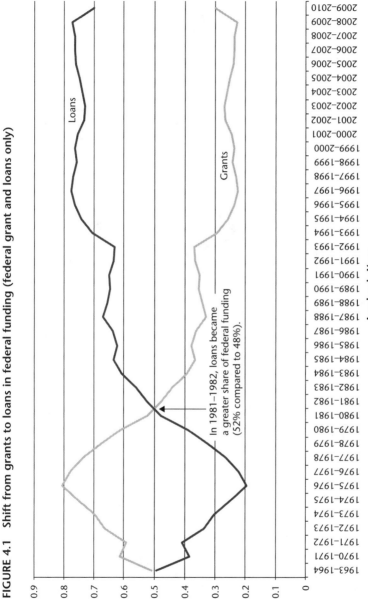

In 1981–1982, loans became a greater share of federal funding (52% compared to 48%).

Academic Year

Source: © 2010 The College Board, www.collegeboard.com. Reproduced with permission.

FIGURE 4.2 Shift from grants to loans (total grants and loans from federal, state, institutional, and private sources)

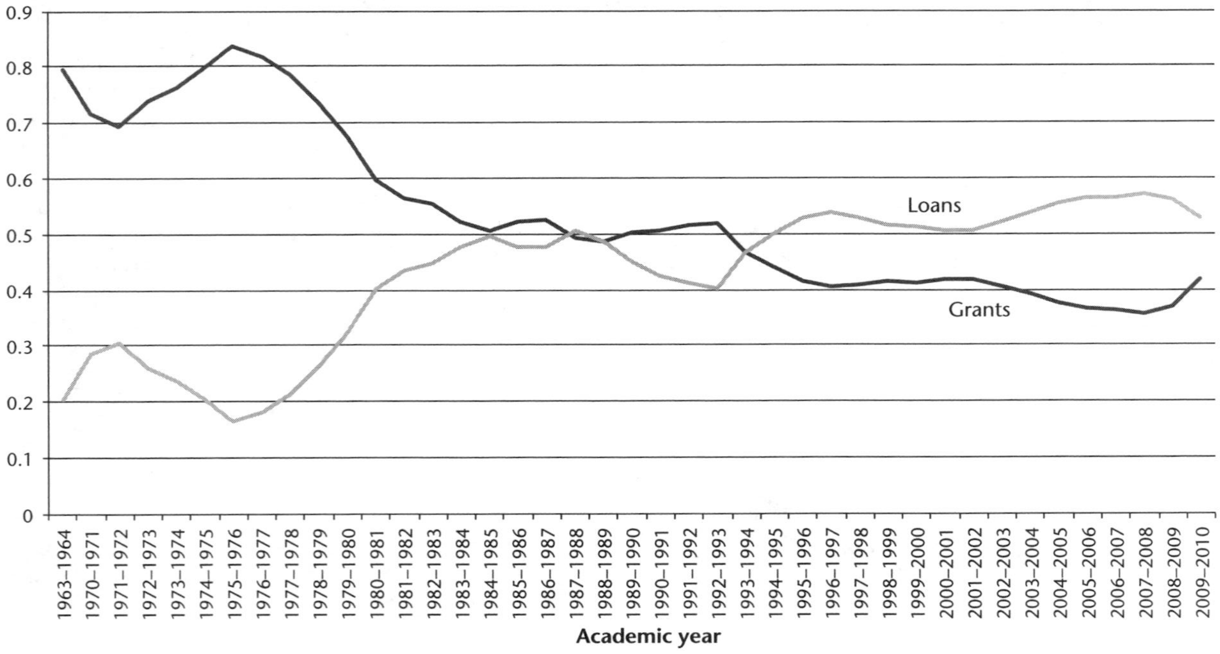
0.9
0.8
0.7
0.6
0.5
0.4
0.3
0.2
0.1
0
Loans
Grants
1963–1964
1970–1971
1971–1972
1972–1973
1973–1974
1974–1975
1975–1976
1976–1977
1977–1978
1978–1979
1979–1980
1980–1981
1981–1982
1982–1983
1983–1984
1984–1985
1985–1986
1986–1987
1987–1988
1988–1989
1989–1990
1990–1991
1991–1992
1992–1993
1993–1994
1994–1995
1995–1996
1996–1997
1997–1998
1998–1999
1999–2000
2000–2001
2001–2002
2002–2003
2003–2004
2004–2005
2005–2006
2006–2007
2007–2008
2008–2009
2009–2010
Academic year

Source: © 2010 The College Board, www.collegeboard.com. Reproduced with permission.

FIGURE 4.3   Federal student aid (in constant 2009 millions)

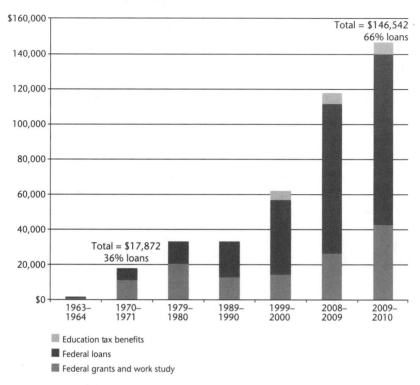

Source: © 2010 The College Board, www.collegeboard.com. Reproduced with permission.

(particularly among the less selective colleges) and the related desire to increase quality and prestige, measured in part by the credentials of the student body. The *U.S. News & World Report*'s rankings of best colleges, by now the best-selling issue of that magazine, continued to fuel the flames of merit aid, because the ranking system gave significant weight to student SAT/ACT scores and rank in high school class. Economic research also stressed the value of "peer effects," the notion that students are more than just an input into educational production but rather are primary contributors to it, as they help to educate each other.[25] The higher the quality of peers, therefore, the higher the quality of education produced in that institution.

Private consulting firms, such as Noel-Levitz, developed techniques for analyzing a college's applicant pool, acceptance patterns, and yield (enrollment) experience, in order to allocate financial aid in the most effective way to attract the most desirable students. The techniques colleges use to manage enrollments, and the use of student aid as a strategic tool in this effort, are well explained by McPherson and Schapiro in their 1998 volume, *The Student Aid Game*.[26] The fact that many of these techniques violate every norm of equity and are distasteful to contemplate helps to explain why college and university leaders would prefer not to discuss these practices or see them described and attributed to them in print. These practices, however, are firmly established and, in a market-driven, competitive system of higher education, are seen as a cost of doing business.

A further blow to the federal priority for need-based grants occurred in 1996–1997, when federal tax legislation, initiated by the Clinton administration, created tuition tax credits in the form of two programs, the Hope Scholarship Credit and the Lifetime Learning Credit, as well as tax-deferred savings plans for educational expenses called Section 529 Savings Plans.[27] The Hope credit applied to the first two years of college and provided a 100 percent tax credit for the first $1,000 of educational expenses and a 50 percent credit on the second $1,000 spent.

The Lifetime Learning Credit applied to anyone taking courses for credit, including continuing education for adults, and was computed as 20 percent of the first $10,000 of educational expenses.[28] Both credits were phased out as family income rose, but neither was *refundable*—that is, the credits only had value to those families with sufficient income to have tax liability. The 529 Savings Plans were (and continue to be) exempt from taxes on earnings in state-sponsored savings plans, and when the funds are withdrawn for qualified educational expenses, they are taxed at the child's usually lower tax rate, although they are the property of parents.[29] These plans, funded with after-tax dollars, are of value only to those families that have substantial discretionary income, and thus are of little use to low-income families. Politically, tax benefits combine the attractiveness of support for college attendance with tax relief for a voting middle-class constituency that has become increasingly anxious about taxes and college costs. However, they cannot be expected to improve college access, since the lowest-income students and families are not eligible. These programs have experienced rapid growth in a relatively brief time since their inception, and because they are embedded in the tax code, the tax benefits are not subject to the annual federal appropriations process (see table 4.1).

During the 1990s, the emphasis on affordability (defined as helping middle- and upper-income families finance the rising price of a college education) gave rise to concerns that the system was moving toward increased stratification by socioeconomic status and family income. These concerns were particularly directed to the selective private colleges and universities, and the handful of selective public universities. The argument was that the nature of the admissions process, with its emphasis on academic quality coupled with the rise of merit aid, would mean that most of the spaces in the elite private and public institutions would go to children of well-educated, higher-income families. These concerns continued to develop in the following decade.

TABLE 4.1
Education tax credits (in constant 2009 millions)

Federal funding for education tax credits	1998–1999	1999–2000	2000–2001	2001–2002	2002–2003	2003–2004	2004–2005	2005–2006	2006–2007	2007–2008	2008–2009	2009–2010	% growth 1999–2010
Undergraduates	$3,360	$4,590	$4,450	$4,440	$5,140	$5,550	$5,910	$5,870	$5,990	$5,890	$5,750	$5,990	78%
All students	$3,920	$5,340	$5,180	$5,170	$5,980	$6,460	$6,880	$6,840	$6,970	$6,850	$6,690	$6,970	78%
Recipients (thousands)	$4,033	$5,492	$5,830	$5,950	$7,725	$8,143	$8,630	$8,519	$8,308	$8,439	$8,132	$8,015	99%
Total dollars awarded	$3,919	$5,335	$5,184	$5,168	$5,979	$6,464	$6,879	$6,844	$6,974	$6,854	$6,687	$6,970	78%
Aid per recipient	$972	$971	$889	$869	$774	$794	$797	$803	$839	$812	$822	$870	–11%

Source: © 2010 The College Board, *Trends in Student Aid*, 2010. www.collegeboard.com. Reproduced with permission.

One measure of what was happening to college participation is captured in the biennial reports of the National Center for Public Policy and Higher Education, in its series known as *Measuring Up: The National Report Card on Higher Education*. In its 2008 report, the center noted that: "The nation as a whole has made no notable progress since the early 1990s in enrolling young adults or working-age adults in education and training beyond high school. Furthermore, participation in education beyond high school still varies by race/ethnicity and annual family income."[30] The National Center also called attention to the growing problem of college affordability for low-income students, which is one cause of the lagging overall participation and completion rates in recent years.

On the demographic front, the traditional college-age population began rising again in the mid-1990s, due to the so-called "echo" baby boom, when the children of the baby boom generation reached college age. This enrollment surge was projected to peak in 2007–2008 and then decline moderately for several years.[31] As a consequence of this demographic trend, college enrollments rose during the 1990s, from 13.8 million in 1990 to 15.3 million in 2000, with most of the increase in the latter half of the decade.[32] Unlike their parents' generation, the echo baby boom cohort was not greeted by new capital drives to expand colleges and universities. The combination of a larger young population and limited facilities and programs gave many existing institutions an opportunity to increase selectivity. Indeed, public colleges and universities as a group did not greatly increase their enrollments over this decade, beginning at 10.8 million students and ending at 11.8 million.[33] The majority of public enrollment growth took place in the less selective two-year community colleges, which grew from 5 million in 1990 to 5.7 million in 2000.[34] Increased enrollment pressure also provided an economic environment in which institutions were able to push through sizable tuition increases, particularly in the latter half of the decade.

Economically, the early 1990s witnessed a period of recession and its aftermath. During these years, higher education experienced an absolute decline in state appropriations—the first time that had occurred since records have been kept (see figure 1.7 in chapter 1 of this volume for the drop in state appropriations per student at this time).[35] The institutional response was a sharp increase in public tuition charges (see figure 1.8 in chapter 1 of this volume). In prior recessions, state support for higher education had declined in many states, but when the economy emerged from recession, appropriations usually increased significantly, giving rise to a boom-and-bust—or roller-coaster—pattern of state support. Harold Hovey, a longtime analyst of state finance, referred to higher education as the balance wheel for state finance, with appropriations for higher education being reduced more sharply than other services when revenues fall, and rising more sharply when revenues recover.[36] The main reason that states can use higher education as a balance wheel is that, unlike other state activities (such as K–12 education, prisons, welfare, and Medicaid), higher education has the ability to tap other sources of support, particularly through tuition increases. A secondary reason is that higher education support is discretionary, unlike many functions that are governed by regulations, entitlement legislation, or court decisions. Thomas Kane, Peter Orzag, and David Gunter note, however, that the rebound from the recession of the early 1990s was different from earlier years: "On a real per capita basis, state appropriations rose rapidly in the mid-to-late 1980s but then fell sharply in the early 1990s. In the late 1990s, state appropriations again increased rapidly, so that by 2001 state appropriations returned to approximately their level in the late 1980s. Note, however, that the 1990s recovery appears quite different than [sic] the 1980s recovery: Appropriations were slower to recover during the 1990s, and they never exceeded their previous peak."[37]

The fact that virtually all states were judged to have *structural deficits* in the late 1990s may help to explain why higher education support did not experience the typical rebound after this recession.[38]

Another unanticipated source of support for higher education at this time was the soaring stock market, as the economic boom in technology and Internet stocks created enormous new wealth. Indeed, the dreary outlook of the early 1990s was rendered moot by this dramatic new source of economic growth. For the universities that were experienced in private fund-raising, this period was a bonanza, not only for new gifts but also for increasingly sophisticated management of endowments, producing annual returns of 15 percent to 20 percent or more. This surge in endowment wealth, while not widely shared among all institutions, may have contributed to the view of some state legislators that higher education could make do with less taxpayer support.

Although shifts in thinking are hard to document, it was during this decade that many public university leaders began to doubt that state support as a share of total institutional revenues would ever return to the levels of earlier decades. As a result, these leaders began to move away from a commitment to low tuition, and toward the view that tuition revenues would have to rise sharply to help offset the drop in appropriations per student that was occurring, even during economic recovery (see figure 1.7 in chapter 1 of this volume). Tuition increases were also supplemented by aggressive private fund-raising and by efforts to encourage faculty to seek increased federal research support. For the first time, people spoke about the "privately financed public university." The privatization of all public services was up for discussion.[39]

As the public watched tuition soar at double-digit rates, college affordability became a prominent political issue in most states again, and at the federal level as well. Anger at higher education spread, putting greater pressure on institutional accountability, in the hope that such pressure would help to slow the rise in prices. State legislatures employed various budgetary techniques to keep pressure on the universities, while some members of Congress used rhetoric, including threats to cut student aid or impose price controls. During this period, federal legislation created a National Commission on the Cost of Higher Education to serve as an independent advisory body to review and report to Congress on the causes of rising college costs and prices.[40] This group commissioned papers, held public meetings, and produced a report that sank without a trace.[41]

As a practical matter, there is little the federal government can do about tuition increases other than to jawbone or to impose price controls, which few support. At the state level, most governors know that when appropriations are cut, the result will be sharper-than-normal increases in tuition. Some economists argue that unit cost increases are inevitable in an enterprise that is essentially a craft with limited opportunity to experience productivity gains.[42] That argument does not quiet the critics, however. At the beginning of the new century, public policies and public support of higher education were as unsettled as at any time in recent memory.

THE CURRENT SITUATION: 2000 TO THE PRESENT

The first decade of the new century was marked by two recessions, terrorist attacks on the World Trade Center and the Pentagon, costly wars in Afghanistan and Iraq, a real estate boom (and speculative bubble), and the worst financial collapse since the Great Depression. The decade opened with a tumultuous recession, as the dot-com market bubble of the late 1990s exploded, with numerous Internet companies closing and the stock market's Dow Jones Industrial Average plunging to a five-year low of 7,286.27 on October 9, 2002.[43] Once again, appropriations for higher education were cut in absolute terms, going from $62.7 billion in fiscal year 2002 to $62.2 billion in fiscal year 2003, and again to $60.7 billion in 2004.[44] Increases in average tuition and fees at public four-year colleges and universities hit double digits again, rising by 13.3 percent in 2003–2004 and by 10.4 percent in 2004–2005. Tuition and fee increases at community colleges were also dramatic, increasing by 14.0 percent in 2003–2004 and 8.9 percent in 2004–2005.[45] These financial developments coincided with continued growth in the number of U.S. high school graduates, which rose from 2.85 million in 2000–2001 to 3.19 million in 2005–2006—a 12 percent increase.[46] Despite the tuition increases, higher education enrollment grew from 15.3 million to 17.5 million during this period, of which 6.8 million were part-time students in 2006. For-profit colleges weighed significantly in this enrollment increase, as their numbers jumped from 450,084 to 1,010,949 from 2000 to 2005.[47] Students and families increasingly viewed higher education as a necessity for a middle-class life.[48]

Issues of global competitiveness took center stage at this time, fueled in part by the publishing success of Thomas Friedman's book, *The World Is Flat*, in 2005.[49] Friedman gave life and human meaning to the dry statistics about outsourcing of jobs, and the growing ability of knowledge workers in India, China, Brazil, Russia, and other countries to perform work online that might otherwise be done in this country. The book also highlighted the declining status of the U.S. education system relative to those of other developed and developing nations. As was mentioned in chapter 1, comparative data published by the Organisation for Economic Co-operation and Development (OECD) have made this point statistically.[50] Combining national data from OECD with U.S. state data from the *Measuring Up* series reveals that 35- to 64-year-olds in the United States are among the best educated cohorts in the world, but that younger U.S. adults (ages 25 to 34) have slipped to tenth place in the percentage with a college degree, falling behind Canada, Japan, Korea, Finland, Norway, Sweden, and Belgium, among others.[51] In essence, the United States embraced broader participation in higher education after World War II—a generation or more before other developed nations did so. This provided the United States with a competitive edge during the past few decades, but other countries have now caught up and in some cases are surpassing our educational performance.

As in the 1990s, concerns have continued to be raised during this decade about the stratification of higher education by socioeconomic factors. Evidence of this trend in highly selective colleges and universities was documented by William Bowen, Martin Kurzweil, and Eugene Tobin in *Equity and Excellence in American Higher Education*, published in 2005. Among many issues covered in this substantial volume is the stark question of whether our elite colleges and universities are "engines of opportunity or bastions of privilege."[52] The authors recommended that highly selective public and private colleges and universities give a helping hand to youth from low-income backgrounds, some of whom achieve solid academic records in high school but are underrepresented in college. They noted that selective colleges give an edge to athletes, legacies (children of alumni), and minority students, but not to low-income students who fit none of those categories. This observation stirred many educational leaders to action, and virtually all of the highly selective institutions have now instituted special programs of financial aid to support the enrollment of such students. The dilemma, however, is that the number coming from a disadvantaged background who can qualify for admission is still very low, so the concerns about access to college and increased social stratification persist.

Efforts to expand accountability of higher education have also remained strong this decade and have taken a variety of forms. On the financial side, tuition increases that exceed inflation as measured by the Consumer Price Index continue to be a target of legislative action. The 2008 Amendments to the HEA, the College Opportunity and Affordability Act, require colleges and universities to explain in considerable written detail any price increases that exceed a certain level. Specifically, if an institution has a large increase in tuition and fees or a large percentage increase in net price over the preceding three academic years, it must describe the major areas in the institution's budget with the greatest cost increases; provide an explanation of the cost increases; and identify the steps it will take to reduce costs. The legislation also contains provisions that penalize states that fail to provide a baseline of support for their public institutions, since cuts in state support have led to sharp tuition increases in recent years. The baseline is not a very demanding one: states must provide public higher education institutions with at least the same level of appropriations as the average they provided over the preceding five academic years (not including for capital or directly funded research). The effectiveness of these measures remains to be seen, but Congress has signaled its unhappiness over financial trends that reduce college affordability and its willingness to use the legislative process to try to rein in large price increases.[53]

Legislators at the national and state levels have also expressed concern about the extent to which some institutions with sizable endowments have very low spending rates from those resources. In several instances before the recent recession, the drawdown rate was well below 5 percent of principal value, which is the minimum required of charitable foundations. Senator Charles Grassley of Iowa, as ranking minority member on the Senate Finance Committee, questioned why colleges and universities with endowments in the billions of dollars should be increasing tuition rather than drawing down some of these resources.[54] Some legislators have called for mandatory spending rates of 5 percent, and state legislators in Massachusetts, home to several highly endowed colleges and universities, have proposed adding a state tax on large endowments. These issues have receded recently, as endowment values have plunged, but they are likely to reemerge so long as legislators remain irritated by increases in tuition and see political benefit in pressing for reform on behalf of students and families. The record of success in limiting tuition increases, however, has not been impressive, whether at the federal or state level.

Beyond these issues of financial accountability, the first decade of the twenty-first century has also seen efforts to define and expand accountability for student learning outcomes in higher education. This thrust, which can be traced to the 1980s, has accelerated in recent years. In 2006, Peter Ewell described the impetus for measuring student learning outcomes in *Making the Grade*, a report prepared for boards of trustees of higher education institutions. He suggested that boards should be able to answer the following questions: "How good is our product? How good are we at producing our product? Are our customers satisfied? Do we have the right 'mix' of products? Do we make the grade?"[55] Ewell purposely used the language of business to frame these questions, arguing not that higher education should be compared directly to business, but rather that students and families contemplating an outlay of $100,000 (or much more in the case of elite private institutions) might reasonably expect an answer to these questions.

The National Center for Public Policy and Higher Education, in its *Measuring Up* series, included student learning outcomes as one of its six graded categories of higher education performance. But the series of reports, published biennially from 2000 to 2008, gave states the grade of "incomplete" in this area due to the lack of relevant data on student outcomes.[56] During the decade, the National Center sponsored research by Margaret Miller and Peter Ewell on how states might develop measures to assess the educational capital of their citizens and reported the results in its 2004 and 2006 editions of *Measuring Up*, as well as in *Measuring Up on College-Level Learning*, which lays out a plan by which data could be assembled for that purpose.[57] To date, however, neither the federal government nor the states has financed this effort. The 2006 report of the Spellings Commission (named for Margaret Spellings, the U.S. Secretary of Education during George W. Bush's second term in office) strongly recommended that "postsecondary education institutions should measure and report meaningful student learning outcomes," indicating a continued federal interest in such data.[58] The public university associations in Washington, D.C., have begun to develop a partial response to that challenge.[59] As these efforts to identify and measure student learning outcomes have generated discussion and some action, three overall purposes appear to be driving this work. The first is to increase accountability of institutions, which some people believe are doing a poor job of producing enough college graduates who are prepared for well-paying careers and the complexities of citizenship. A second motive is to improve consumer knowledge and understanding by providing better information to students and families who are making educational choices in selecting a college or university. The third derives from a motivation to improve public policy by seeking measurable information on the educational capital of citizens. In relation to these three purposes, the direction of this movement remains uncertain at this time.

As the nation emerges from the first decade of the twenty-first century, the financial picture remains bleak. After the recession of the early years of the decade, a new economic bubble arose in the housing market, as the Federal Reserve Board kept interest rates low and new debt instruments, based on subprime mortgages, were packaged (securitized) as collateralized debt obligations and sold to Wall Street, at huge volume.[60] As with all economic bubbles, this one exploded in 2006–2007, with the impact spread through all credit markets that rely on securitization, thus hitting automobile loans, credit card loans, and student loans. Investors suddenly reassessed the risk of holding securitized debt, and financial markets locked up, as no one wanted to buy or hold these instruments of uncertain value. The ensuing credit crisis took down the investment banks Bear Stearns and Lehman Brothers; the brokerage giant, Merrill Lynch; several large banks, including IndyMac and Wachovia; and forced the Federal Reserve and Treasury Department to take over Fannie Mae and Freddie Mac, heretofore quasi-governmental organizations that held trillions of dollars worth of home mortgages. The U.S. Department of Education also had to intervene in the student loan market to assure that loans remained available.

During the real estate boom from 2004 to 2007, the stock market soared, state revenues were strengthened, the economy grew rapidly, and inflation was largely contained. State and local support for higher education thus rebounded, reaching nearly $72 billion in fiscal year 2005.[61] The National Bureau of Economic Research (NBER), official arbiter of recessions, announced in late 2008 that a recession had begun in the final quarter of 2007—a downturn that has since become known, due to its severity and length, as the Great Recession.[62] By 2008, the economy was growing very sluggishly; unemployment was rising; the price of oil had reached a record high of $145 per barrel; gasoline prices had soared, driving up transportation costs and thereby affecting virtually all sectors of the economy; and state revenues were falling sharply again, as two-thirds of states projected budget shortfalls totaling $40 billion in 2009.[63] States have been slow to recover and, as of the end of fiscal year 2011, no longer benefit from American Recovery and Reinvestment Act stimulus funds. Midway through 2011, budget shortfalls appeared in fifteen states. Thirty-five states have projected budget gaps in 2012, and twenty-four states anticipate budget shortfalls in 2014.[64] Thus, the short- and intermediate-term outlook for state support of higher education is grim.

During the first half of the decade, student financial aid grew rapidly, with the total from all sources rising from $102.2 billion in 2000–2001 to $155 billion in 2005–2006 (in 2009 dollars). Pell Grants increased from $9.9 to $14 billion during this period, federal loans climbed from $42.9 to $63.9 billion, and private loans added another $17.6 billion in 2005–2006. Loans accounted for 70 percent of federal student aid in 2005–2006, while grants made up just 22 percent.[65] Higher education today is increasingly provided and sold as a private good, its purchase heavily reliant on debt financing.

In 2009, the American Opportunity Tax Credit (AOTC) modified the existing Hope Tax Credit for 2009 and 2010. AOTC made the Hope Tax Credit available to a broader range of taxpayers, including many with higher incomes and those who owe no tax. As a result, education tax expenditures expanded at the end of the decade, continuing a trend that began during the Clinton administration (see table 4.2).

Also in 2009, President Barack Obama articulated his national goal for higher education: by 2020, the United States should rank first in the world in the share of its population with a college degree. This overall objective was later revised to focus on the educational attainment of 25- to 35-year-olds, the age group that had lost the most ground in comparison with their peers in other developed nations. To reach and surpass the leading nations for this age group, the United States will need to achieve approximately a 4 percent *annual*

TABLE 4.2
Education tax expenditures* (millions of dollars)

	2009	2010
Exclusion of scholarship and fellowship income (normal tax method)	2,080	2,160
HOPE tax credit	2,920	0
Lifetime Learning tax credit	3,860	2,910
American Opportunity tax credit	2,460	13,590
Education Individual Retirement Accounts	40	60
Deductibility of student-loan interest	1,250	1,260
Deduction for higher education expenses	1,790	520
State prepaid tuition plans	1,200	1,390
Exclusion of interest on student-loan bonds	440	400
Exclusion of interest on bonds for private nonprofit educational facilities	1,780	1,610
Credit for holders of zone academy bonds	190	220
Exclusion of interest on savings bonds redeemed to finance educational expenses	20	20
Parental personal exemption for students age 19 or over	4,440	2,710
Deductibility of charitable contributions (education)	4,170	4,290
Exclusion of employer-provided educational assistance	660	690
Special deduction for teacher expenses	180	160
Discharge of student loan indebtedness	20	20
Qualified school construction bonds	20	110
Total	27,520	32,120

Source: Office of Management and Budget, 2011 Budget, Supplemental Materials, Tax Expenditures Spreadsheet, http://www.whitehouse.gov/omb/budget/Supplemental.
*Total income tax expenditures

increase through 2020 in the proportion of young adults with an associate or a bachelor's degree.[66]

In support of this goal, the president proposed major initiatives to streamline and strengthen federal student financial assistance, as well as new federal programs to improve access to college, raise college graduation rates, and strengthen community colleges. In addition, the American Recovery and Reinvestment Act of 2009 (ARRA) provided states with federal stimulus dollars that could be allocated for higher education. States appropriated $5.9 billion of federal ARRA funds to operating support for colleges and universities in 2009 and 2010. In 2009, these federal resources accounted for 3 percent of state and local support of higher education. However, these federal investments were not linked to the president's goals or policy strategies.[67]

In 2010, Congress enacted the Health Care and Education Reconciliation Act, which included higher education provisions that were considerably more modest than the president had initially proposed. As the administration had advocated, the new law enacted a major change in federal student financial aid: eliminating federal guaranteed student loans supplied by banks and other financial institutions and shifting to direct federal loans, with a projected savings of $61 billion over ten years. The law allocated $36 billion of the savings to increase Pell Grants (raising the maximum grant to $5,550 in 2010 and to $5,975 by 2017) and to index the grants to inflation (that is, to the Consumer Price Index) beginning in 2013. Indexing Pell Grants to inflation promises to regularize the rates of increase, thereby dampening the volatility of adjustments, which has plagued the program for most of its history. Since the early 1970s, the Pell Grant (initially called Basic Educational Opportunity Grants) has been the foundation program for equality of opportunity in higher education. But adjustments to the maximum grant level awarded to the students with the greatest financial need have been sporadic (see figure 4.4). Consequently, the portion of college costs covered by the grants has fluctuated with long periods of erosion of purchasing power between adjustments (see figure 4.5).

FIGURE 4.4   Actual maximum Pell Grant over time

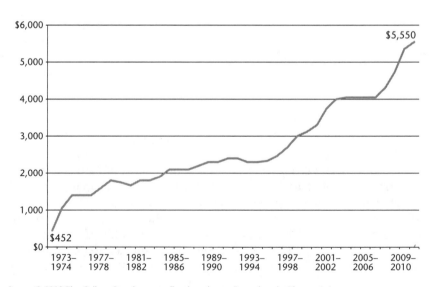

Source: © 2010 The College Board, www.collegeboard.com. Reproduced with permission.

FIGURE 4.5   Pell Grant per recipient as a percentage of average annual tuition
and fees at public four-year colleges (in current dollars)

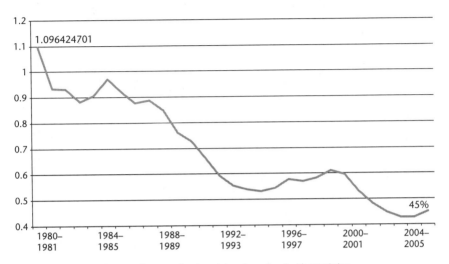

Source: © 2010 The College Board, www.collegeboard.com. Reproduced with permission.

In addition to making changes in Pell Grants, the Health Care and Education Reconciliation Act streamlined the application process for student
financial aid. The law also invested another $1.5 billion to lower the cap on
repayments of federal loans from 15 percent to 10 percent of monthly discretionary income after 2014. But the $12 billion that had been designated in
the original Obama proposal to support new programs for community colleges through the American Graduation Initiative and the $2.5 billion aimed
at improving college completion through the College Access and Completion
Innovation Fund were shifted to health-care reform in the final version of
the law. In place of these initiatives, $750 million was allocated to the exist-
ing College Access Challenge Grant program and $2 billion was directed to
the Department of Labor for a previously authorized competitive grant program for educational and career training in community colleges.[68]

With the 2010 legislation, the Obama administration succeeded in streamlining and improving support for key federal student aid programs and shifting substantial public subsidies from financial institutions to these programs.
But at the end of the decade, the overall thrust of federal support for students
was still strongly in favor of loans as compared with grants. As of 2009–2010,
preliminary federal spending on grants totaled $29.8 billion, compared with
$105.2 billion for loans and almost $7 billion for education tax benefits (see
table 4.3).

TABLE 4.3
Major federal financial aid programs

Program	Description	Student eligibility	Preliminary spending 2009–2010 (millions)	2010 recipients (thousands)
Grant programs*			**$29,835**	**9,896**
Pell Grants	Grants to undergraduates based on financial need.	Undergraduate, financial need.	$28,213	7,738
Supplemental Educational Opportunity Grants (SEOG)	Institutions must match a portion of federal funds.	Undergraduate, exceptional financial need.	$758	1,303
Leveraging Educational Assistance Partnership (LEAP)	Federal government assists states in providing aid to students with financial need. Aid can be in the form of grants or work-study.	Student eligibility differs from state to state, but the student must demonstrate "substantial financial need" as determined by the state.	N/A	N/A
Academic Competitiveness Grants	1st or 2nd year, must have completed rigorous secondary school program.	Pell recipient.	$503	716
SMART Grants	3rd or 4th year, majoring in certain scientific, technical, or high demand fields and have at least a 3.0 GPA.	Pell recipient.	$361	139
Loan programs			**$105,201**	**18,945**
Perkins Loans	Schools administer funds and must contribute matching funds. Undergrads and grads with exceptional financial need.		$1,106	521

Program	Description	Student eligibility	Preliminary spending 2009–2010 (millions)	2010 recipients (thousands)
Subsidized Stafford	Basis of financial need, undergrads and grads who are enrolled at least half-time. Federal government pays interest costs while student is in school and 6 months after graduation. Student repays after graduation.	Financial need.	$36,741	8,855
Direct			$14,190	3,523
Guaranteed			$22,551	5,331
Unsubsidized Stafford	Undergrads and grads who are enrolled at least half-time. Federal government does not pay interest costs.		$44,689	8,507
Direct			$16,721	3,398
Guaranteed			$27,968	5,109
PLUS	Loans made to parents on behalf of students enrolled at least half-time. Borrower pays for all interest.	Loan amounts limited to cost of attendance less other aid.	$14,165	1,063
Direct			$5,934	504
Guaranteed			$8,231	560
Other loans			$8,500	N/A
Education tax benefits			**$6,970**	**8,015**
Hope Tax Credits		Student must be at least half-time and in the first 2 years of enrollment. Credit amount depends on income level.	N/A	N/A
Lifetime Learning Tax Credits	Available to part-time students and graduate students.	Undergrad or grad. Credit amount depends on income level.	N/A	N/A

continued

TABLE 4.3 *continued*

Program	Description	Student eligibility	Preliminary spending 2009–2010 (millions)	2010 recipients (thousands)
Tuition tax deductions		Students must be enrolled at least half-time. Deduction amount depends on income level.	N/A	N/A
Education savings accounts	For each child under 18, families may deposit money into an Education IRA—earnings will accumulate tax free and no taxes will be charged upon withdrawal if used for higher education expenses.	Phased out for higher income families. A taxpayer cannot withdraw from an Education IRA in the same year as the benefit from a HOPE or LLC is used.	N/A	N/A
Federal work study	Money earned while attending school—part-time jobs.	Financial need.	$1,417	930

Sources: U.S. Department of Education, Federal Student Aid, *Federal Student Aid at a Glance,* www.FederalStudentAid.ed.gov/pubs; U.S. Government Accountability Office GAO-05-684, Student Aid And Postsecondary Tax Preferences: Limited Research Exists on Effectiveness of Tools to Assist Students and Families through Title IV Student Aid and Tax Preferences, July 29, 2005; The College Board, *Trends in Student Aid* 2010.

N/A = Not available.

Note: Spending numbers are in current dollars and represent disbursements. Loan recipients total does not include recipients of "other loans."

*Grant programs do not include certain veterans, military, and other grant programs administered outside of the Department of Education. The 2009 recipients do not include LEAP recipients.

CONCLUDING OBSERVATIONS ABOUT THE HISTORY
OF HIGHER EDUCATION

We can draw several important observations from the brief history of higher education finance provided in this and the previous chapter. First, in the post-World War II years, the United States, through a series of fortuitous and almost accidental decisions, moved toward mass higher education earlier than other nations, and this gave the United States an enormous economic edge for at least one generation. That edge has largely evaporated, and we now face many developed and developing nations whose citizens are achieving high rates of postsecondary (or "tertiary") education. This presents the United States with severe challenges in a knowledge-based world economy.

Second, over the last fifty years, the federal government has assumed an increasing role in supporting college opportunity for students and families. The extent and magnitude of that policy shift are reflected in the increased costs and numbers of students served by federal programs over the past half-century (see table 4.4, and figure 4.6). This development would have been inconceivable in the first century and a half after the adoption of the U.S. Constitution.

A third broad observation concerns the steady shift in perceptions of some policy makers and higher education leaders of higher education as a private benefit rather than a public good. The policy implication of this transformation is that more of the costs of college have been transferred away from general taxpayers and toward individual students and families. Under these conditions, further expansion of enrollments and participation rates in college will require significant expansion of student debt—at a time when credit markets have been contracting and when student debt has reached unprecedented levels, causing many to wonder if students can carry and service the debt after graduation. Furthermore, many first-generation college students and their families are reluctant to incur debt, and many will not borrow for what is, to them, an uncertain educational investment opportunity. In this environment, alternative finance mechanisms will most likely need to be considered.[69]

A fourth observation concerns the difficulties of coordinating federal and state policies, in part because each of the fifty states has its own approach to finance, while the federal government operates primarily in its own sphere, unable to assume that state practices will remain stable.[70] This practice will need to change if overall system performance is to be improved with limited resources. As one example, what is now the Pell Grant program was originally enacted at a time of nearly universal low public tuition, but as states have shifted funding patterns toward higher tuition, the original hope that Pell Grants could ensure access has been dashed. The absence of a national education ministry has often been seen as a strength of U.S. higher education, but we must also acknowledge that there are costs associated with our highly decentralized nonsystem of higher education.

TABLE 4.4
Federal spending on higher education and number of recipients by program type

Program	1963–1964	1970–1971	1979–1980	1989–1990	1999–2000	2009–2010
Federal grants and work study	$0.8	$11.4	$20.8	$12.5	$14.3	$42.7
Federal loans	$0.8	$6.5	$12.2	$20.6	$42.4	$96.8
Education tax benefits	$0.0	$0.0	$0.0	$0.0	$5.3	$7.0
Total federal student aid	$1.6	$17.9	$33.0	$33.1	$62.1	$146.5

Number of grant, loan, and tax recipients (academic year, thousands of borrowers)

Program Type	1980–1981	1989–1990	1999–2000	2009–2010
Grants				
Pell Grants	2,708	3,322	3,764	7,738
Federal SEOG	717	728	1,170	1,303
Academic Competitiveness Grants	—	—	—	716
SMART Grants	—	—	—	139
Total of selected grant programs	3,424	4,050	4,933	9,896
Work-Study	819	677	733	930
Loans				
Perkins Loans	813	696	655	521
Federal Direct Student Loans				
Stafford Subsidized	N/A	N/A	1,403	3,523
Stafford Unsubsidized	N/A	N/A	884	3,398
PLUS	N/A	N/A	166	504
Federal Family Education Loans				
Stafford Subsidized	N/A	N/A	2,771	5,331
Stafford Unsubsidized	N/A	N/A	1,796	5,109
PLUS	N/A	N/A	294	560
Total of selected loan programs	N/A	N/A	7,968	18,945
Federal education tax benefits	—	—	5,492	8,015

Source: The College Board, Trends in Student Aid, 2010. © 2010 The College Board, www.collegeboard.com.
Reproduced with permission.
N/A = Data not available.

FIGURE 4.6 Total federal student aid (in constant 2009 dollars)

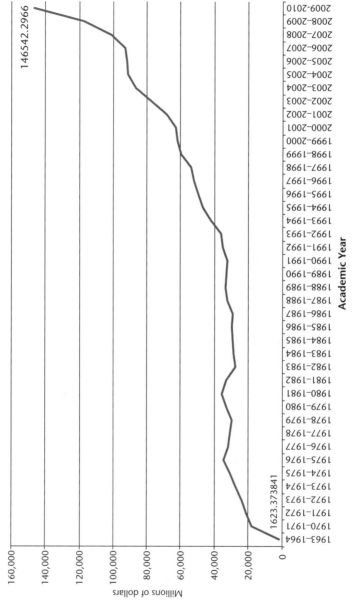

Source: © 2010 The College Board, www.collegeboard.com. Reproduced with permission.

Fifth, the record of the last sixty-five years shows that colleges and universities, far from being sluggish and incapable of change, are remarkably adaptable and able to adjust to shifting economic, demographic, technological, and political environments. Despite some initial reservations, these institutions managed to provide mass higher education to the GIs after World War II and to the baby boom generation in the 1960s and 1970s. During the difficult enrollment years of the 1980s and early 1990s, they broadened their reach to include adult and part-time students, and, initially in the private sector, they developed the art of price discrimination, using financial aid for enrollment management. When it became increasingly clear that the share of state support devoted to higher education was not likely to return to the levels of the 1960s, they aggressively sought other revenues, including higher tuition, increased private fund-raising, more aggressive endowment investment strategies, and the privatization of professional schools, such as in law and graduate business. Through all the ebbs and flows of financial and political support noted in this and the previous chapter, enrollments have continued to rise and few colleges have closed their doors. Few industries, if any, can point to a comparable record.

Sixth, the Great Recession beginning in 2007 and its extended aftermath has caused some higher education leaders and policy makers to talk for the first time about a new normal for higher education, recognizing that the economic environment has changed in fundamental ways to which institutions must adapt.[71] Many observers question the sustainability of the prevalent business model of the enterprise—that is, constant sharp increases in tuition and reliance on private fund-raising to maintain ever-growing revenues. There are increasing calls for cost containment, the streamlining of programs, the adoption of cost-saving instructional technology, and the identification and support of core educational programs and courses rather than less central activities. Chapter 7 focuses on these issues in greater detail, as they represent the central challenges facing higher education in the years ahead.

Finally, nothing in this history would lead one to believe that the demand or need for higher education is likely to diminish in coming years. We may be approaching an impasse, however, as our ability or willingness to pay for higher education, individually or collectively, appears to be declining, at least in the absence of changes in how higher education operates. The perennial questions, first posed by the Carnegie Commission—*Who Pays? Who Benefits? Who Should Pay?*—will continue to be with us in ever more pressing form for the foreseeable future.

CHAPTER 5

State Higher Education Policy

The provision and oversight of higher education is effectively reserved to the states by omission from the U.S. Constitution. In practical terms, the states are responsible for their public systems of higher education and oversee, to a greater or lesser degree, the entire postsecondary enterprise within their borders, while the federal government is limited primarily to the support of research and financially needy students. As a result, when the United States seeks to achieve national goals for higher education, the federal government must work with the fifty states, which are diverse in the challenges they face and in the ways they organize higher education.

In this chapter, we examine the diversity of the states in higher education policy and finance, and we identify key policy levers available to states to improve their performance in higher education. Based on our analysis, we propose several groupings of states (i.e., a typology) according to their common characteristics and challenges, and we identify policy approaches that are appropriate for addressing their specific needs and goals. Later, in chapter 7, we broaden our approach to propose several areas where federal and state policies can be better aligned to assist the nation and the states in achieving substantial increases in degree attainment and equity.

THE ROLE OF STATES IN HIGHER EDUCATION POLICY

The states finance and oversee the public colleges and universities that enroll about three-fourths of all college students in United States. States also provide financial aid to students in the amount of some $9 billion per year.[1] A significant part of this state student aid, more than one-third, goes to students

This chapter was coauthored by William Doyle, associate professor of education, Vanderbilt University.

attending private colleges and universities, both nonprofit and for-profit institutions.[2] The states also provide umbrella policy or governance structures that, to varying degrees, license private institutions, monitor and regulate them, and seek to, at least loosely, coordinate their activities with those of public institutions.[3]

In terms of finance, the states provided about 54 percent of total educational revenues for higher education operations in fiscal year 2010 and a substantially larger share if research universities are excluded.[4] However, this 54 percent aggregate figure for 2010 masks wide variation among the states, from around 20 percent provided by the state in Massachusetts to nearly 90 percent in New Mexico. States also have substantial influence over student tuition and fees, which comprise the other major revenue source for public colleges and universities.[5] A few states provide modest direct funding to some of their private colleges and universities, and nearly all states give financial aid to students attending accredited private institutions.[6]

Given the support they provide to higher education, states have a central role in increasing the degree output of the nation's colleges and universities. But inducing states—along with institutions themselves—to take effective steps to increase degree output is a major challenge. Even before the sharp economic downturn that began at the end of 2007, states faced serious fiscal challenges in funding higher education. In every state, the costs of major services (such as K–12 education, higher education, Medicaid, and corrections) were projected to exceed revenues through 2016 under current laws governing program eligibility and at current tax rates, thus producing structural budget deficits that are difficult to correct through either tax increases or service reductions.[7] The 2007–2009 recession and its aftermath have only worsened the fiscal position of the states, and the damage is not likely to be repaired quickly. States had to close budget imbalances totaling $230 billion nationally between fiscal years 2009 and 2011, and the immediate fiscal future does not look bright, as federal stabilization funds are withdrawn.[8] If higher education is to meet the nation's needs in such an environment, the nation must give careful thought to using resources efficiently and productively.

Variation Among States

In addition to the challenges associated with state fiscal duress, the wide differences among the states—in their higher education systems, demographic and geographic characteristics, resources, and attitudes relevant to policy making—complicate the achievement of ambitious policy goals. States range from enrolling virtually all of their college and university students in public institutions (Wyoming) to educating more than half their students in the private sector (the District of Columbia and Massachusetts, with several others above 40 percent) (see table 5.1).[9] The private sector is not directly under

TABLE 5.1
Sector shares of higher education enrollment by state, autumn 2008.

	% share of public 4-year and post-baccalureate	% share of public 2-year	% share of private not-for-profit*	% share of private for-profit	Total
Alabama	51.9%	26.9%	8.8%	12.4%	310,941
Alaska	91.7	3.2	2.6	2.4	30,717
Arizona	18.1	28.9	1.1	51.8	704,245
Arkansas	54.4	34.4	9.6	1.6	158,374
California	24.8	59.6	10.1	5.5	2,652,241
Colorado	47.2	25.1	9.9	17.8	325,232
Connecticut	36.7	27.7	33.8	1.7	184,178
Delaware	45.3	28.1	26.6	0.0	53,088
District of Columbia	4.4	0.0	59.1	36.5	126,110
Florida	47.7	25.3	15.9	11.2	972,699
Georgia	49.3	29.7	14.0	7.0	476,581
Hawaii	40.5	35.9	19.2	4.4	70,104
Idaho	59.7	16.3	21.5	2.4	80,456
Illinois	23.7	41.6	25.8	9.0	859,242
Indiana	53.4	20.5	21.1	5.0	401,956
Iowa	24.1	30.7	19.7	25.6	286,891
Kansas	49.5	37.3	12.2	1.1	198,991
Kentucky	46.3	34.8	12.8	6.0	257,583
Louisiana	60.4	25.5	10.5	3.6	236,375
Maine	49.3	21.7	26.5	2.4	67,796
Maryland	45.0	37.8	15.5	1.7	338,914
Massachusetts	23.6	19.5	55.7	1.1	477,056
Michigan	44.8	36.1	17.8	1.3	652,799
Minnesota	32.3	30.2	17.5	20.0	411,055
Mississippi	44.4	45.5	8.8	1.3	160,441
Missouri	34.4	23.3	37.1	5.2	396,409
Montana	71.4	19.6	8.9	0.0	47,840
Nebraska	43.0	33.4	22.0	1.7	130,458
Nevada	79.7	10.4	1.4	8.5	120,490
New Hampshire	40.9	18.0	35.6	5.6	71,739
New Jersey	40.1	40.0	18.3	1.5	410,160
New Mexico	40.6	52.8	1.8	4.8	142,413
New York	31.0	23.7	41.6	3.6	1,234,858
North Carolina	40.8	41.5	16.5	1.3	528,977
North Dakota	74.1	12.2	10.9	2.8	51,327
Ohio	45.4	27.4	21.3	6.0	653,585
Oklahoma	56.4	29.8	10.4	3.4	206,757

continued

TABLE 4.3   *continued*

	% share of public 4-year and post-baccalureate	*% share of public 2-year*	*% share of private not-for-profit**	*% share of private for-profit*	*Total*
Oregon	40.2	42.1	13.7	4.0	220,474
Pennsylvania	36.6	18.1	38.7	6.6	740,288
Rhode Island	29.8	21.0	48.9	0.3	83,893
South Carolina	42.8	38.4	16.6	2.2	230,695
South Dakota	68.4	10.4	14.8	6.5	50,444
Tennessee	43.6	26.1	23.2	7.2	307,610
Texas	43.0	44.7	9.6	2.8	1,327,148
Utah	53.0	19.8	23.1	4.1	217,224
Vermont	46.2	13.3	38.9	1.6	42,946
Virginia	41.1	35.4	16.9	6.6	500,796
Washington	39.4	46.7	11.5	2.5	362,535
West Virginia	54.6	16.1	9.7	19.6	125,333
Wisconsin	50.0	29.5	18.0	2.5	352,875
Wyoming	33.6	62.2	0.0	4.2	35,936
United States	38.4%	34.8%	19.2%	7.7%	19,102,814

Source: U.S. Department of Education, National Center for Education Statistics, 2008 Integrated Postsecondary Education Data System (IPEDS), Spring 2009. (This table was prepared May 2010), Table 225.
*Includes two-year and post-baccalureate enrollments.

state control, but it can be influenced by state policy incentives. Enrollment in private colleges and universities, as compared with public institutions, tends to cost the state much less per state resident enrolled, even though some of these students receive state student aid.[10]

Several states (California, New Mexico, and Wyoming) enroll more than half their students in two-year colleges, while others have proportionally small two-year sectors (Alaska, Nevada, the Dakotas, and Vermont). Two-year colleges spend much less per enrolled student than baccalaureate colleges and universities, but transfer rates between these two types of institutions are low and raising them has been a challenge, which in turn limits the completion of bachelor's degrees.[11] Also, there is considerable variation by state in the prominence of research universities as compared with less costly comprehensive universities and baccalaureate-only colleges.[12] These structural differences in state higher education sectors are important to consider in developing policies to increase degree output and equity in an era of constrained resources.

State performance in higher education also varies widely. Participation rates—that is, the percentage of 18- to 24-year-olds enrolled in college-level education—range from a high of 50 percent in Rhode Island to 18 percent in Alaska.[13] Degree attainment varies as well: in Massachusetts, 41 percent of the adult population has a bachelor's degree or higher; in West Virginia, only 18 percent do.[14] To some extent, these differences in participation and attainment correlate with demographic and income differences in state populations. In general, states with lower participation rates tend to have larger populations of ethnic minorities (as a share of the overall population) and slightly higher poverty rates. States with lower median income also generally have lower participation rates, but the relationship between median income and college participation is not as strong as the relationship between ethnic population and college participation. Unless poverty and ethnic-based disadvantages in the lagging states are addressed, it is likely that these disparities will be perpetuated.

Demographics, after all, are not static. Nationally, the number of high school graduates is thought to have peaked at 3.34 million in 2008 and is projected to decline by a modest 4 percent by 2013 before increasing gradually to 3.36 million in 2021. There remains, however, a sizable minority of states experiencing substantial growth in high school graduates and thus in demand for college spaces, with much of the growth in nonwhite ethnic groups and in populations with low or moderate incomes. Between 2009 and 2021, eight states are projected to have at least a 20 percent increase in the number of high school graduates, and five more expect at least a 10 percent increase.[15] These states will need to find ways to accommodate additional traditional-age students in higher education, while also serving older workers seeking more education.

In contrast, eight states are expecting a decrease in the number of high school graduates, and most states expect only modest increases.[16] In the majority of states without strong population pressures, there will be an opportunity to increase higher education participation rates without having to cope with growing cohort sizes. This will require new approaches to attracting and retaining students of color and those from lower-income backgrounds. In addition, efforts to increase higher education attainment will likely need to reach beyond the youth cohort to the adult working-age population, particularly in these states.[17]

There are also large differences among states in wealth and income and in their inclination to tax themselves to provide public services, including access to higher education. Annual personal income per capita ranges from a high of about $55,000 in Connecticut to about $28,500 in Mississippi. Meanwhile, the "tax burden," which measures taxes per capita, ranges from $3,600 in Vermont to $1,430 in South Dakota.[18]

The physical size of states and their population distribution are also relevant to higher education policy. States that include large geographic areas with sparsely populated regions will need different policy approaches for higher education than smaller states dominated by densely populated metropolitan regions. Since many states have both rural and urbanized regions, they need to tailor their mix of policies accordingly.

The extent and limits of gubernatorial powers vary considerably across states and can be expected to influence priorities for higher education.[19] For example, earlier research suggests that governors can serve an important role in raising higher education's profile on state policy agendas.[20] Having a governorship with extensive powers in relation to the state legislature may not be essential and does not guarantee success in raising the profile of higher education, but it can be helpful.

Finally, the political culture of each state influences the kinds of policies enacted in the public sphere, including higher education.[21] It appears that grouping states by region can help in distinguishing common approaches to governance of higher education. Zumeta found, for example, that most states in the Great Plains and Rocky Mountain West tended to employ laissez-faire policy approaches for their private (nonprofit) college and university sectors, while states in the Northeast and upper Midwest were more inclined toward central planning that encompasses both public and private sectors. In contrast, many southern and lower Midwest states tended toward policies that favor market forces in distributing students and state subsidies.[22]

POLICY LEVERS AVAILABLE TO STATES

Most of the basic state characteristics described are either relatively constant or shift very slowly. A state cannot alter its basic geography, nor can it increase its wealth or alter the structure of its higher education system rapidly. Yet there are policy levers that states can employ to pursue their goals for higher education more immediately. The following sections describe the most readily available tools state policy makers can use to influence the performance of higher education systems. The applicability of each lever depends upon the state, as we will elaborate in the subsequent section of the chapter.

State Higher Education Governance Structures

Employing a framework first suggested by Lyman Glenny, state governance arrangements for higher education are usually classified by contrasting two main types of state-level bodies: governing boards and coordinating boards. The distinction is based on whether the board has line management authority over the public institutions in the state (as in Georgia, North Carolina, and Wisconsin, for example) or is authorized only to coordinate their activities in some fashion and make recommendations to state policy makers (as in California, Indiana, and Washington).[23] A further distinction is often made between those coordinating boards with budgetary authority and those without. In addition, a number of states have separate boards for two-year and baccalaureate-granting institutions. Beyond this, the specific powers of different coordinating boards vary, and some states have several multicampus systems with system-level governing boards overseen by a statewide coordinating board.[24]

Given this complexity, it is difficult to make generalizations across states, but we can make several useful observations. Since governing boards are designed to lead systems of public institutions, they tend to perceive private colleges and universities as competitors. As a result, coordinating boards tend to be better equipped structurally to address the role of private institutions in helping to meet state higher education goals.[25] Similarly, having separate system boards for two-year and baccalaureate institutions can create impediments to smooth transfers between these two types of colleges.

Research on the various forms of state governance of higher education has not yielded clear answers as to which of the wide variety of arrangements is best for all circumstances. A recent five-state comparative study by Richard Richardson and Mario Martinez, however, provides several plausible suggestions.[26] These authors examined the relationship between state policies in higher education—which they call "rules in use"—and the performance of state systems on such outcomes as student preparation for college, participation and completion rates, and research prowess. They found the following: (1) states that develop clear public goals and priorities for higher education and pursue them through consistent, intentional strategy can achieve improved performance; (2) states that lack a strong interface agency operating between higher education institutions and state government (that is, a coordinating or governing board with real influence) are at a disadvantage in achieving public goals; (3) states that have a significant private higher-education sector and that include this sector in their policy portfolio can improve performance; (4) need-based student aid programs can improve performance; and (5) states that constrain aspirations of non- or limited-research institutions to develop or expand their research mission (commonly referred to as "mission creep") can achieve better overall performance.

To achieve statewide goals, it appears that state-level leadership and the development of mechanisms to align institutional goals with statewide goals are necessary.[27] Depending upon the state's governance arrangements, however, the mechanisms for effective influence will vary. For example, a statewide governing board overseeing both two-year and baccalaureate institutions can use more direct means to improve transfer rates than can a coordinating board that seeks to influence these rates by developing financial incentives or by convening interinstitutional committees.

Appropriations Levels for Higher Education

Extensive research concerning the link between spending and performance in higher education suggests that the manner in which funds are spent matters at least as much as the amount spent.[28] The level of funding historically provided for higher education is a factor in setting the stage for state policy making. Yet the level of funding is consistently perceived as more important to performance than it actually is. National Center for Higher Education Management Systems research shows that levels of performance vary widely at any given level of per-student funding, suggesting that resources provided for institutions do not directly or solely determine the level of performance.[29] This finding holds across multiple performance outcomes, including undergraduate degree production, graduate degree production, and research productivity.

Despite the lack of a direct causal link between appropriations and performance, overall levels of appropriations do affect the kinds of policies that are available at any given time. In states that have historically provided low levels of appropriations per student (such as New Hampshire and Vermont), requests for programs that require substantial new or increased state spending are unlikely to receive a hearing. On the other hand, requests for programs that require relatively little spending while leveraging private or out-of-state resources are likely to be taken more seriously. In states with relatively high levels of appropriations per student (such as New Mexico), reallocating ample resources that are already in place may be the only route to improved performance in a time of budget restraint. In the coming years, few states are likely to have extensive new resources to invest in higher education, so it will be important to use available resources productively.

Even when economic conditions improve, achieving better performance will depend upon *how* any new resources are directed and linked to incentives for improved performance. For example, creating budget incentives that are linked to completion and equity goals—that is, to degree output and to who gets degrees—can be powerful levers that are readily understood and should be supported by policy makers and many stakeholders who are committed to achieving these goals.

Tuition and Financial Aid Policies

A substantial body of evidence has demonstrated that, as economic theory predicts, lowering the net price (tuition less financial aid) of higher education results in increased enrollment, other things being equal.[30] In addition, low-income students are more responsive to changes in net price than their middle- and high-income peers.[31] Well-designed financial aid policies can help close long-standing participation gaps between low-income and other students.[32] Thus, tuition and financial aid policies can substantially affect the level of enrollment in a state as well as equity across groups.

In theory, there are several ways that states can affect the net price of higher education, but few states are in a position to completely redesign their tuition and financial aid systems. Incremental changes in existing systems are likely to be more feasible for most states, and these changes, if structured well, can affect both overall enrollment levels and gaps in enrollment rates between groups. Many states with proportionally large public higher education systems have sought to maintain tuition at low or moderate levels in relation to income. Some of the goals of a low-tuition policy are to maintain access for needy students and to enhance political support from middle- and upper-class families. However, a low-tuition policy requires a relatively high level of state support per student, and therefore, states that wish to expand access to broader populations of students while maintaining or improving completion rates and safeguarding quality would need to provide more funding to colleges and universities (which seems improbable given recent fiscal conditions), or institutions would need to become more cost-effective, or some combination of the two.

Many states with relatively large private sectors have adopted a high-tuition policy for public colleges and universities. In seeking to improve access to needy students, many of these states accompany their higher public tuition prices with generous student aid funding, awarded primarily on the basis of need. This aid can be provided by the state directly to students, which contributes to equity statewide, or the state can require institutions to provide the aid (for example, in return for the state's continued support of high-tuition policies).

Some states, mostly in the South, have resisted providing much aid based on student need and have favored instead merit-based aid, which is usually tied to the student's high school grades and test scores.[33] Compared with a need-based approach, merit-based aid is much less efficient in helping low-income and minority students, since much of the aid goes to more affluent, white students who tend to perform better on grades and tests. As a result, merit-based aid is problematic on equity grounds, yet it seems to have raised overall enrollments in several states, and it may have resulted in improving the academic exertions and focus of high school students.[34] In those states for which politics ensure the continuation of such programs, the development of "need-within-merit" funding—whereby needy students with merit receive larger grants—could yield additional results for qualified low-income students.

A few states have successfully employed policy innovations that link academic and financial aid policy in order to increase college participation rates, especially of underrepresented populations. A prominent example is Indiana's Twenty-First Century Scholars Program, which has demonstrated that financial incentives (in the form of an early guarantee to the needy of aid for college) for high school students to enroll and succeed in a rigorous college preparatory curriculum can substantially improve their academic performance, high school graduation rates, and college matriculation rates.[35] As this program has been implemented, Indiana's continuation rate of high school to college nearly doubled, to 62 percent in 2004, and its rank among the states jumped from twenty-eighth to tenth.

As several studies have pointed out, however, tuition, financial aid, and appropriations policies can be a barrier to achieving state strategic goals if they are not tightly linked via explicit institutionalized mechanisms.[36] Changing any one of the three in isolation will likely lead to undesirable results. For instance, simply increasing appropriations to higher education without articulating explicit goals for tuition or student aid does not necessarily lead to improved access for needy students, as institutions might use the increased appropriations without restraining tuition increases. Similarly, tuition increases that are not accompanied by more financial aid are likely to result in diminished access, particularly among low- and moderate-income students. Unfortunately, since 1990, there has been a steady decoupling of decisions about appropriations from those on tuition and financial aid, with the result that tuition has climbed far faster than family incomes or, in most states, student aid. This has seriously undermined the affordability of higher education.[37] Achieving better performance in college participation and attainment will require these policy alignment issues to be addressed.

Accountability Policies

Many states have budgeting and accountability processes in place that are designed to provide incentives for institutions to accomplish key objectives. According to Joseph Burke, there are three types of approaches that states use toward this end. *Performance funding* makes the delivery of specific resources dependent upon institutional results on specific indicators.[38] When states use this approach, the resource levels are usually modest: only a few percent of state higher education appropriations. In contrast, *performance budgeting* refers to the use of institutional performance data in a more general way by state policy makers when allocating resources to higher education. This approach typically can influence a wider range of state resources than performance funding, but its influence is harder to pinpoint. *Performance reporting* merely requires that institutions provide information to the state about progress toward goals. While the research base is growing, it is not established that these programs change underlying performance.[39]

One key weakness in policies that link state funding to performance is that states tend to offer modest levels of new funding as incentives for gains in performance, yet cut the new funding when a recession occurs.[40] In general, the incentives for performance have not been substantial enough to produce changes in how colleges and universities expend their base budgets. States might consider offering larger funding amounts that are tied to performance on course completion, degree production, equity in outcomes, and other state policy goals. To increase degree output substantially, however, these policies would need to provide serious and consistent incentives to broad-access institutions (community colleges and regional or comprehensive schools) that serve the large majority of students in most states. Thus far, it is the elite research universities that have showed the most interest in such "performance compacts" with states.[41]

Structures and Policies for Linking K–12 and Postsecondary Systems

A great deal of recent work on higher education policy has focused on K–16 issues, the set of policy linkage problems that occurs as students transition between secondary school and higher education. This research has revealed that many students do not complete their educational objectives because the two systems have very different standards, with little useful communication between them.[42] Students leaving high school expect to be prepared for higher education, only to find in many cases that their education is not sufficient for college-level studies, necessitating frustrating and costly remedial work at the postsecondary level.[43] Michael Kirst and Andrea Venezia, who have done some of the most important thinking in this area, summarize the key state policy requisites as follows: (a) aligning postsecondary placement standards with K–12 exit standards; (b) linking secondary curriculum with general education curriculum at the postsecondary level; (c) expanding concurrent enrollment opportunities (that is, college credit course work while the student is in high school); and (d) linking data systems within and across sectors of education in order to track student progress and the effectiveness of policies.[44] More effective K–16 linkage policies are needed in virtually all states but are particularly important in states that are lagging in preparation of high school graduates for postsecondary education.[45] Over the long run, tighter coupling between the two major education sectors has the potential to improve system performance and efficiency substantially. However, not all states are active in this domain.

Policies to Link Two-Year and Four-Year Institutions

Another important challenge to improving college access and completion involves the effectiveness of articulation between community colleges and baccalaureate-granting institutions. Community colleges have seen the largest enrollment growth among higher education sectors in the postwar period, and, as noted earlier, some states' higher education systems depend heavily upon them. Nearly 80 percent of community college students enter higher education with the goal of completing a bachelor's degree. However, only about 20 percent do so within six years.[46] Many never transfer to a four-year institution or even complete a degree or certificate at a two-year school.[47] Also, research has shown that many students depart from higher education *after* transferring from community college. Among students who transfer to a four-year college or university, those who have fewer community college transfer credits accepted by their higher education institution are much less likely to graduate, compared with those who have more transfer credits accepted.[48]

Over the past quarter-century, states have used both academic and financial policies in an attempt to improve the progress and completion of transfer students. The academic policies include common course numbering, sector-level course and program articulation agreements, and even state-mandated articulation policies. Common course numbering is designed to ensure that all colleges and universities in a state share a common framework for course content, particularly at the general education level. Sector-level articulation agreements obviate the need for cumbersome institution-by-institution agreements, with entire sectors (such as community colleges and universities) agreeing on the courses that all their institutions will accept from transfer students. If voluntary efforts among higher education institutions and systems fall short, as is often the case, states can potentially mandate articulation, such as requiring that all public universities accept an entire transfer sequence, but such a step is much harder to accomplish in some states than others.[49]

Another promising idea for improving articulation is the development of low-cost, online advising systems that clarify for community college students which courses at their college count for which majors at various prospective baccalaureate institutions. Likewise, community college students can benefit from the creation of course bundles that are well publicized at their college and that are specific to each major (for example, science, technology, engineering, and mathematics [STEM] majors). The idea is to prepare students efficiently during their community college years for transfer directly into upper-division majors. In addition, some community colleges have begun working more closely with private and for-profit institutions on articulation and transfers; in some states, transfers to these types of colleges and universities are growing faster than those to public four-year institutions.

Financial policies to support successful transfer can focus on students or institutions. Some states, such as Arizona, have financial aid packages targeted to assist transfer students. Others, such as Maryland, reserve a fixed percentage of university enrollment slots for transfer students (40 percent at the University of Maryland).[50] These policies provide strong incentives for successful transfer and can be cost effective for both the state and the students. Through these policies, for example, the state takes advantage of the lower per-student costs at its community colleges, and the students pay the lower community college tuition for their initial years, while being aware that the higher costs coming later will be, at least partially, covered by need-based aid. Similarly, finance polices could provide incentives for baccalaureate institutions to accept transfer students and for community colleges to send them better prepared, but these types of finance policies are generally not in place currently.

Despite the myriad of policy and administrative remedies that seek to improve transfer from two-year to four-year colleges, few states have succeeded in increasing transfer rates substantially over time. Student completion data recently available from the National Student Clearinghouse shows that states with large community college sectors (such as California, Florida, and Texas) have widely varying rates of transfer and completion of baccalaureate degrees by those who do transfer.[51] Of these three large states, Florida has been more successful in having its community college entrants complete bachelor's degrees. Notably, Florida uses a systemwide common-course numbering system, mandates that community college transfer students earn an associate's degree prior to transfer, and requires that these credits count toward the bachelor's degree at public baccalaureate institutions. Better data are becoming available in many states to track and understand state transfer rates.[52] Particularly for states with large two-year college systems, examining transfer patterns and identifying public policies that work effectively to support transfers are key pieces of any policy strategy to improve college completion rates cost effectively.

Finally, in states where poor rural access to baccalaureate opportunities is a major challenge, one potential solution is to have baccalaureate institutions develop programs on community college campuses (or their satellite sites), since these campuses tend to be more widely distributed geographically. Such programs are not easy or inexpensive to operate at a high level of quality, but distance-learning components can help. In addition, some fast-growing states (such as Florida and Washington) are allowing community colleges to develop their own baccalaureate programs.[53] While this approach may appear to be cost effective in the short turn, it raises questions that remain to be answered about the possible distortion of the two-year colleges' basic mission and about their ability to provide high-quality bachelor's programs.

Distance Learning Policies

The use of distance learning—teaching via technologies that permit students and the instructor to be in different locations and even working at different times—has grown dramatically in the past decade. Students enrolled in distance education courses, the vast majority of which are delivered via the Internet, now constitute approximately 29 percent of all enrollments in higher education in the United States.[54] Distance education has evolved considerably from the days of correspondence courses, educational television, and videoconferences. New technologies allow course designers and instructors to utilize Web-based resources and applications via collaboration technologies that either stand alone or can be blended with face-to-face course components. A U.S. Department of Education study contrasted online with face-to-face instruction in a number of courses and fields from 1996 to 2008.[55] The authors concluded that students who took all or part of a course online in general performed modestly better than those taking the same course through face-to-face instruction.

Many students use online courses to supplement standard classroom-based courses rather than enrolling exclusively online. The advantage for states is that more students can be reached and educated without large new expenditures for "bricks and mortar," although the costs of technology infrastructure, faculty training, updates, and ongoing support must be considered carefully.[56] States can provide incentives for institutions to deliver more courses and online programs to groups that might not otherwise have access to higher education, particularly in geographically isolated regions, as well as to provide instruction more cost effectively.[57] Thoughtful start-up efforts and incentives are necessary since most senior faculty are not inclined to initiate efforts in this domain without infrastructure, training, and support. Younger faculty, however, are more likely to be responsive to incentives in this area, so the future of online offerings is promising. Also, community colleges and for-profit institutions, which are higher education's major growth sectors, have been the most active in developing and expanding online offerings.

Policies to Involve Private Higher Education

As noted earlier, states vary widely in the size of their private nonprofit sectors of higher education as well as their historic interest in taking this sector into account in state policy making.[58] Where the sector is significant in size and the goal is to increase enrollments and degree completion, it makes sense for state policy makers to consider providing financial incentives to willing private colleges and universities to increase enrollments of state residents. This applies especially to students from underrepresented groups or those seeking to study in fields where the state has needs and private institutions have capacity (for example, in certain K–12 teaching specialties, health professions, or engineering). Most states have financial aid programs that permit students to enroll in private institutions within the state, but these are often small or offer weak financial incentives, especially for studies in demanding, high-need fields such as science, engineering, technology, and mathematics (STEM fields). Strengthening the incentives for students to enroll in the private sector may be more cost effective for a state than providing full student subsidies and/or building new capacity in its public higher education sector. States vary, though, in the degree to which public financial support of the private sector is politically viable.[59]

When its laws and politics permit, a state can use more direct means to create capacity by offering capital and/or operating subsidies or contracts to private institutions for additional desired capacity, rather than using incentives to students to indirectly achieve similar aims.[60] In such an arrangement, a state could allow qualified public and private institutions to offer proposals to expand particular targeted state capacities, and then fund the most attractive and cost-effective ones. Research shows that policies involving the private sector are more likely to be taken seriously where private-sector interests are structurally represented in state governance and planning processes.[61]

Quality Assurance Policies

Quality assurance in higher education is an important but relatively unheralded role for state policy. Many state higher education agencies have responsibilities for ensuring a minimum level of quality for instruction, but most have devoted few resources to such oversight. They generally defer to accrediting bodies, a practice that has worked satisfactorily for traditional colleges and universities up to a point, but has been less effective for some for-profit providers. State policy can and should respond flexibly to new providers and new modes of instructional delivery, while at the same time ensuring reasonable academic standards and institutional performance, regardless of an institution's for-profit or nonprofit status. It makes sense to encourage innovative institutions that are responding appropriately, at little cost to the state, to educational demands that are not being met by traditional providers or forms of delivery.

The majority of states now allow resident students who attend accredited for-profit institutions to receive state student aid.[62] Once state funds are involved, the state's interest in quality assurance is even greater. Ideally, quality assurance efforts could move beyond simple rule-based approaches to include assessment of academic outcomes, such as program completion. Accrediting agencies appear to be moving in this direction, but states with burgeoning for-profit sectors may especially need to take further steps in the interim to ensure that enrolled citizens (and the state) receive the benefits these institutions advertise.[63]

Information Systems to Track Students Across Systems

The success of most state policies described cannot be evaluated fully without information on students and their academic progress. Until recently, data collection and reporting focused almost exclusively on institutions, through such systems as the federal Integrated Postsecondary Education Data System (IPEDS). However, to truly understand the success of various policies, state student information systems need to track students at and through all types of institutions: from K–12 into postsecondary education and from two-year to public and private baccalaureate institutions. This requires tracking students through state relational, or unit-record, databases. In addition, since significant numbers of students cross state lines to attend higher education, state data systems should be linked to one another across states. In 2007, Peter Ewell and Marianne Boeke reported that forty states had state-unit-record databases that covered at least all of public higher education and that seventeen of these had at least some coverage of private nonprofit institutions within their borders.[64] They also identified a positive trend in the increasing number and expanding coverage of these databases, but there remains considerable opposition to such comprehensive data systems in some states and in the U.S. Congress. Some further progress has been made in the last few years with the aid of substantial federal grants and through the advocacy of the Data Quality Campaign, which was founded with philanthropic support but now also has federal funding.[65] There remains much to do, however, to make these data systems fully operational and useful for policy analysis. In addition, there is no guarantee that the federal aid that has provided an important boost to these efforts will continue.

ANALYSIS: POLICY CHALLENGES FOR STATES

The previous section summarized the major policy tools available to states for improving higher education performance. In this section, we identify the key challenges facing states and match the policy tools to the challenges that states face. The variation in state policy environments suggests that no one solution can be universally applied effectively in all states or under all circumstances. As a result, we identify different combinations of tools that are appropriate for specific types of state contexts.

We organize this section around four challenges that are crucial for state policy makers to address in substantially increasing levels of educational capital and dramatically improving equity of opportunities and outcomes. The first challenge can be characterized as a contextual condition, while the other three are state policy goals central to achieving these overarching objectives.

- *Changes in the population of young people.* Some states face substantial growth in the numbers of young people expected to be ready for higher education in the near future, others face a declining young population, and the majority of states expect slow growth. In the fast-growing states, the primary challenge is to find resources to at least meet the increased growth-driven demand.[66] In those states with little or no growth in the youth population, two key challenges emerge: to increase the numbers of college graduates by reaching deeper into the populations of youth and younger adults, and to focus available resources more effectively on those enrolled, in order to improve graduation rates.
- *Improving low participation rates.* Few state policy makers today would argue that too many people are going to college. Rather, international comparisons reveal that many states are at a serious disadvantage in global economic competition because too few people have acquired the skills necessary to compete for available jobs.[67] Some states are farther behind than others, partly because of poor high school graduation rates or weak preparation of those who do graduate from high school.
- *Equitable participation in postsecondary education.* Virtually all states have inequities across population groups in college participation. Beyond this challenge, if states are to increase overall participation rates, many of them

will need to increase access for the fastest-growing segments of their young population—that is, those groups that have historically been underserved by higher education traditionally, including low-income students, under-represented minorities, students from rural areas, and those from disadvantaged communities in urban centers. Again, weak precollege preparation and low high school graduation rates play an important role.

• *Low postsecondary completion rates.* In many states, educational attainment has not improved, even as a larger percentage of young people attend higher education. The key reason is that too few students complete their educational objectives once enrolled. There is wide variation across states in postsecondary success measures.[68]

In the next sections, we examine each of these challenges in turn, describing the nature of the problem and the kinds of policy approaches that are likely to be most promising for particular types of states, depending upon their specific challenges and their structural characteristics and policy cultures.

The First Major Challenge: Changes in the Population of Young People

According to the Western Interstate Commission for Higher Education, sixteen states will experience greater than 10 percent growth in the number of high school graduates between 2009 and 2021, while thirteen states will see more modest growth and twenty-one will experience declines, some of which will be substantial (see figure 5.1). When it comes to minority high

FIGURE 5.1   Percentage change in public and private high school graduates, 2009 to 2021

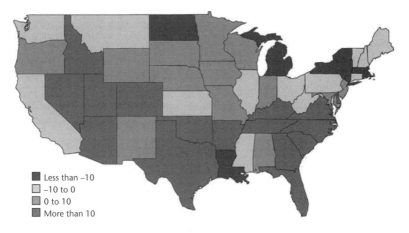

Less than –10
–10 to 0
0 to 10
More than 10

Note: Alaska = –12.7 percent; Hawaii = –5 percent.

Source: Western Interstate Commission for Higher Education (WICHE), *Knocking on the College Door: Projections of High School Graduates by State and Race/Ethnicity* (Boulder, CO: WICHE, 2008).

school graduates who are underrepresented in higher education, however, most states will see some increase and sixteen will see increases of more than 10 percent.[69]

Given states' fiscal limitations, accommodating the growth in youth populations requires the effective use of existing higher education structures, and the key structural characteristics we focus on for high-growth states involves making use of existing institutional capacity. States with large community college capacity will need to leverage the flexibility and low costs of these institutions while improving transfer rates to baccalaureate institutions. In states where the four-year collegiate sector is dominated by research universities, a priority would be to direct additional undergraduate enrollments primarily to the less expensive comprehensive and baccalaureate-only institutions. Where there is substantial private higher education capacity, state policy makers should consider financial incentives for these institutions to enroll more state residents, as long as this is cost effective for the state.

This line of analysis is depicted in table 5.2. In all states, it will be crucial in this era of constrained resources to emphasize accountability for outcomes, especially regarding student persistence, graduation and transfer, and

TABLE 5.2

Policy challenge: High levels of projected growth

Major structural characteristics	Example states	Key policy levers
Large community college system	Arizona, California, Florida, North Carolina, Texas, Virginia, Washington	Financial incentives to matriculate at community colleges, with state funding following students.
		Policies encompassing both two- and four-year institutions to improve articulation, transfer, and completion rates for those transferring.
		K–16 policies and accountability (including longitudinal unit-record data systems) to ensure high school graduates are prepared for college.
Large public 4-year sector	Arkansas, Colorado, Georgia, Nevada,	Tightened control of "mission creep" to avoid creating more expensive research-oriented institutions.
		Undergraduate growth directed to baccalaureate and comprehensive four-year institutions, with state funding following students.
		Expansion of two-year sector and use of privates to help accommodate growth.
Relatively large private sector	Florida, Georgia, North Carolina, Virginia	Expansion of student aid programs and, where feasible, provision of contracts providing incentives for private institutions to enroll state residents, where cost effective.

progress toward equity across population groups. The capacity to reach these goals can be enhanced by the further development of student unit record data systems.

The Second Major Challenge: Low Participation Rates

States vary in their rates of youth participation in higher education—that is, in the percentage of 18- to 24-year-olds enrolled (see figure 5.2). This definition of participation, drawn from the National Center for Public Policy and Higher Education's *Measuring Up* series, is preferable to other measures because it takes into account both the rates of graduation from high school and the rates of these graduates' enrollment in higher education. In some states, enrollment rates among high school graduates are fairly high, but overall participation is low due to low graduation rates from high school. In South Carolina, for example, college participation of high school graduates is relatively high, with 64 percent going on to college, but only 56 percent of students in the state graduate from high school within four years.[70]

There are three drivers of low participation rates: a lack of student supply from the K–12 system (such as low graduation rates from high school); policies and practices at the postsecondary level that discourage participation, including poor affordability; and, finally, a lack of strong demand for highly educated individuals in a state's labor market. Most states are not facing problems with the third driver, as market demand for highly educated individuals has been increasing over the last thirty years.[71]

FIGURE 5.2   Postsecondary participation rates for 18- to 24-year-olds, 2007

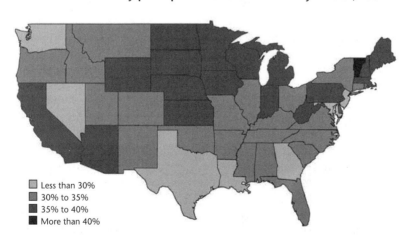

Less than 30%
30% to 35%
35% to 40%
More than 40%

Note: Alaska = 18.5 percent; Hawaii = 30.3 percent.

Source: U.S. Bureau of the Census, *American Community Survey: Percent of Population 18–24 Enrolled in Higher Education* (Washington, DC: 2009).

The U.S. high school completion rate for 18- to 24-year-olds stood at 89 percent in 2007, a figure that includes students who obtain alternative certifications such as the GED (General Educational Development diploma), but excludes the incarcerated population, which is considerable.[72] The high school completion rate varies, however, across racial and ethnic groups: 72.7 percent of Hispanic youth had completed some kind of high school credential, while 93.5 percent of white students had done so.[73] The data also show high levels of variation across income groups.[74] Students who do not complete high school have little chance of participating in or graduating from college.

States with low participation rates among 18- to 24-year-olds face different challenges depending on the success of their K–12 systems in graduating students and preparing them for college. States with poor high school preparation should consider efforts to strengthen linkages of higher education to the K–12 system, especially those focused on improving college readiness.[75] Promising K–16 linkage policies include improving preparation of K–12 teachers and alignment of standards, curricula, and assessments through the grades and across the divide between high school and college. Also important are comprehensive outreach efforts—focusing on college preparation and how to access financial aid—targeted to students, families, and communities where college participation rates have been low. In many cases, this outreach will need to be focused on low-income communities and communities of color and the schools within them. Through investments, incentives, and accountability, states can improve the coordination and effectiveness of this outreach.[76]

Many states with low participation rates have postsecondary structures that are poorly suited to the needs of incoming students. For example, a state with low college participation rates may lack adequate capacity in open-access institutions, which are the entry points for most underrepresented and first-generation students. Developing more effective remediation programs at these institutions is important, at least until K–16 efforts to improve college readiness bear fruit. States that are dominated by large research universities may find it important, but more difficult, to develop low-cost opportunities for larger numbers of students. Finally, if large proportions of students graduate from high school and are ready for college, yet relatively few actually enroll, then state policy makers may need to focus on better connecting postsecondary programs to the state's economic opportunities.[77]

Policies that make college more affordable for families can also improve participation rates in higher education. For example, states can design financial aid programs to ensure that aid is focused on those students who need it most; research demonstrates that students, especially low- and moderate-income students, are responsive to the price of higher education that they actually pay. As explained earlier, there are two basic routes to improve affordability: the historic one of keeping tuition in public institutions as low as possible for all students (low tuition, low aid), or an approach that includes higher tuition but also features student aid that is linked to students' financial needs (high tuition, high aid). In the latter approach, state subsidies are more targeted on the most needy.[78]

Table 5.3 summarizes our analysis of key policy levers for states challenged by low participation rates of 18- to 24-year-olds in higher education. The first row of the table includes states with low participation rates where performance in preparing high school students for college is mixed and affordability is poor. By "mixed" performance in high school preparation, we mean that relatively few students are prepared to go to college, based on indicators such as the proportion of students completing high-level courses while in high school and the performance of high school students on the National Assessment of Educational Progress. By affordability, we refer to the state scores as reported in *Measuring Up 2008*, which measures the average net price of higher education (after student aid is considered) relative to family income across states.[79] In Rhode Island and South Carolina, for example, a greater focus on encouraging qualified but financially marginal students to attend college could be helpful in improving participation rates. In many states, such a focus might include an increase in need-based financial aid,

TABLE 5.3

States challenged by low participation rates of 18- to 24-year-olds, by levels of preparation and affordability

Preparation and affordability	Example states	Key policy levers
Preparation: Mixed Affordability: Poor	Alaska, Florida, Georgia, Nevada, Rhode Island, South Carolina	More need-based aid for undergraduates, with very moderate tuition growth.
		Outreach efforts directed to eligible students as well as K–16 policies to improve preparation.
Preparation: Poor Affordability: Moderate	Arizona, Louisiana	Increased emphasis on K–16 policies to improve preparation.
		Tuition increases limited to growth in personal income in the state.
Preparation: Mixed Affordability: Moderate	California, Idaho, Texas, Utah, Washington	K–16 policies to improve preparation.
		Incentives to institutions for increased undergraduate enrollment, including via distance learning.
		Tuition increases limited to growth in personal income in the state.
		Support for community colleges and transfer policies to increase degree attainment cost effectively.

while in others it might mean providing a low-tuition option for students. The choice each state makes on this matter is likely to be influenced by factors such as existence of a substantial public two-year college sector or a history of strongly supporting need-based student aid.

The second row of the table focuses on states, such as Arizona and Louisiana, with low participation rates where preparation for college is poor and affordability moderate. In these states, comprehensive deployment of K–16 policies and outreach could help improve student preparation and interest in college. Meanwhile, the moderate affordability of postsecondary education should not be allowed to deteriorate if a state wishes to increase college access as preparation improves.

In the third row of the table are states with low participation rates, mixed scores on preparation, and moderate affordability. Most of these are large states geographically in the Western United States that face strong population growth and demographic changes. K–16 policies can help improve preparation for college in such states, and affordability efforts can improve access. Due to enrollment pressures, physical distances, and fiscal constraints, most of these states can benefit from incentives for colleges and universities to expand distance-learning enrollments and policies to expand the use community colleges (with strong transfer policies) and private institutions, depending upon the structural characteristics of each state's system.

The Third Major Challenge: Inequitable Participation

Many states not only face challenges in increasing their overall rates of postsecondary enrollment, but also have large gaps in participation by ethnicity and income (see figures 5.3 and 5.4). In Colorado, for example, 41 percent of white 18- to 24-year-olds are enrolled in higher education, compared with 19 percent of Hispanic young people of the same age. Among 18- to 24–year-olds in Wisconsin, 44 percent of whites are enrolled, compared with 21 percent of African Americans.[80] Participation rates are also uneven nationally. Among 18- to 24-year-olds in the United States, 45 percent of whites are enrolled in postsecondary studies, compared with only 38 percent of blacks and 28 percent of Hispanics.[81]

In terms of income, figure 5.4 reports the college attendance rates in 2006 for students who were high school sophomores in 2002. As shown, the overall chance of enrollment is strongly correlated with income: among students whose family income was less than $20,000, 52 percent enrolled in some kind of postsecondary education, while among students whose parents made more than $100,000, 90 percent enrolled in college. Figure 5.4 also shows that enrollment is stratified by college sector. Among low-income students who went to college, the majority (52 percent) attended a community college. Among higher-income students who went on to college, 77 percent attended four-year institutions. This difference in starting points puts the low-income

FIGURE 5.3   Percentage point gap in college participation between white young people and largest minority group in state

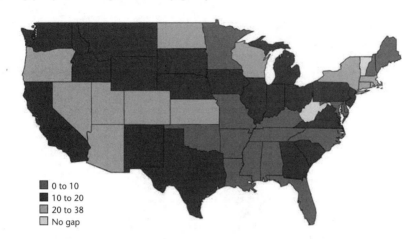

0 to 10
10 to 20
20 to 38
No gap

Note: Alaska = 22.73; Hawaii = –13.63. In Hawaii, the participation of the largest minority group (Asian/Pacific Islander) is higher than participation among the white population.

Source: U.S. Bureau of the Census, *American Community Survey: Percent of Population 18-24 Enrolled in Higher Education* (Washington, DC: 2009).

students at a serious disadvantage in terms of their chances for completing a baccalaureate degree.[82] There are no state-by-state data on the extent to which low-income students enroll in higher education—a glaring gap in our knowledge regarding the variation in state performance in providing higher education opportunity. But it is likely that no state has fully solved the problem of low enrollment of low-income youth.

States seeking to close gaps in postsecondary participation rates can build on efforts to reduce disparities in K–12 educational achievement, particularly those school reforms that focus on improving preparation for college. In addition, improving equity in postsecondary participation requires colleges and universities to provide better signals to high school students about how to prepare for and succeed in college, including efforts to smooth transitions between high school and college.[83]

Many states face different problems in improving participation rates for their urban versus rural populations. For young people in urban settings, the most promising interventions often involve outreach from urban college campuses to nearby high schools, including information and exposure to college readiness requirements for teachers, students, and parents. Also, some high schools are finding that preparing and supporting students in taking college classes while in high school—that is, through concurrent or dual enrollment—can assist in helping students gain experience in passing

FIGURE 5.4   College attendance rates in 2006 for high school sophomores in 2002, by income and sector attended (in thousands)

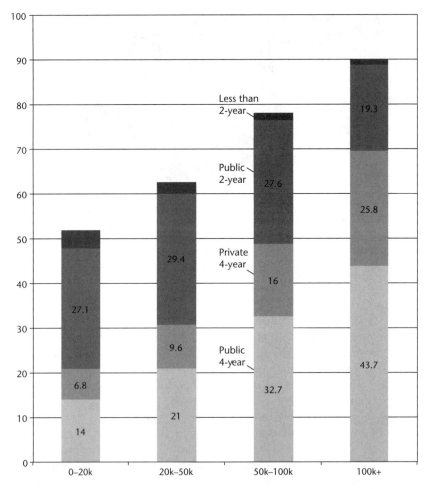

Source: R. Bozick and E. Lauff, *Education Longitudinal Study of 2002: A First Look at the Initial Postsecondary Experiences of the Sophomore Class of 2002* (Washington, DC: National Center for Education Statistics, 2007), table 3.

college classes and can help to clarify college readiness standards for high school students. These programs can also help to encourage alignment of curriculum and assessments across systems, which makes a substantial difference in preparing students for college. Indeed, efforts are emerging to replace the general high school track of minimum graduation requirements with a universal focus on preparing students for postsecondary education and the workforce—on the theory that most decent-paying twenty-first-century jobs will require at least some postsecondary training, whether academic or vocational.[84] The specifics of such an approach involve some controversy, but it is clear that better signals about postsecondary readiness—and a broader distribution of opportunities for students to achieve it—are important if degree production is to increase substantially.

For students in rural settings, the primary challenge involves providing more opportunities for postsecondary education near where students live. The majority of students travel less than twenty miles to attend higher education, and participation rates decline sharply with greater distance.[85] Creative combinations of community colleges, satellite campuses, and distance education can bring higher education at all undergraduate levels within reach of most students in a state. The distance-learning consortium run by Northern Arizona University is an example of one such approach. This model combines learning centers at satellite campuses with instruction delivered by a number of means, including video and online instruction, to reach people across its vast service area (which is the entire state outside metropolitan Phoenix and Tucson).[86]

Many of the gaps in enrollment rates by population group can be traced to large gaps in achievement at the K–12 level. Although this is only starting to be fully recognized, higher education has an important role to play in reducing these gaps by virtue of its teacher preparation role and by establishing clear standards for admission and placement that are tied to curriculum and assessments at the K–12 level. Of course, states and school districts also need to provide appropriate incentives and professional development for recruitment and retention of quality teachers in high poverty and predominantly minority schools.

Table 5.4 summarizes our analysis of key policy levers for states with highly inequitable college participation rates across population groups.

The Fourth Major Challenge: Low Postsecondary Completion Rates

Solving the problem of college access is not sufficient if enrolled students do not complete degrees in a timely manner. Improving student success has been the Achilles' heel of the American higher education system. Of the students who enrolled in college in 1995 with the goal of obtaining a bachelor's degree, only 53 percent had done so by 2001.[87] States vary tremendously in the percentage of first-time, full-time freshmen who graduate from their first four-year institution within six years (see figure5.5).[88] In Massachusetts, 68 percent of first-time freshmen who began in 2001 graduated within six years, while in Alaska, only 22 percent did so. Fourteen states have six-year graduation rates above 60 percent, while sixteen states are below 50 percent. Nevada and Alaska fall below 40 percent.

TABLE 5.4

States with highly inequitable participation rates

Structural characteristic	Example states	Key policy levers
Inequity within large urban centers	California, Illinois, Massachusetts, New York	Regional strategies, including local K–12 outreach and dual enrollment.
Inequity across geographic regions	Arizona, Colorado, North Dakota, Utah	Widespread use of focused satellite campuses and distance education.
		Costly expansion of standard comprehensive campuses discouraged.
Large gaps across population groups in K–12 education	Connecticut, New York, Pennsylvania, Tennessee	Increased articulation of K–12 schools and higher education; teacher preparation to reduce gaps; incentives for teacher recruitment and retention in needy schools.
		Emphasis on broad distribution of curricular and other opportunities for preparation for postsecondary matriculation and success.

Figure 5.5 includes both public and private institutions, and many of the high-performing states on this measure have sizable private higher education sectors. Figure 5.6 shows six-year graduation rates for first-time, full-time freshmen at public institutions only. Based on these comparisons, both Delaware and Virginia have relatively high graduation rates at their public four-

FIGURE 5.5 Percentage of first-time, full-time freshmen in 2001 who graduated with a bachelor's degree within six years (public and private institutions)

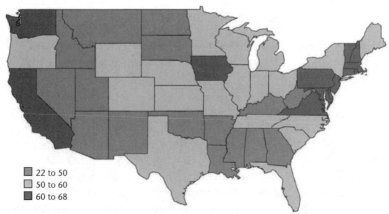

22 to 50
50 to 60
60 to 68

Note: Alaska = 22.4 percent; Hawaii = 45.9 percent.

Source: National Center for Education Statistics, Integrated Postsecondary Education Data System, Peer Analysis System, Electronic Resource (Washington, DC: 2009), http://nces.ed.gov/ipeds/datacenter/.

FIGURE 5.6   Percentage of first-time, full-time freshmen in 2001 who graduated with a bachelor's degree within six years (public institutions only)

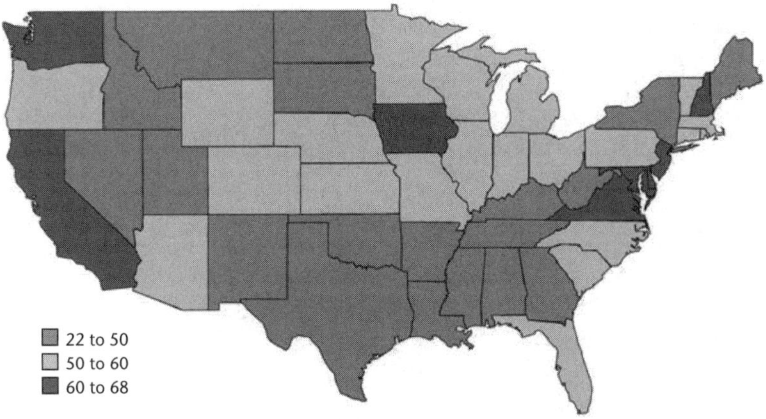

22 to 50
50 to 60
60 to 68

Note: Alaska = 24.6 percent; Hawaii = 43.1 percent.

Source: National Center for Education Statistics, Integrated Postsecondary Education Data System, Peer Analysis System, Electronic Resource (Washington, DC: 2009), http://nces.ed.gov/ipeds/datacenter/.

year institutions, while Alaska and Nevada are low no matter which types of institutions are included.

States with low completion rates need to prioritize efforts to improve student success, for increasing participation alone will not produce much higher attainment otherwise. Yet even the best-performing states on this measure have substantial room for improvement, as they do not compare well with global competitors—especially when the large numbers of part-time students with even lower completion rates are included. As noted in chapter 1, the United States continues to benefit from some of the highest overall levels of educational attainment among developed countries. But it has fallen behind in the educational attainment of younger working-age adults (ages 25 to 34), an ominous trend in an increasingly knowledge-driven global economy.[89]

Measuring the percentage of full-time students who begin at a four-year institution and complete a bachelor's degree there within six years (that is, figures 5.5 and 5.6) provides a good overall indicator of students moving through the system in a reasonable period of time (at least those covered by the federal graduation measure). Examining the total number of degrees and certificates completed per 100 undergraduate students in both two- and four-year colleges provides a measure of the total degree productivity in a state, capturing the impact of community college and part-time students as well (see figure 5.7). As with completion rates, performance on degree productivity likewise shows considerable variation by state.

The literature on why students do not complete their higher education studies reveals that once students enroll, their continued success is related to

FIGURE 5.7   All certificates and degrees per 100 undergraduate students enrolled, 2006

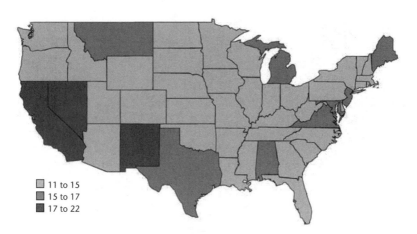

☐ 11 to 15
▨ 15 to 17
■ 17 to 22

Note: Alaska = 10.6; Hawaii = 16.3.

Source: National Center for Public Policy and Higher Education, *Measuring Up 2008* (San Jose, CA: author, 2008), www.highereducation.org.

a variety of factors, including their background and the ability of the campus to engage them intensely in their educational pursuits. Financial aid is a necessary but insufficient condition for student success. Students who engage in active learning and feel their campus is invested in their success have higher degree completion rates than those who are not actively engaged in their education.[90] Colleges can improve student engagement by better targeting, coordinating, and aligning their services to meet student needs.

In addition, a performance-based set of state funding policies can be helpful in improving student success at all levels of postsecondary education. The vast majority of institutions are funded on the basis of student enrollment in courses. This is typically measured a few weeks into the term, on the "census" date for each campus. Changing to a system that provides funds at least in part on the basis of student completion of courses could transform incentives considerably on many campuses.[91] Some states are beginning to move cautiously in this direction. A similar option is for states to consider funding institutions in part based on degree completion. Most institutions receive the same amount of state funding per student whether or not that individual graduates. Performance-funding systems can provide incentives for campuses to increase graduation rates.

As with other types of outcome-based funding, however, these approaches should be risk adjusted to take into account the specific challenges a campus may face, given the student populations it serves. Without appropriate safeguards, performance-based incentives might encourage some institutions to lessen their commitments to open access or even erode academic standards. It is crucial not to reinforce these tendencies, particularly since student populations that have been underrepresented in the past are the very groups the country now most needs to educate at higher levels. Still, the current funding systems in most states reward initial enrollment too heavily relative to subsequent student success.

Table 5.5 groups states facing the challenge of low college completion rates by the type of higher education governance structure in the state. As addressed earlier, improving completion rates involves coordinating campus activities more effectively and aligning incentives to reward institutions that make comprehensive efforts to engage students in their own learning. Different policy solutions must be emphasized depending upon the ability of the state governance structure to influence these changes on individual campuses.

POLICY CHALLENGE: LOW BACCALAUREATE GRADUATION RATES

The first row of table 5.5 includes states with low graduation rates and centralized governance structures. In these systems, governance bodies can make institutions directly accountable for their students' success and can work to better align the postsecondary system both from within (spanning both two-year and baccalaureate institutions) and across sectors (with K–12 schools). Centralized governing structures are in a better position to under-

TABLE 5.5
Policy challenge: Low baccalaureate graduation rates

Structural characteristics	Example states	Key policy levers
Unified or centralized governance	Alaska, Arizona, Idaho, Montana, Nevada, West Virginia	Coordinated policies and accountability across two-year and four-year institutions.
		Accountability within systems.
		Increased articulation with K–12 and other sectors.
		Unit-record data systems to track students across institutions and systems.
Coordinating board without budgetary authority	New Mexico	Strategic initiatives, led by governor or legislative committee, to provide incentives for student success.
		Unit-record data systems to track students.
Coordinating board with budgetary authority	Arkansas, Louisiana, Oklahoma	Use of budgetary performance incentives to accomplish objectives.
		Unit-record data systems to track students.

take these direct steps, although alignment with the K–12 sector remains outside of their authority.

The second row of table 5.5 offers ideas for states with low graduation rates that have coordinating boards without budgetary authority for higher education. Since these types of boards are limited in the actions they can take, policy changes in these states probably need to begin with initiatives led by the governor or by relevant legislative committees (though initiatives led by the governor tend to be less cumbersome). For these states, legislatively directed financial incentives that reward effective interinstitutional coordination and articulation should help support a focus on student success and efficient transfer. For example, full financial credit for a student who transfers from a community college to a baccalaureate institution might be provided only after the student achieves specific milestones at the baccalaureate institution—in order to encourage both institutions to take responsibility for adequate preparation and course alignment.

The last row of table 5.5 depicts states that have low graduation rates and coordinating boards with budgetary authority over higher education institutions. Boards in these types of states can themselves implement strong student-tracking systems, combined with financial performance incentives to reward campuses and intercampus initiatives for student success.

Finally, it is important to note that private nonprofit colleges and universities, in general, have higher completion rates than public institutions that serve similar student populations. In many instances, state policies that encourage more state residents to attend such private colleges may help to improve the state's degree completion and attainment rates—though policy makers need to ensure that these policies remain cost effective for the state. Typically, states with coordinating boards are best positioned to achieve progress in this regard.[92]

CONCLUSION

In this chapter, we have sought to describe the key challenges that states face and the types of policy levers they can use to increase substantially their undergraduate degree production and reduce gaps across population groups—at a time when student demographics are changing and resources are seriously constrained. Our framework recognizes the wide differences among states both in terms of challenges they face and the types of policy tools they can readily use. In particular, our analysis takes into account the structure of a state's higher education system—most prominently the role of two-year versus four-year institutions and the relative size of the private collegiate sector—and the nature of state-level governance arrangements, as well as its historic tuition and financial aid policies.

It is important to note, however, that states have much in common with respect to some policy tools. For example, there are substantial differences across states in levels of per-student appropriations, but these differences are not likely to change dramatically, and research strongly suggests that they need not change in order for performance to improve. Rather, it appears that the incentives associated with the deployment of funds are more crucial than their level—although additional state funding certainly could, if used skillfully, facilitate change and enlarge possibilities. Thus, virtually all states should consider developing budgetary incentives for institutions to enroll more students from underserved populations and graduate them successfully and efficiently. Similarly, although some are well ahead of others, virtually all states have progress to make in building data and accountability systems that facilitate analysis of problems and track the impacts of implemented remedies. For example, states should know: How does each high school fare, with the student population it serves, in terms of the percentage of its students going on to postsecondary education and doing so without needing remedial classes? How successful are community colleges, considering their populations of students, in supporting student completion of certificates and degrees and, where students so desire, transfer to baccalaureate institutions? And how well are four-year colleges and universities performing, considering their populations of students, in supporting the success of their students, including transfer students? Some states are ahead of others in developing information and accountability systems, but most can do a better job.

Similarly, virtually all states have far to go in improving linkages between their K–12 and postsecondary education systems, so that many more students, particularly those from low-income families and underrepresented ethnic groups, complete high school and prepare for some form of postsecondary education. Better linkages in such areas as teacher preparation, curriculum and testing alignment, support services, and financial aid awareness are essential for achieving the performance that the nation, and virtually every state, needs in order to compete internationally.

Finally, all states need strong policy leadership that recognizes the urgency of the challenges we face and that is willing to marshal and sustain the needed support and resources. Particularly in today's tight fiscal conditions, state leaders must be willing to persist in the difficult task of developing a policy agenda and goals—despite budget crises and political distractions—to educate many more people at the postsecondary level for the twenty-first-century work force.

CHAPTER 6

Educational Capacity in American Higher Education

The central arguments of the foregoing chapters might be condensed into two propositions: First, our nation needs a significant increase in the number of educated men and women in order to remain competitive in a global, knowledge-based economy. Second, the financing of American higher education, if not completely broken, is under severe stress and, as currently structured, is unlikely to address the needs of our society effectively. If one accepts these propositions, then the challenges facing the country in the next decade are serious and daunting. If we do not resolve these issues, economic decline will likely define our future.

In the preceding chapters, we focused primarily on student demand for higher education, including enrollment trends, affordability, labor market demand for graduates, the rate of return for a college degree, the role of state governments in providing subsidized tuition and responding to state-specific needs, and the federal role in providing direct student grants and guaranteeing student loans.[1] Indeed, most of the literature on the economics of higher education emphasizes the demand side of the market, largely ignoring the supply of higher education, which is generally assumed to be infinitely elastic in response to student demand and therefore not a constraint.

Overlooking the supply side of institutional capacity is no longer acceptable, however, for the financial pressures on institutions cast doubt on the notion that the system's capacity can expand sufficiently to meet the degree-output targets that have been called for recently—for example, by the Obama administration, the Lumina Foundation, and others who seek a sharp increase in certificates and degrees.[2] While rising tuition charges and diminished affordability have dominated the discussion, constraints on the availability of places for additional students pose an equally important challenge. The prospects for building new campuses in the nonprofit public or private sectors seem minimal at best, leading to the question of whether we can expect existing colleges and universities to increase enrollments significantly, given the current and foreseeable financial environment.

INSTITUTIONAL CAPACITY

The National Center for Education Statistics (NCES) reports that in academic year 2009–2010, there were 4,409 two-year and four-year institutions of higher education in the United States, made up of 652 four-year public universities, 1,024 two-year public community colleges, 1,537 four-year and 92 two-year independent colleges and universities, plus 530 four-year and 574 two-year for-profit colleges.[3] In fall 2009, these institutions collectively enrolled 20.4 million students, of whom 57.1 percent were female, 62.3 percent attended full-time, and 37.7 percent attended part-time. Public two-year and four-year colleges and universities enrolled 72.5 percent of the total, independent (private nonprofit) colleges and universities enrolled 18.4 percent, and for-profit colleges enrolled 9.1 percent.[4]

Over the past three decades, there has been modest growth in the number of public four-year colleges and universities and no net growth in the number of public two-year colleges (some of this reflects conversion of two-year into four-year institutions). (See table 6.1.) The number of private nonprofit four-year colleges increased somewhat in the 1990s and early 2000s, but declined in the later part of the decade; the number of private two-year colleges has declined sharply. In contrast, there has been explosive growth in the number of for-profit institutions, both four year and two year. Many of these four-year institutions offer two-year and lower degrees and certificates.

TABLE 6.1
Number of institutions, by year and type of control

	Public		Private		For-profit	
Year	Four-year	Two-year	Four-year	Two-year	Four-year	Two-year
1993	600	1,024	1,569	445	76	266
1998	615	1,092	1,694	663	166	484
2003	631	1,081	1,835	621	297	494
2008	653	1,032	1,532	92	490	553
2009	652	1,024	1,537	92	530	574

Source: National Center for Education Statistics (NCES), *Digest of Education Statistics*, 2010 (Washington, NCES), table 275.

TABLE 6.2

Enrollment percentages, by year and type of control

Year	Public four-year	Public two-year	Private two- and four year*	For-profit two- and four-year
1993	40.9%	37.3%	20.2%	1.6%
1998	40.6%	36.2%	20.7%	2.5%
2003	39.3%	36.7%	19.8%	4.2%
2008	38.4%	34.8%	19.2%	7.7%
2009	37.7%	34.8%	18.4%	9.1%

Source: Calculated from NCES, *Digest of Education Statistics,* 2010 (Washington NCES), tables 197 and 198.
*Two-year institutions account for a very small proportion of the total for private nonprofit institutions.

In examining enrollment percentages (market share) for public, private, and for-profit institutions over the same time period, several key trends stand out (see table 6.2). Public four-year colleges and universities have seen their market share decline over the past two decades—as have private nonprofit institutions. Public two-year colleges have also slightly declined in market share. Meanwhile, the for-profit sector has seen substantial growth, mirroring the sharp increase in the number of for-profit colleges noted in table 6.1. A crude extrapolation might suggest that the for-profit sector is likely to gain further market share over the next fifteen years, not necessarily at the expense of reduced enrollments in the other sectors, but simply through capturing an increasing share of the growth of higher education as a whole.

On average, institutions have increased enrollments across all higher education sectors over the past fifteen years (see table 6.3). From 1993 to 2009,

TABLE 6.3

Average undergraduate enrollment per institution, by year and type of control

Year	Public		Private		For-profit	
	Four-year	Two-year	Four-year	Two-year	Four-year	Two-year
1993	9,243	4,507	1,841	514	N/A	N/A
1998	9,515	4,888	1,736	100	1,130	368
2003	9,337	4,853	1,797	71	1,553	489
2008	10,183	6,017	2,367	384	2,395	535
2009	10,332	6,097	2,427	378	2,768	671

Source: NCES, *Digest of Education Statistics,* 2010, Tables 202 and 275. For enrollment numbers for 1993, 1998, and 2003, see earlier editions. Enrollments include both full-time and part-time students.

public four-year institutions increased average enrollment by 11.8 percent, public two-year colleges by 35.4 percent, private nonprofit two- and four-year colleges by 19.1 percent, and for-profit four-year colleges by a striking 129.6 percent (for-profit change is between 1998 and 2008 as 1993, data are unavailable). The sharpest percentage increases came from colleges with a smaller initial enrollment base, but the public institutions remain the central workhorses in this industry because of their larger size. If one assumes that the number of public and private nonprofit colleges and universities is not likely to change much over the coming decade, then the ability to increase enrollments per institution will be a critical factor determining the capacity of the system to serve more students. The numbers indicate that a relatively mature set of institutions have been able to increase enrollments, which could auger well for the future.

In terms of the numbers of associate and bachelor's degrees awarded, the institutions have, on average, produced more graduates over the past two decades (see table 6.4), which is consistent with the increase in enrollments described. Unfortunately, we do not have time-series data on degrees produced by the for-profit sector, but those numbers are, most likely, rising, given the increase in institutions and enrollments in that sector.

The ratio of enrollments to degrees produced provides a crude measure of inputs (enrollments) in comparison with outputs (degrees). In general, the smaller the ratio, the greater the output per unit of input—that is, smaller ratios are desirable. This measurement is imperfect primarily because it does not track or account for cohorts over time, so the enrollments measured do not match precisely with the degrees awarded. For example, changes in the numbers of degrees awarded tend to lag behind changes in the numbers of students enrolled. In periods of enrollment growth, therefore, the ratio tends to exaggerate the numbers of enrollments required to produce a degree.

TABLE 6.4

Associate and bachelor's degrees awarded per institution, by year and type of control

Year	Public four-year	Public two-year	Private two- and four year	For-profit two- and four-year*
1993	1,309	420	231	N/A
1998	1,275	417	214	N/A
2008	1,388	461	248	N/A
2008	1,526	561	455	N/A
2009	1,565	582	474	N/A

Source: Calculated from NCES, *Digest of Education Statistics*, 2010 (Washington NCES), tables 275 and 287.
*NCES does not report degrees awarded by the for-profit sector.

Considering the inherent limitations of the crude measure, the ratios of enrollments to degrees by institution type may suggest some small efficiency gains, but otherwise do not show clear trends over time (see table 6.5). The ratio for public four-year institutions decreased slightly, and unevenly, from 1992–1993 to 2008–2009, which indicates somewhat greater output per unit of input. For public two-year colleges, the measure has increased and decreased during this period. Both public four-year and two-year institutions experienced a decline in efficiency between 1993 and 1998, but have experienced overall efficiency gains from 1998 to present. The ratio for private colleges and universities has shown a more consistent decline from 1993 to 2009. Given the scope of the challenges facing the nation, the small efficiency gains suggested by this measure are insufficient to increase degree output sharply.

In summary, based on trends over the past decades and the current fiscal outlook for states and the federal government, it appears that traditional sectors of higher education are unlikely to see large-scale changes in the numbers of institutions, although a few private nonprofit colleges or universities may open their doors in the coming decade, and there may be some closures. The number of institutions in the for-profit sector is likely to continue to increase, however, unless regulatory constraints or limitations on the availability of federal student financial aid to that sector are imposed by the federal government. In addition, the enrollment share of for-profit colleges has increased notably over the past decades and may continue to grow.

However, average enrollment per institution grew over the past fifteen years and could continue to increase. For public colleges and universities, the increases would likely depend on financial support and decisions made by college governing boards, state coordinating boards, governors, and state legislators. Much of this also depends upon the will of citizens and taxpayers. If financial support for public higher education continues to stagnate or

TABLE 6.5
Enrollments per degree, by year and type of control

Year	Public four-year	Public two-year	Private two- and four year
1993	7.06	10.73	6.22
1998	7.46	11.73	5.84
2003	6.73	10.53	5.41
2008	6.67	10.73	4.91
2009	6.60	10.47	4.83

Source: Calculated from NCES, *Digest of Education Statistics*, 2010 (Washington NCES), tables 202 and 287. For enrollment numbers for 1993, 1998, and 2003, see earlier editions. Enrollments include both full-time and part-time students.

decline, many institutions may be unwilling to enroll more students, as we discuss in the next section. Facility size and other constraints on physical space may limit enrollment growth at some institutions, and capital funding has been scarce in recent years.

Finally, it appears that we can expect the number of degrees awarded to increase if student enrollments increase, but probably not in a lockstep or mechanical fashion. If financial support continues to decline, the link between enrollment levels and degrees awarded could weaken—that is, completion rates could drop. Such a decline is more likely as colleges and universities enroll larger numbers of students with weak academic preparation and limited financial resources, particularly in the absence of funding and policies that support improved completion rates for these groups of students. However, weak academic preparation is not the only challenge to degree efficiency. One study found that completion rates decline as the size of the entering class increases, largely because funding does not increase at the same rate as enrollment. When enrollment booms and educational resources per student decline, some students are crowded out of course sections and support services; degree attainment appears to suffer.[5] Relative to this, it appears that the output of associate and bachelor's degrees did not improve substantially over the prior decades, based on crude measures of the ratio of enrollments to degrees awarded. This suggests that the system has not to this point experienced the large efficiency gains that we need to increase degree attainment rates significantly.

FACTORS INFLUENCING INSTITUTIONAL DECISIONS ABOUT ENROLLMENT

The public, private, and for-profit sectors of higher education respond to different incentives in determining how many students to enroll. Within each of these sectors, incentives for individual institutions vary in establishing their enrollment capacity in a given year or over the course of several decades. Despite these differences, there are patterns in decision-making processes by sector that are important to identify in order to understand the capacity challenges facing higher education in the United States.

Public Two-Year Colleges

Public community and technical colleges are deeply committed to maintaining open enrollments, as their mission and philosophy are to provide opportunities for postsecondary education or training to virtually all interested local residents at low cost. Some students enroll part-time or full-time in technical fields where the associate degree is a terminal credential, some enroll in shorter certificate programs, and some enroll in academic programs designed for transfer to four-year colleges and universities. Many incoming students are not prepared for college-level courses and are required to undertake remedial programs in reading, writing, or mathematics, which do not carry college credit. The typical two-year college strives to be "the community's college," where virtually every citizen can find some offering of value and interest.[6]

Community colleges in nearly half the states receive local property tax revenue, but their core functions are supported increasingly by state appropriations and tuition. In many states with large community college systems (such as Arizona, California, and Florida), the prevailing goal is to encourage enrollment by keeping tuition as low as possible. As state funding for community colleges has slowed or declined in most states, however, tuition increases have not fully offset the colleges' losses in state and local revenues, and this erosion of their funding base appears to be limiting their ability to meet their open-enrollment objectives. Two consequences have been a reduction in class sections and limits to enrollment in programs that are resource intensive, such as nursing. In these cases, students might be able to enroll in the college but cannot gain entry into particular courses or areas of study. To reduce costs, most two-year colleges have also sharply increased reliance on adjunct faculty, as compared with full-time professors on the tenure track, thereby reducing the number of faculty available for counseling, mentoring, advising, and generally assisting students to advance toward their goals. This can hinder efforts to improve degree productivity.

The educational philosophy that guides community colleges requires them to strive to enroll all who seek admission, but many community college leaders and other observers worry that resources are being stretched beyond the point where quality and opportunity begin to suffer.[7] In some states, such as California, the dire financing situation has led to denials of admission, reductions in enrollment by hundreds of thousands, and many closed sections.[8] As tuition in the four-year public sector has soared in recent years, more transfer-oriented students are enrolling as freshmen at community colleges, which increases enrollment pressure on this sector. Historically, transfer rates from community colleges to four-year institutions have been much lower than many had hoped or assumed when these "2+2" systems were designed to provide the first two years of general education courses at community colleges followed by two years of upper-level courses at a baccalaureate institution. In general, articulation arrangements among two-year and four-year colleges are poorly developed, and this is not primarily the fault of the two-year sector. Several states are addressing this problem, but concerns remain as to the effectiveness of the transfer route and the extent to which it can significantly increase the number of college graduates. Due to their large enrollments and the broad populations of students they serve, community colleges will be central players in the educational landscape over the next decade, but their ability to increase the number of college graduates at the baccalaureate level substantially remains unclear.

Public Four-Year Comprehensive Universities

From the 1950s to the 1980s, public colleges and universities in many states were financed by enrollment-driven funding models, a method commonly used for setting institutional appropriations. For every additional one hundred students enrolled, for example, the college might have a claim on the state treasury for so many dollars per additional student.[9] During the 1980s and 1990s, however, states began to move away from this form of budgeting, often in response to revenue shortfalls caused by periodic recessions. Many universities continued to keep track of the amount of funding they should have received based on enrollments, but this was a hollow exercise in most cases, since the institutions increasingly received support unrelated to enrollment levels.

In most state budgets, funding for higher education is discretionary and thus loses ground relative to activities covered by statutory or related requirements (for example, Medicaid, K–12 education, and corrections), which generally have been perceived as higher priorities for state funding in recent years. One institutional response has been to increase tuition. As with community colleges, however, tuition increases at four-year institutions have usually failed to fully offset the reduced state support (especially when some of the increased revenue is used for student aid). As a result, the incentives provided by enrollment-driven funding models for institutions to maintain or increase enrollment have diminished, and college leaders, concerned about quality, have begun to consider factors such as educational resources per student in their decision making. Adding a hundred additional students with only the resources provided by tuition payments requires the university's resources to spread more thinly over a larger student body. If one roughly measures quality by resources per student, then spreading the resources more thinly is perceived as a decline in quality. We may need to question this definition of quality in this new era, but academic decision makers subscribe to it.

Public comprehensive universities occupy an important and intermediate place in the supply side of higher education, as these institutions typically offer a wide range of bachelor's, master's, and professional degrees, but without the emphasis on doctoral programs and research found in most land-grant and flagship universities. The American Association of State Colleges and Universities (AASCU) represents these institutions and provides the following statement of identity and purpose:

> AASCU's 430 public college and university members are found throughout the United States, and in Guam, Puerto Rico and the Virgin Islands. AASCU institutions enroll nearly 3.5 million students, representing more than half of all students enrolled in the nation's public four-year institutions.
>
> We range in size from 1,000 students to 44,000. We are found in the inner city, in suburbs, towns and cities, and in remote rural America. We include campuses with extensive offerings in law, medicine and doctoral

education—as well as campuses offering associate degrees to complement baccalaureate studies. We are both residential and commuter, and with online degrees as well.

We believe that through this stewardship and through our commitments to access and opportunity and to our students, public colleges and universities effectively and accountably deliver America's promise. In so doing we honor and fulfill the public trust.[10]

AASCU universities operate under the regulatory, budgetary, and governance structures established in each of the fifty states, with no two states exactly alike. In some states, the AASCU institutions are part of a statewide system with a single governing board whose members are either appointed (typically by the governor) or elected at large. In other states, a coordinating board oversees the public colleges and universities, which often have their own institutional governing boards. States also differ in how public tuition levels are set and by whom. In some cases, the universities have autonomy in setting tuition, with limited oversight by the governing or coordinating board; in others, the governor or state legislature is the ultimate authority on tuition rates. In most states, the institutions receive their own tuition revenues, but a few states treat tuition charges as general revenue for the state and do not necessarily return them dollar for dollar to the campuses. Fees, however, are usually under direct control of the institution and can be substantial. Tuition at AASCU institutions is fairly low compared with research universities.

Capital budgets are normally handled separately from operating budgets, and states differ on how they manage these arrangements for public colleges and universities. Campuses have been increasingly encouraged to do their own fund-raising to support new building construction, but states may also issue general obligation bonds for that purpose. Some buildings, such as student dormitories, have their own revenue sources, but others must be financed from state or institutional general funds. Any campus seeking to increase enrollments significantly will normally have to generate a capital plan, including a financing plan, for new construction and have it approved by the state before putting the first shovel in the ground. Apart from the constraints on enrollment increases posed by uncertain operating budgets, capital budgets pose further financial hurdles to overcome. State policy could provide incentives for more intensive use of existing capital facilities.

While many AASCU universities are open-enrollment institutions, either by design or through practice, administrators can use many techniques to limit enrollment, if they choose. Increasing academic requirements for admittance is one method, and closing the admissions window early is another. Many private colleges and universities limit the size of their entering classes, and this is another option open to some public campuses. The result can be to increase the academic credentials of the class, which in turn can provide the campus with bragging rights and possibly raise its place in the *U.S. News*

& *World Report* rankings of colleges and universities. When additional enrollments are perceived as being underfunded by the state, this is a tempting strategy for institutional decision makers.

With such variety among the AASCU institutions across the fifty states, it is impossible to know whether these universities will be willing and able to enroll many more students, whether their leaders will be motivated to operate more efficiently, whether serious efforts will be made to increase completion rates, whether the universities will aggressively explore distance learning techniques as a way to increase enrollments, or whether they will collaborate more effectively with community colleges in encouraging transfer.[11] What we can say with confidence is that increased uncertainty and volatility of operating and capital budgets may cause some leaders to be conservative in launching new programs or taking in larger enrollments, particularly with no promise that new resources will accompany such decisions. This conservative response appears likely unless governing boards, state leaders, the business community, foundations, and leaders within higher education itself can generate offsetting policies to ensure that qualified students are not turned away from higher education. Whether the country has the political will and wisdom to ensure college opportunities for the coming generation is a central question addressed by this book. Currently, the answer to this question is uncertain, both for the public four-year comprehensive universities and for the community colleges.

Public Research Universities

No universally accepted definition exists for public research universities, and thus their exact number is subject to debate. Research universities are at the pinnacle of the pecking order among institutions of higher education, and thus many universities aspire to that label. Furthermore, there exists no national association analogous to AASCU devoted exclusively to public research universities, although two associations bracket most of the contenders: the Association of American Universities (AAU) and the Association of Public and Land-grant Universities (APLU).[12] The former organization, which elects its own members, includes thirty-five public and twenty-eight private universities, while APLU includes several institutions that few would consider research universities. A review of the APLU membership list indicates that thirty-three institutions that are not members of AAU could reasonably be added to the thirty-five public AAU members, for a total of sixty-eight public research universities. A number in this range is, if anything, a generous count for this category.

Public research universities garner the lion's share of media attention given to colleges and universities, primarily because of their prominent roles in graduate and professional education and research and their high visibility in NCAA Division 1-A sports. As a result of this attention, it is understandable that the public and many policy makers exaggerate their role in undergraduate education. As visible as they may be, these universities serve a modest percentage of undergraduates enrolled in U.S. higher education, and thus they are unlikely as a group to be a major source of growth of bachelor's degrees. Furthermore, many of these institutions enjoy selective admissions and thus are able to control with considerable precision the number of students in each entering class. In general, institutions that are selective tend to set enrollment targets and meet them, unlike the majority of colleges, which are effectively open-enrollment institutions that sometimes struggle to meet their targets. The priorities set by most research universities are research first and graduate education second, with undergraduate education a distant third. These priorities suggest that efforts to increase undergraduate enrollments will not rank highly in decision making on these campuses, unless the research universities are forced to change by external incentives or other pressures, which is unlikely and probably undesirable. The most that we can expect from these universities are more serious efforts to improve undergraduate completion rates and to develop better articulation for transfer students, particularly those from community colleges. Many who care deeply about undergraduate education tend to be critical of research universities for the relatively low priority they assign to this function. A wiser course for the nation, however, would be to focus energy and resources on comprehensive public universities and community colleges. Within the public sector, it is in these institutions where meaningful increases in undergraduate enrollments and degrees are most likely to occur.

Private, Independent Colleges and Universities

The private, independent sector is made up of a highly diverse set of institutions, ranging from two-year colleges through renowned research universities. Although the number of private nonprofit four-year colleges and universities (1,537) vastly exceeds the number of public four-year institutions (652), their much smaller average size keeps their enrollment share at approximately 30 percent of the total at baccalaureate-level institutions. The independent sector also contains several hundred small liberal arts colleges that enroll only undergraduates seeking a bachelor's degree, a type of institution that is almost nonexistent in the public sector. Most private colleges and universities were originally founded by church denominations. Many still maintain this link, while others have declared themselves independent of church affiliation.

Apart from differences in mission, the primary differentiating factors among private colleges and universities are wealth and selectivity, which are highly correlated. For our purposes, there are three relatively small groups within the private sector that will play little, if any, role in helping the nation increase the number of college graduates: private two-year colleges, the leading private research universities, and the most selective private liberal arts colleges.[13] The two-year colleges, as noted earlier, have been declining in number and enrollments for many years, and are relatively insignificant in terms of degrees they produce. There is little chance that they will either expand or increase in number, and thus can reasonably be set aside for policy purposes. The top private research universities, those included within the AAU as well as a few others, are focused heavily on research and graduate education. While many deliver excellent undergraduate education, few are likely to expand their enrollments significantly. These universities have many more applicants than places in each class and thus are able with great precision to determine exactly how many students to admit and enroll. They prize their selectivity and limited size, and prefer not to have their endowment revenues spread more thinly over larger student numbers. Similarly, the top fifty or so highly selective liberal arts colleges, while focused exclusively on undergraduates, also value selectivity and tightly controlled enrollment to ensure quality and maintain attractiveness to academically talented students. We do not expect enrollment increases of any magnitude from these institutions. With these exclusions, about fourteen hundred private colleges and universities remain for consideration.

As one works down the wealth and selectivity scale, the revenue structures for private colleges increasingly depend upon tuition, as large endowments are highly concentrated in the top 5 percent to 10 percent of these institutions. In the last decade or so, as tuitions have risen sharply in this sector, more and more colleges have had to resort to tuition discounting in order to fill their entering classes.[14] When done effectively, discounting can increase net tuition revenue for colleges that would otherwise face empty places in the entering class, but the practice also means that many private colleges are taking in considerably less tuition revenue than their posted "sticker prices" might suggest. Discount rates of 45 percent or more are not unusual, although most colleges strive to keep that rate as low as possible, subject to the need to meet enrollment targets. Thus, the approach these colleges take to affordability serves to limit the number of potential students who choose to enroll in the independent sector. Making matters worse, our "system" of financial aid is complicated and confusing, and many students and families do not understand how it works. Consequently, even students who might be eligible for substantial institutional aid to supplement state and federal grants and loans do not bother to apply to private institutions because of the high sticker price. Even though many of the less selective private colleges and universities might be able and willing to increase their enrollments, the challenge would be to successfully encourage more students to apply and, for those who are accepted, to find resources to make their enrollment affordable for both the student and college. Despite these challenges, a recent analysis of enrollment patterns reveals that the private nonprofit sector has expanded, increasing enrollments by over 1.5 million (1996 to 2007).[15] Because enrollments in other sectors (particularly the for-profit sector) have increased faster than in the private sector, however, the market share of the private sector has decreased from about 20 percent to about 18 percent over the past two decades(see table 6.2).

State governments should incorporate the private sector into their inventory of potential capacity for increased student enrollments, but without substantial increases in financial aid from states and the federal government, many of these potential slots may go unfilled. While every effort should be made to use the educational resources of the independent colleges to maximum effect, it is unlikely that their contribution to enrollment expansion will be substantial.[16]

For-Profit Colleges and Universities

As noted earlier, the for-profit sector is growing rapidly, numbering over eleven hundred institutions by 2009–2010, roughly 25 percent of the total. Proprietary schools offering vocational and technical training have been in existence for decades, and most of these used to be small, locally owned and managed institutions with programs that were relatively short in duration and that did not offer degrees. In the last decade or so, however, a new breed of for-profit college emerged: degree-granting, well-capitalized institutions with stock listed on the exchanges, accredited either regionally or nationally and usually operated as a chain with multiple locations. Major names include the Apollo Corporation (parent of the University of Phoenix), DeVry, Strayer, Kaplan, Corinthian Colleges, and the ITT Technical Institutes.

In stark comparison with public and private nonprofit higher education, it is in the for-profit sector where we can expect substantial continued growth in the number of institutions and enrollments—barring obstacles that we will note shortly. The business model for these institutions requires only the continued presence and growth of federal Title IV student grant and loan programs, for which their students are eligible so long as the institutions are accredited by a recognized regional or national body. Indeed, nearly 90 percent of the revenues received by the typical for-profit college come from these federal student aid programs.[17] These institutions do not receive state appropriations. They only require from states a favorable regulatory environment that allows them to grow as rapidly as they wish, which they lobby to secure.[18] Several of these large corporations have received regional accreditation, most frequently from the Higher Learning Commission of the North Central Association of Colleges and Schools, while others have chosen national accreditation by the Accrediting Commission of Career Schools and Colleges or the Accrediting Council for Independent Colleges and Schools.

In general, the companies listed on stock exchanges have been highly profitable, and thus have been able to secure investment capital. Continued access to capital, however, will require continued strong enrollment growth. To trim costs, these institutions typically lease office space for classes rather than building and maintaining expensive campuses; keep instructional costs very low by hiring part-time professional practitioners as faculty; realize economies of scale through large enrollments, the use of common instructional materials, and the employment of common back-office procedures; provide educational programs in fields that typically have low costs; and make heavy use of distance learning. Campus learning centers (as opposed to libraries) are often fully electronic and are designed to support course work rather than research or scholarship. Most of the institutions do not have dormitories or many of the other facilities and services required for a full-time, residential population. Their purpose and marketing strategies focus on careers and jobs rather than general education or breadth of knowledge. Many of these colleges primarily serve older, part-time adult students, and they emphasize convenience, plentiful parking, short courses, and the ability to begin a course of study at almost any time of year. One of their real strengths is providing college opportunity to adult students who are not well served by traditional colleges and universities. In addition, they serve students of modest means and from underrepresented minority groups disproportionately. They tend to be student-centered rather than faculty-centered institutions.[19]

Recently, the media and the U.S. Congress have severely scrutinized for-profit colleges, partly because of allegations that students have not acquired marketable skills in the areas studied, partly because of the institutions' rapid growth and high profitability (fueled by very aggressive student recruiting tactics), and partly because of the colleges' heavy draw on Title IV student aid funds and high levels of student debt. For example, *Time* and *Business Week* ran critical stories about the industry, and a report on National Public Radio announced: "For-profit educators were under the microscope at a hearing on Capitol Hill Thursday. A Senate report says the industry reaps huge fees, delivers substandard education and profits from federally backed student loans. The industry says it is ramping up to meet demand that nonprofits cannot provide, and is fighting back."[20]

Much of this negative attention was triggered by a critical analysis that Steven Eisman of FrontPoint Partners delivered on May 26, 2010, at the Ira Sohn Conference, a gathering of Wall Street investment analysts. Eisman, who received favorable national attention in *The Big Short*, a book about the subprime mortgage market and the abuses that prompted the financial meltdown of 2007–2008, began his remarks by stating: "Until recently, I thought that there would never again be an opportunity to be involved with an industry as socially destructive and morally bankrupt as the subprime mortgage industry. I was wrong. The for-profit education industry has proven equal to the task."[21]

Because of his prominence provided by the Lewis book, Eisman's remarks set off a firestorm of controversy and led to his being a star witness at a hearing of the Senate Committee on Health, Education, Labor, & Pensions on June 24, 2010, where he repeated many of his earlier allegations.[22] Further hearings have taken place, and it is clear that for-profit colleges are now under the microscope in Congress. Among other issues, the members have been exploring improper recruitment practices, excessive borrowing by students for degrees that are worth little in the marketplace, misleading information provided to students by recruiters, and low completion rates. It is premature to judge the outcome of this and related investigations, but one of the key concerns for members of Congress is that for-profit colleges, with well under 10 percent of enrollments, are drawing nearly 25 percent of the federal Title IV student aid funds.[23] In August 2010, the Government Accountability Office published the findings of an undercover investigation into the recruitment practices of for-profit colleges. The investigation of fifteen colleges uncovered that all engaged in deceptive or questionable recruitment tactics and that four encouraged outright fraud (including falsifying financial aid forms).[24]

If the for-profit industry were to garner an increase of 1 percent per year of market share, it would enroll roughly 20 percent of all students in postsecondary education by 2020, a troubling outcome given its alleged improprieties. It is far from clear that accreditation is an adequate safeguard for students, and regulations in most states are weaker than needed for an enterprise with this size, growth potential, and lack of transparency to students regarding the quality and value of services. Public hearings in 2009 began a flurry of activity and debate about the role of for-profit colleges. Specifically, the Department of Education revised several controversial regulations on the definition of a credit hour, incentive compensation for recruiters, and whether vocational schools prepare graduates for "gainful employment." This last issue has been especially controversial, with the for-profit sector maintaining that it provides a necessary and valuable service, while others have argued that graduates' salaries are insufficient to pay off the massive debt they have accrued.[25] Although the federal regulations on gainful employment were issued in June 2011, the debate about the sector is continuing.[26]

We do not take a stand for or against for-profit higher education per se, primarily because we see these institutions as serving an important role in adult education and career preparation. We are concerned, however, about their explosive growth and heavy reliance on federal student aid. We are also concerned that those institutions that are operated by publicly traded companies may be under such pressure to achieve enrollment growth that they leave themselves open to abuse, particularly in light of the lack of effective oversight and regulatory resources devoted to this industry. Properly regulated, these institutions could provide many of the new spaces that will be required by an economy increasingly dependent on a well-trained work force.

Technology, Distance Learning, and Competency-Based Assessment

The greatest potential for increasing educational capacity lies in technology and distance learning, and much can be learned from fairly recent developments and research. An analysis of online learning studies by the U.S. Department of Education examined more than a thousand empirical studies of online learning from 1996 through July 2008, including entirely online learning compared with "blended instruction" or "hybrid learning," two common terms that refer to online instruction that is combined with face-to-face instruction.[27] The techniques for online learning overlap with those for distance education, but are more extensively developed than those that were characteristic of earlier correspondence courses and televised instruction.

Most of the studies examined in this comprehensive government analysis focused primarily on undergraduate education, although a few focused on K–12 or graduate education. As part of the analysis, researchers screened for fifty independent and comparable effects related to technology and learning. The findings revealed that "students in online learning conditions performed modestly better than those receiving face-to-face instruction."[28] The authors also found that students participating in hybrid or blended learning formats performed better than those participating in purely face-to-face or purely online instruction.[29] The researchers noted that online and face-to-face instruction can differ on various dimensions—including the time the learner spends on task and the structure of the curriculum—and that each of these factors may influence student learning.

In general, the analysis suggests that the interactive and better-developed Web-based tools available today are particularly important to achieving gains in student outcomes through online or blended instruction. The authors noted several important trends: (1) videos and online quizzes do not appear to affect students' learning outcomes; (2) online learning is enhanced by built-in interactions where learners control the media and reflect on their work; and (3) techniques that provide guidance for groups of learners are less effective than those that provide guidance tailored to individual learners.[30] These findings suggest that expansion of online instruction may be an important factor in assessing the future supply of higher education opportunities.

In addition to the Department of Education's recent analysis, a series of annual surveys over an eight-year period speak directly to the question of increased educational capacity through online learning. The survey results, summarized in a 2010 report published by the Sloan Consortium, found rapid growth in the number of students taking at least one online course, compared with enrollment growth generally at the same institutions (see table 6.6).The annual growth in online course taking was relatively modest from fall 2006 to fall 2008, but expanded again substantially in 2009, by almost a million students—the largest numeric annual increase since the surveys began in 2002. As the authors point out, the growth from 1.6 million students taking at least one online course in fall 2002 to 5.6 million students in fall 2009 translates into a compound annual growth rate of 19 percent for this period—a much higher rate than the 2 percent annually for enroll-

TABLE 6.6

Total and online enrollment in degree-granting postsecondary institutions, fall 2002 through fall 2009

Year	Total enrollment	Annual growth rate total enrollment	Students taking at least one online course	Annual growth in online enrollment	Online enrollment as a percent of total enrollment
Fall 2002	16,611,710	NA	1,602,970	NA	9.6%
Fall 2003	16,911,481	1.8%	1,971,397	23.0%	11.7%
Fall 2004	17,272,043	2.1%	2,329,783	18.2%	13.5%
Fall 2005	17,487,481	1.2%	3,180,050	36.5%	18.2%
Fall 2006	17,758,872	1.6%	3,488,381	9.7%	19.6%
Fall 2007	18,248,133	2.8%	3,938,111	12.9%	21.6%
Fall 2008	18,698,630	2.5%	4,606,353	16.9%	24.6%
Fall 2009	19,036,860	1.2%	5,579,022	21.1%	29.3%

Source: I. Elaine Allen and Jeff Seaman, Class Differences: Online Education in the United States (Newburyport, MA: Sloan Consortium, 2010), 8. http://sloanconsortium.org/publications/survey/pdf/class_differences.pdf.

Note: Based on annual surveys of participating colleges and universities.

ment growth generally.[31] It is important to note that the Sloan report, unlike the Department of Education's analysis, does not consider blended or hybrid models as "online education."[32] Therefore, any forecast of available supply relying on the Sloan studies alone may be an underestimate.

In their 2009 annual report, the authors noted that chief academic officers believed that online enrollment growth was reaching a plateau. In the 2010 edition, however, the authors found, "There is no compelling evidence that the continued robust growth in online enrollments is at its end." Still, they do describe some "clouds on the horizon." For example, they report that recent growth in online enrollments has resulted primarily from the expansion of existing offerings rather than from the development of new programs.[33] The difference in forecasts between the 2009 and 2010 reports illustrates the difficulties in predicting the supply of online and/or blended education. It is also possible that the recent economic recession has contributed to the upward projections in the 2010 Sloan report, as institutions and students look for more economical educational offerings.

The authors note a consistent pattern throughout the survey years: that the largest institutions offer considerably more online education than institutions of any other size. In general, as the size of the institution increases, online enrollments increase. Institutions with fifteen thousand or more total enrollments accounted for about two-thirds (64 percent) of online course taking by students. This group of institutions, however, offered only 14 percent of all online courses.[34]

In terms of attitudes about online learning, the institutions with higher online enrollments had a much more favorable opinion of the learning outcomes for online courses than institutions without online offerings. In addition, about 76 percent of the leaders of public institutions reported that online learning is as good as or better than face-to-face instruction, compared with 55 percent of private nonprofit leaders and 67 percent of those from for-profits who felt the same way.[35] In comparing demand for face-to-face programs versus online programs, nearly half of institutions surveyed reported that the economic downturn had increased demand for the former, while about 75 percent of institutions reported it had increased demand for the latter.[36]

Increasing capacity for online education requires resources. Nearly 20 percent of all institutions included in the 2009 Sloan survey said they did not provide training to faculty who were teaching online. The report found that large institutions were more likely to have training courses and the very smallest (with fifteen hundred or fewer enrollments) were the least likely, possibly because smaller institutions may lack the resources for training. Institutions with enrollments over fifteen thousand generally had the most robust array of courses for training faculty.[37]

Promising Practices in Online Learning and Competency-Based Assessment

Many institutions are developing more online and blended education models. Three initiatives stand out as promising both for their potential for scaling these nontraditional models to larger numbers of students and for their efforts at assessment: Carnegie Mellon University's "Open Learning Initiative"; the course redesign work of the National Center for Academic Transformation; and the model employed by Western Governors University (WGU). All of these initiatives are able to provide data related to learning outcomes and costs. WGU has also developed and tested methods for assessing students' prior learning at considerable scale.

Open Learning Initiative. In the first example, Carnegie Mellon's Open Learning Initiative (OLI) provides online courses and related materials to the public for free, and to other higher education institutions for a nominal fee. OLI courses are designed as learning modules to allow faculty to select the modules that their students need or to deliver the full sequence as designed. OLI courses have been broadly disseminated.

The OLI uses "intelligent" tutoring systems, virtual laboratories, simulations, and frequent opportunities for assessment and feedback, with the data and outcomes from student activities used to adjust instruction. One of the most powerful features involves the extent to which assessment is embedded into everyday Web-based instructional activities, with pertinent student outcomes available to students, instructors, course designers, and learning science researchers for continuous evaluation and improvement. As instruction is delivered, Carnegie Mellon University also collects real-time interaction data on all student users.[38] These are some of the features identified in the Sloan studies as important for improving learning outcomes.

In addition, Carnegie Mellon has received funding for and initiated collaboration with state agencies and national associations to establish a consortium of community colleges that will enact a large-scale systems-change process that increases efficiency in the way instruction is developed, delivered, evaluated, and improved. The far-reaching goal of the consortium is to demonstrate a 25 percent improvement in course completion rates for students from disadvantaged populations, with a focus on "gatekeeper" courses—that is, the introductory courses critical to academic program entry and eventual graduation success. Within three years, the Community College OLI will include forty community college partners and reach an additional fifty to one hundred classrooms.[39]

National Center for Academic Transformation. A second well-known and promising initiative is the National Center for Academic Transformation (NCAT), which is directed by Carol Twigg. The center's original purpose was to demonstrate how colleges and universities could redesign their instructional approaches using technology to achieve improved student learning outcomes as well as cost savings. Initially, the center focused its activities, through its Program in Course Redesign (PCR), on large-enrollment gatekeeper courses that are common in many colleges and universities. Key components of the PCR, which lasted from 1999 to 2003, were online tutorials, Web-based discussion groups, on-demand support and group activities, and automated assessment of class exercises, quizzes, and tests. Individual courses in the PCR required students to meet specified learning objectives instead of requirements for seat time, thus allowing for flexibility in the times and places of student engagement while maintaining structure in the course format to ensure students stayed engaged with the course and reached educational milestones.[40]

Twenty-five of the original thirty redesign projects showed significant increases in student learning; the other five showed learning equivalent to traditional formats. Of the twenty-four projects that measured student retention, eighteen reported a noticeable decrease in drop or failure rates, as well as higher course completion rates. Most dramatically, all thirty institutions reduced their costs, by 37 percent on average, and produced a collective annual savings of about $3 million. Other positive outcomes included better student attitudes toward the subject matter and increased student and faculty satisfaction with the model of instruction. The institutions that participated in the project found that using online formats to deliver selected course components enabled them to use classroom space more efficiently. For adult students, the convenience and flexibility of technology-enhanced instruction stood out as a prominent benefit.[41]

NCAT sought to build upon and expand the successes of the PCR program by initiating a Course Redesign Program (CRP) for states and systems. The program included a three-year, three-phase process involving three partners: (1) states, systems, or regional compacts that championed the program and provided funding for the effort; (2) NCAT staff who managed the program and provided expertise to successful redesign participants; and (3) local faculty, staff, and administrators who participated in an initial education and commitment-building phase, a well-structured planning phase, and a comprehensive implementation phase on their campuses. As with the PCR, the expanded redesign program generally focused on large-enrollment, introductory courses that have the potential to reach many students and generate substantial cost savings.[42]

One of the strengths of the NCAT methodology is the data collected through the course redesign process. For example, the Virginia Tech Math Emporium eliminated all class meetings in several courses and replaced them with faculty-developed, Web-based resources such as interactive tutorials, computational exercises, an electronic hypertext book, practice exercises with video responses to frequently asked questions, applications of concepts learned, and online quizzes. The course material is organized into units that students cover at a rate of one or two units per week, each one ending with a short, electronically graded quiz. Multiple sections are treated as single courses. Faculty, graduate teaching assistants, and peer tutors provide support to students and answer questions. A computer lab with five hundred workstations is open twenty-four hours per day, seven days a week. The redesigned courses allow students to choose when to access course materials, what types of learning materials to use, and how quickly to work through the course material within the fifteen-week term. Instant feedback is provided to students through practice quizzes and tests. In addition, computer-based testing provides faculty with comprehensive, continuous data on individual students, so that the faculty can adjust instruction and provide individualized help.

For participants in the project, overall learning outcomes improved. The percentage of students completing a course by achieving grades of D– or better improved from an average of 80.5 percent in the two fall semesters preceding the redesign to an average of 87.25 percent in the subsequent four fall semesters, a statistically significant difference. In addition, instructors' time was reduced by 73 percent from the traditional model. Overall, the cost per student credit hour declined $70, from $91 in the traditional format to $21 in the redesigned model.[43]

In addition to the traditional gatekeeper courses, NCAT's recent work has focused on developmental mathematics at community colleges: basic math, elementary algebra and intermediate algebra. The Tennessee Board of Regents has partnered with NCAT in this initiative. Using the Math Emporium model, participating students at Cleveland State Community College in Tennessee met one hour in class and two hours in a large computer lab each week of the term. The one-hour class meetings were held in computer labs to allow students to work online; instructors provided individual student assistance and reviewed student progress. All course materials were organized into modules, which students completed at a rate of one or more modules each week. All homework and testing were done online. Students completing a developmental math course before the end of the term were allowed to begin the next developmental course immediately. Online testing provided students with immediate diagnostic feedback and continuous assessment using low-stakes quizzes, to help students understand which areas to focus on in order to improve their outcomes.

As a result of the course redesign, participating students in basic math, elementary algebra, and intermediate algebra showed significant improvement when compared with earlier cohorts as measured by performance on common exam items. The percentage of students earning a C grade or better improved significantly in two of the three courses. The course completion rate for elementary algebra increased from 50 percent before the redesign to 68 percent after the redesign. The completion rate for intermediate algebra jumped from 57 percent to 74 percent. Initial success rates for students in basic math, however, were not maintained during the subsequent semesters, and the Cleveland faculty team plans to revisit its redesign process to improve basic math grades and course retention.

Beyond the promising outcomes described, NCAT has documented other positive impacts on students, including: improvement in student attitudes about math anxiety; faster progress within the developmental math sequence (for students who complete courses before the end of a term and can thereby move on without waiting until the next semester); an increase in students passing at least one developmental math class; an increase in students enrolled in college-level math courses; and an increase in students starting in developmental education who successfully complete a college-level course.

Significant cost savings have been realized as well. For example, in the traditional model, Cleveland State Community College offered fifty-five developmental math sections of twenty-four students each in the fall and spring semesters (a total of 1,320 students). Forty-five of the sections were taught by full-time faculty at a cost of $256,275, and ten were taught by adjuncts at a cost of $14,400. The total cost of the traditional course was thus $270,625. In the redesigned model, the college offered seventy-seven sections of eighteen students each in fall and spring (a total of 1,386 students), all of which were taught by full-time faculty at a cost of $219,258. NCAT reported total savings of $51,418 or 19 percent, while accommodating 5 percent more students. This amount represents substantial savings, particularly for a small institution like Cleveland State. Faculty productivity in these courses rose by 23 percent, as evidenced by the increase in faculty to student ratios (FTE per teacher increased from 21.2 to 26).In the traditional model, faculty taught five sections per semester. In the redesigned model, faculty members taught ten to eleven sections, which means that they handled more than a hundred-fifty students each semester and worked eight to ten hours per week in the lab.[44]

Due to the success of the redesign project, the math department at Cleveland State Community College has expanded course redesign to three college-level courses: college algebra, finite math, and introductory statistics. The project's findings—in terms of student outcomes and cost savings—have important potential implications nationally, due to the large numbers of students required to take developmental math courses.

In addition to the projects described, NCAT is continuing to redesign courses in many disciplinary fields at many colleges and universities (both public and private, two-year and four-year). Through its work, NCAT has identified the following five principles as important in course redesign efforts: (1) redesign the whole course rather than a single class or section; (2) encourage active learning; (3) provide students with individualized assistance; (4) build in ongoing assessment and prompt, automated feedback; and(5) ensure sufficient time on task and monitor student progress.[45] As faculty experience in course redesign increases and more data are collected about its efficacy, it may be that increasing numbers of faculty will gain confidence in online instructional formats.

Western Governors University. A third example of an initiative with potential to diversify the supply side of education is Western Governors University (WGU), which was founded in 1995 by nineteen state governors, each of whom agreed to contribute $100,000 in state funds for start-up costs. WGU now has twenty-two member governors and is able to sustain its operation on tuition revenues. WGU's tuition is slightly under $2,900 for six months of study ($3,250 for its nursing and MBA programs). WGU targets adult students, many whom have families and are less likely than younger students to leave their state to pursue education. Many adult students are not eligible for most state financial aid programs, but they are eligible for federal Pell Grants if they are financially needy and enrolled at least half time. As a result, WGU costs little to states and requires little infrastructure to support adult education (as explained later). WGU offers more than fifty accredited degree programs in four high-demand areas—teaching, health care, information technology, and business—and, after a slow start, enrolls over twenty-three thousand students from all fifty states and the District of Columbia.[46]

One of the key innovations of WGU is its "competency-based" approach to education that measures and rewards what students know without regard to where or when they learned it. As WGU president Robert Mendenhall states: "We hold the learning constant and let the time vary, as opposed to the traditional approach, which holds the time constant and lets the learning vary."[47]

As with NCAT's emphasis on students meeting learning objectives rather than logging in seat time, this approach enables students to receive credit for knowledge and skills they already have, as well as to learn at their own pace and in a range of settings, including online. As a result, this approach to assessment has the potential to assist in shortening the time to completion for some students and thereby increasing the supply of education for others.

As WGU grows and is able to demonstrate educational effectiveness and efficiency, it becomes a viable option for states to consider to increase their educational capacity. In November 2010, Indiana Governor Mitch Daniels joined the board of WGU and created WGU Indiana. Because Indiana ranks forty-fifth in the nation in terms of the percentage of adults with a bachelor's degree or higher, Daniels saw WGU as an option for providing education to more Indiana adults for relatively low tuition and with no direct state support. Daniels now refers to WGU Indiana as Indiana's "eighth university."[48] In addition, with funding from national foundations, WGU Indiana has announced a $1 million marketing campaign that extends well beyond the Internet to billboards, buses, print, radio, and television. The governor appears on the WGU Indiana Web site to appeal to adults to return to college by stating that "Indiana needs more college grads. And you deserve the greater opportunities that a college degree can bring."[49] Under WGU Indiana, the national WGU offices in Utah govern the new branch through its existing board of trustees, with guidance from an advisory board of Indiana officials and prominent state leaders.[50] It remains to be seen whether large numbers of adults in Indiana will enroll in WGU Indiana, but it appears that the political climate is ready for this kind of alternative educational opportunity.

With enrollments growing at a rate of 30 percent annually, WGU predicts it will grow from twenty-one thousand students thirty thousand students within the next few years.[51] Other states are joining the conversation about using WGU or a similar model to increase educational capacity. A 2010 report from California's legislative analyst recommended that the state legislature create a task force to pursue a public-private partnership with WGU as one strategy for accommodating more students in higher education.[52]

These three initiatives—the Open Learning Initiative, NCAT's course redesign model, and WGU—suggest that states may be able to increase their higher education capacity by using alternative educational opportunities, including online learning. Looking beyond U.S. borders, Great Britain's Open University (UKOU) offers another model for distance learning on a large scale that addresses the challenges of accessibility, cost, and quality. Established more than four decades ago as a public open-admissions institution, the Open University serves about a hundred eighty thousand students through centrally developed curricula and tutorial support, using a range of electronic media that encompasses BBC radio and television, audio and video cassettes, e-mail, and the Internet. By the mid-1990s, after twenty-five years of operation: the university accounted for more than a third of all part-time students in the United Kingdom. Its costs to the government approximated 40 percent of the average per-student cost of other British universities. The teaching quality of a high proportion of its programs was categorized as "excellent" according to national standards, which places the university in the top tier of British institutions. An effort by the Open University to establish an American counterpart was not successful, but American public and private institutions have adapted some aspects of its model.[53]

CONCLUSION

Based on this overview of the supply side of American higher education, it appears that increased capacity in American higher education has been a responsibility shared across higher education sectors in the past—and this will likely continue to be the case. For example, for-profit colleges will likely continue to increase their market share. Yet it is the broad-access public colleges and universities that the nation and the states should look to primarily to meet the challenges of increased college participation and attainment, since it is these institutions that serve the largest numbers of undergraduate students, particularly those populations that have traditionally been underserved by higher education. Innovations in the design, delivery, and assessment of higher education will be critical to increasing substantially the number of Americans who enroll and successfully complete high-quality college programs.

Given the fiscal challenges facing states, however, the leaders of public colleges and universities in the United States face increased uncertainty and volatility of operating and capital budgets, which may cause many of them to be cautious in launching new programs or taking in larger student enrollments. This conservative response appears likely, unless state, civic, business, and education leaders can generate offsetting policies to ensure that qualified students are not turned away from higher education.

CHAPTER 7

Financing Higher Education in an Era of Global Challenge

An Agenda for the Nation

We begin this final chapter by reviewing our essential arguments and guiding principles. We then offer a framework for identifying the primary policy questions and issues that the United States must address if it is to achieve substantial increases in the share of its population with a college degree. Our framework includes suggestions for key changes in higher education policy at the state and federal levels, but does not offer a comprehensive blueprint. Such an attempt would be presumptuous and unrealistic, considering the wide variation in state circumstances and approaches, as described in earlier chapters. Our intention is to help stimulate a national debate on the restructuring of higher education finance, which we believe will be required if the nation and the states are to make substantial advances in degree attainment and equity. We do not claim to resolve the debate. Rather, our primary purpose is to make clear the urgency of raising degree attainment levels in today's knowledge-driven society and economy, and to illuminate the critical role of finance policy in reaching this goal. Although major changes in finance policy are necessary, we are optimistic that the system can be reoriented so that substantially more American citizens can achieve the higher levels of education the nation needs.

GUIDING ASSUMPTIONS AND PRINCIPLES

The Goal Is Substantially Higher Degree Attainment and Greater Equity

In earlier chapters, we described the nation's needs for increasing significantly the numbers of students graduating from college (at both the bachelor's and associate degree levels). To meet these needs, the increase in college graduates must exceed the rate of population growth, which has accounted for most of our small gains in college graduates recently. The United States is underperforming in the accessibility of higher education, in the rates of college completion, and in the educational attainment levels of young adults. In light of the nation's recent relative decline in international rankings of college attainment, President Barack Obama set the ambitious goal of returning the United States to first place in the world on this measure by 2020. Major foundations and associations working in the field of higher education have established similar goals (see appendix A), which suggests broad and influential support for increasing educational attainment levels in the United States.

To achieve this goal, colleges and universities need to enroll and graduate a much larger share of underrepresented populations than they have in the past. These populations include low- and moderate-income students (those in the lower two-fifths of the income distribution) and traditionally underrepresented minority groups. In addition to the equity imperative that has been a major policy consideration since the civil rights movement, these populations are growing so fast that improvements in their educational performance is imperative if the nation as a whole is to improve its college attainment rate. As reported by the Carsey Institute (based on U.S. Census data), the number of minority youth (age nineteen and younger) increased by 4.8 million, or 15.5 percent, from 2000 to 2008, and Hispanics accounted for 3.9 million, or about four-fifths of the increase. The number of African Americans declined by almost a percentage point (–0.9 percent) over this eight-year period, while other minorities such as Asians and mixed-race individuals grew by 985,000 (18.2 percent). Non-Hispanic white youth declined by 2.6 million (–5.3 percent). In July 2008, blacks, Hispanics, and other minorities constituted well over two-fifths (43 percent) of the nation's 82.6 million youth.[1]

The United States cannot succeed in substantially increasing its degree attainment rates without achieving large gains among the population groups that have been poorly served by our education system in the past (as witnessed by their lower graduation rates from high school, their lower college enrollment rates among those who do graduate, and their poorer degree completion rates for those who enroll in college). Cumulatively, these lower success rates along the educational pipeline result in poorer college degree completion rates among low- and moderate-income students and among minority population groups such as Hispanics, African Americans, and Native Americans.[2] If not successfully addressed, these trends will severely restrict the nation's ability to improve the capacities of its work force and citizenry. In a world where knowledge and skills are increasingly important, marked disadvantages in educational attainment consign lower-income and minority populations to limited opportunities for social and economic mobility.[3]

Current Policies Cannot Achieve the Goal

We have argued that existing policies and practices in higher education will not accomplish the desired increases in college degree production, especially given the resource limitations that governments face for the foreseeable future. High school graduation rates are below international norms and are not improving much.[4] Even among high school graduates, roughly half of those entering higher education are not fully prepared for college-level work, and the share is likely higher at broad-access institutions.[5] While the causes of these failures in college preparation are complex, higher education and state policies play an important role in addressing some of them. Examples include policies that articulate standards across the K–16 divide and those that encourage the development of cross-sector, longitudinal data systems. Well-designed finance policies can serve a constructive role in providing incentives for cross-sector planning and integration in both of these areas, for example, by linking some resources for both baccalaureate institutions and community colleges to successful transfer and baccalaureate degree completion. In addition, college persistence and completion rates are low by international standards and have been stagnant over time.[6] This is partly attributable to weak student preparation but is also affected by the declining affordability of college for students and their families—an issue that can be influenced by tuition and student aid policies. In sum, the restructuring of higher education finance in ways that align it with national needs and priorities is pivotal if the United States is to achieve substantially higher rates of educational attainment.

The two major expansions of higher education in the post-World War II era—for the GIs and later for the baby boomers—occurred when the American economy and the public sector were growing rapidly. As Clark Kerr noted, the higher education expansion of the post-World War II period was enabled by the dramatic gains in the productivity of the American economy in the 1950s and 1960s; these have not been matched in any subsequent decade.[7] In contrast, the contemporary challenge to significantly expand college access and attainment must be addressed in the context of more problematic national economic growth and severe constraints on federal and state budgets over the next decade. The default response to the budgetary shortfalls and cuts of recent decades has been to shift costs to students through tuition increases that have exceeded rates of inflation and growth in family incomes. College affordability for most American families has eroded, and the indebtedness of college students and graduates has grown to unprecedented levels (see table 7.1 for a snapshot of college affordability by income level during 2008). Grants are less focused on those with greatest financial need. In addition, a larger share of financial aid is loans rather than grants: between 1980–1981 and 2009–2010, the proportion of total aid provided through loans has risen from 39 percent to 51 percent according to College Board data (see table 7.2). From 2004 to 2008, average debt levels for graduating seniors with student loans rose 24 percent, to $23,200. In 2008, graduating seniors who were Pell Grant recipients had an average debt of $24,800—about $1,600 more than the average for all seniors graduating with loans.[8]

Higher education's share of state and local budgets has been declining for several decades. Demands from the other major state budgetary categories—health care, elementary and secondary education, criminal justice, and transportation—show no signs of letting up, and many enjoy legal protections that higher education funding (often categorized as "discretionary") lacks. The largest two categories of spending in state budgets are K–12 education (improvements there would eventually help higher education) and health-care expenditures—including Medicaid, long-term care for the "medically indigent," and public employee health care—which are likely to continue to grow faster than state revenues as the population ages.[9] In addition,

TABLE 7.1

Percent of income needed to pay net college cost

	Community college		Public four-year		Private non-profit four-year	
	2000	2008	2000	2008	2000	2008
20% of the population with the lowest income	40	49	39	55	151	197
20% of the population with lower-middle income	22	29	23	33	58	79
20% of the population with middle income	15	20	18	25	37	50
20% of the population with upper-middle income	10	13	12	16	25	33
20% of the population with the highest income	6	7	7	9	15	20
40% of the population with the lowest income	27	35	28	40	84	113

TABLE 7.2
Student aid and college prices (in 2009 dollars)

	1980–1981	1984–1985	1989–1990	1994–1995	1999–2000	2004–2005	2008–2009	2009–2010	% change, 1981 to 2010
Student aid									
Pell Grants	$6,216	$6,316	$8,271	$8,010	$9,312	$14,952	$17,907	$28,213	354%
Total federal grants	$17,572	$10,203	$11,339	$11,781	$13,132	$20,991	$25,182	$41,321	135%
Total federal loans	$16,110	$17,661	$20,576	$33,876	$42,444	$62,338	$84,892	$96,834	501%
Total federal aid	$35,400	$29,199	$33,064	$46,756	$62,101	$91,440	$117,853	$146,542	314%
State grant programs	$2,086	$2,528	$2,976	$4,024	$5,250	$7,520	$8,224	$8,722	318%
State-sponsored loans	$0	$0	$0	$0	$650	$910	$880	$800	N/A
Institutional grants	$4,220	$5,300	$8,570	$14,030	$19,780	$24,620	$29,710	$33,380	691%
Private and employer grants	$0	$0	$2,130	$4,110	$6,890	$9,690	$11,710	$10,550	N/A
Private sector loans	$0	$0	$0	$0	$4,520	$14,780	$10,080	$7,700	N/A
Total funds used to post-secondary expenses	**$41,706**	**$37,027**	**$46,740**	**$68,920**	**$99,191**	**$148,961**	**$178,457**	**$207,694**	**398%**
Pell Grants as % of total funds used to finance postsecondary	15%	17%	18%	12%	9%	10%	10%	14%	
Average tuition									
Private not-for-profit four-year	$9,419	$11,494	$14,997	$17,006	$20,047	$22,792	$24,649	$26,129	177%
Public four-year	$2,094	$2,540	$2,936	$3,925	$4,343	$5,828	$6,453	$7,050	237%
Public two-year	$1,018	$1,208	$1,456	$1,901	$2,130	$2,364	$2,322	$2,558	151%

Source: The College Board, *Trends in Student Aid,* 2010 and *Trends in College Pricing,* 2010. © 2010 The College Board, www.collegeboard.com. Reproduced with permission.

it appears that the federal government's substantial, long-term budget imbalances rule out thoughts of any broad-based federalization of higher education finance, save perhaps for temporary assistance in periods of cyclical macroeconomic decline.

It is highly improbable that the nation and the states can afford major expansion of college opportunity without significant improvements in cost effectiveness. For example, the National Center for Higher Education Management Systems has estimated that achieving President Obama's goal of international leadership by 2020 would require increasing undergraduate enrollments at two- and four-year public colleges and universities by 33 percent beyond current projections. Assuming current levels of tuition, inflation, and expenditures per student, an increase of 31 percent in state and local appropriations would be required over the next decade to serve all the students—a very unlikely scenario (see figure 7.1).[10] While it is clear that strategic public investment will be needed if the nation is to raise substantially its levels of college access and attainment, it is not realistic to expect that this investment will be commensurate with historical patterns, such as those during the post-World War II era. Similarly, tuition increases are likely to continue. But the pattern of tuition growth that consistently outstrips family income (and inflation) and that absorbs new student financial aid resources with little or no improvement in college access or affordability must be altered.

FIGURE 7.1   Percent increase in state and local appropriations needed above current levels to meet 2020 goal

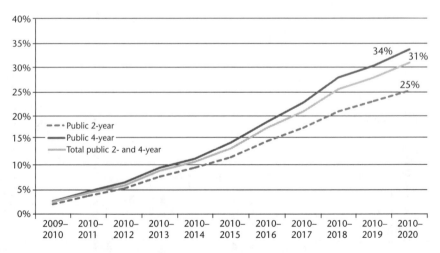

Source: Calculation based on data from National Center for Higher Education Management Systems.

Based on these conditions in higher education, public finance, and college affordability, we conclude that the patterns of public expenditures and tuition growth of recent decades are not sustainable. The consequences of maintaining current financing policies and practices are that the national and state needs for major improvements in higher education opportunity and attainment will not be met, with serious negative implications for competitiveness in the global economy and for equity in American society. This is the core of our argument for a fundamental rethinking of higher education finance. The need for restructuring public finance of higher education was apparent to many before the onset of the Great Recession, though the depth and length of the sluggish economic aftermath have brought the need into much sharper focus than "normal" times would have. Entrenched policies and practices are notoriously difficult to change—but change they must. Sometimes a crisis, particularly an extended one, can provide the perspective and impetus needed to catalyze transformation.

In the longer term, there are grounds for guarded optimism, we think, if changes are forthcoming. As we will explain, we see a stalemate in higher education policy and finance—between those who ask for more public resources to be poured into the current system and those who recognize other claims for scarce resources and do not trust the current arrangements to produce the results they seek, even with additional resources. The strategic rebalancing of priorities through changed incentive structures, along with increased openness to new delivery modes, can serve to increase public and policy-maker confidence in higher education, once better results are apparent, and thereby make increased investment at least thinkable. Much is now known about innovations with potential to improve educational effectiveness while reducing costs, although many successful approaches have not yet been implemented systemically or at scale.[11] As the economy eventually improves and some additional resources become available for higher education, strategic investments that leverage improved educational and cost effectiveness must be the highest priority.

Finance Is a Means to Other Policy Ends

Public policies regarding higher education finance, broadly construed to encompass tuition and student aid policies, as well as direct funding of institutions by states, are critical to achieving attainment and equity goals. Finance policies, however, provide means to the broader goals and are not ends in themselves. As society's needs and goals change, finance policies should adapt.

Finance policies must be a key part of the overall strategy for several reasons. First, clearly public resources are, and likely will continue to be, very tightly constrained. As just explained, improvements in attainment levels cannot be achieved simply by funding more enrollments and graduates in the traditional ways. Fortunately, unlike in the postwar years of great enroll-ment pressure, the physical infrastructure to educate more students is, for the most part, already in place, although it needs to be maintained more effec-tively and utilized more efficiently. As a result, finance policy for higher edu-cation does not need to focus so much on building new infrastructure but must use finance levers strategically to alter performance. The ways in which resources are allocated and incentives created to pursue public policy goals should now be the major concerns of higher education finance.

Second and closely related, we believe that the nation and the states will need to make additional investments in order to educate more students, but these additional investments will likely be modest by historical standards and will need to be "earned" first by the higher education enterprise. This will require refocusing higher education's efforts squarely on meeting pub-lic needs and policy objectives, and being far more transparent, accountable, and performance-oriented in doing so. Third, policies regarding the fund-ing of institutions must be coordinated effectively with tuition and student aid policies, with the latter involving the federal government as well as the states. We cannot educate more people, especially when many are from low-income and underrepresented backgrounds, if state funding shortfalls con-tinue to automatically lead to large tuition hikes that absorb most state and federal increases in student aid.

A National Policy Can Be Developed Within American Federalism

Higher education operates—and should continue to operate—within a fed-eral context that provides extensive powers and responsibilities to states. Americans do not believe in a fully authoritative national government, espe-cially concerning education. Thus, the states' constitutionally based policy role in higher education must be recognized. As we discussed in chapter 5, the states are diverse: in the evolution and histories of their higher educa-tion "systems"; in their reliance upon public versus private institutions and on two-year compared with four-year institutions; in their structures for pub-lic policy and for higher education governance; in their demographic and economic configurations; in their needs and available resources; and in the effectiveness of their public schools, colleges, and universities.

Nonetheless, the scope of the emergent degree-production shortfall and the inefficient cross-purposes at which current federal and state policies operate call for a serious effort to develop and sustain policies that comple-ment rather than checkmate one another. In framing this line of thinking, we conceive of the goal of producing substantially more college graduates as a *national* rather than a *federal* one, with related state goals negotiated volun-tarily, based on broad involvement within each state. It is very much in states' interest to develop these goals, since each will reap the primary benefits from better educating its people. Thoughtfully designed federal incentives developed out of a national policy dialogue must be part of this picture. Only then can we have a viable national higher education strategy that is broadly owned and therefore sustainable and adaptable to diverse state circumstances. Many of our global competitors have been able to mount national efforts, and in the modern knowledge age, America needs to keep up. For the United States, however, effective national policy must take into account the size, scope, and institutional diversity of American higher education, and the strengths as well as the constraints of American federalism.

Increasing Attainment Is a Political Challenge

Like most complex public policy problems, deciding to produce substantially more graduates and organizing to accomplish this goal are political challenges in the best sense of that term: mounting collective action at a national scale to address a public need. The nation needs to recognize the importance of the goal, resolve to make the changes at various levels that are necessary to address it, and follow through in pursuing the goal over time. The follow-through will be challenging in the face of inevitable political leadership turnover, economic ups and downs, and some likely pushback from those who feel threatened by the changes or who simply find entrenched ways of thinking hard to break. We will suggest ways to address these difficulties. From the start, however, meeting the overall political challenge will require broad public awareness of the need, determined political leadership, and an energetic and well-coordinated effort to institutionalize changes rapidly. We recognize that this is a tall order in a diverse, democratic nation that is organized federally. That is why we emphasize the importance of building broad awareness of the need to increase the educational attainment of the population. One key goal of this book is to raise public and policy-maker awareness of this need; another is to identify how the challenges can be met, so that a coherent national strategy can emerge.

All Hands Will Be Needed

Public policies that seek to increase educational attainment levels substantially must address all parts of the higher education system, including the private collegiate sector, its fast-growing for-profit subsector, and all modes of instructional delivery such online learning and competency certification. Given the scope of the challenge and the limited availability of new resources, the country will truly need all hands on deck. Policies will need to encourage innovative approaches to preparing people for work and life. Both state and federal policies are implicated here.

Despite the need to involve all higher education sectors, we think that for this particular challenge the broad-access institutions of higher education, both public and private, will play the most important role. As we discussed in the previous chapter, community colleges, comprehensive colleges and universities, less-selective private nonprofits, and for-profit schools are the sectors best positioned for substantial growth. Research universities serve other important roles in providing research capacities and graduate and professional education, which could be jeopardized by significantly increasing their numbers or sizes to accommodate more undergraduates. Moreover, research universities are the most expensive institutions to expand and generally are not enthusiastic about doing so at the undergraduate level. Although we offer suggestions as to how research universities can contribute, we believe that the policy challenges and potential solutions on which we focus here can be addressed most effectively by the broad-access sectors, which are best positioned for undergraduate growth. These institutions generally receive too little attention in the media and in discussions about higher education policy.

ACHIEVING SUBSTANTIALLY INCREASED DEGREE ATTAINMENT: A PUBLIC POLICY AND FINANCE FRAMEWORK

Setting the Stage

One of the most fundamental steps in increasing degree attainment is building and sustaining awareness of the scope of the challenge and the rationale for taking it up. It is vital that the public as well as state and federal policy makers become aware of the essential relevant facts: our growing global disadvantage in degree attainment; the consequences of it for international economic competitiveness and the American standard of living; and the changes in policy and practice that will be required to address this situation. Broad awareness among the public and key stakeholders is the best hope for sustaining policy-maker attention to the problem over time. Recent public opinion research shows that this is a message the American public is ready to hear; the proportion of Americans who believe that college "is necessary to be successful in today's work world" has grown steadily and sharply—from 31 percent to 55 percent over the past decade.[12]

President Obama's recognition of the problem and his establishment of a national goal to regain international leadership in educational attainment are important first steps that have catalyzed some promising actions in a limited number of states (see appendix B). In general, however, too little has been accomplished since he established the national goal in July 2009, particularly on the part of states and institutions.[13] It is essential that the president and his successors use the bully pulpit not only to articulate the goal and its rationale but also to lead the development of a federal-state partnership that creates and implements coordinated policies to achieve the overall target.

One way to begin this process is to convene a presidential commission along the lines of the Truman Commission on Higher Education of the late 1940s. As we described in chapter 3, this group articulated and legitimated the need to educate many more Americans to college degrees in the aftermath of World War II. To accomplish the task, the commission identified a set of promising ideas that were ultimately quite influential. For example, it was the Truman Commission that called for the expansion of the community college sector that soon emerged, as well as for the expansion of federal scholarships and fellowships, which were, at the time, almost nonexistent. Today, a similar presidential commission could, if managed correctly, provide a vehicle for building a broad national understanding of the importance of increased college degree attainment for the country's future and a range of coordinated steps to achieve it.

The federal government has an important role to play, but it is principally the states and institutions of higher education that must rise to this challenge. Whether or not there is a Truman-like presidential commission to lead the way, it will be necessary for the president to convene the nation's governors, legislative leaders, major philanthropies, representatives of higher education, and key stakeholders (such as the business community) to negotiate meaningful state goals. As part of this process, there must be commitments from the federal government and philanthropy to assist in achieving the goals. In light of the scope of the challenge and the financial plight of both the federal government and the states, assumptions about innovations in delivery, productivity per dollar spent, cost containment, and tuition and student aid policies will be an important part of this conversation. If the groundwork is laid properly and the effort is met with sustained presidential attention and some modest but strategically targeted new resources, it should bring home to many opinion leaders the overall need and the challenges involved, including the need for new ways of thinking and acting. With public support and a presidential mandate endorsed by many governors, it would become increasingly difficult for more reluctant states to opt out or to back away from agreed-upon goals.

In the remainder of this chapter, we describe first the federal and then the state policy priorities that are necessary to meet national goals for increased college degree attainment.

FEDERAL POLICIES

Most importantly, federal policies need to stop inadvertently encouraging actions by states and colleges and universities that increase costs and that discourage student enrollment and completion. Federal policies in several spheres have these effects, including student aid, regulatory efforts, and the awarding of research and development support. We consider each of these in turn.

Perverse Incentives in Federal Student Aid Policies

In its signature achievement to date in higher education policy, the Obama administration in March 2010 engineered an end to the bank-based, federally guaranteed student loan program and redirected substantial portions of the subsidies formerly paid to lenders into increases in Pell Grants to low-income students. The additional funds for this purpose are expected to total more than $36 billion over ten years (if they survive intense pressures to reduce federal spending).[14] The maximum award under the Pell program is scheduled to rise from $5,550 in 2010 to $5,975 in 2017 and will be indexed to inflation in the latter years.[15] Ceilings on student borrowing in the loan programs also were raised recently, after a number of years during which they remained unchanged.[16]

In taking these steps, federal policy makers sought to make college more affordable for students and families. Unfortunately, their actions are being vitiated by large tuition increases at the state and institutional levels.[17] For public colleges and universities, the states' fiscal woes have played an important role in inducing hefty increases in tuition, a problem we address under the state policy section later. It is common knowledge among those who work with state legislatures that, in a fiscal crisis, higher education is often the least painful target for deep cuts. Unlike the children served in K–12 education, the inmates in prison, or the indigent needing Medicaid or public assistance, college students can be asked to pay more for the services they receive. Tuition increases become even easier to justify when they coincide with increases in federal funding for student financial aid, particularly when the aid programs are sensitive to tuition in calculating student eligibility for funds.

College and university leaders in the private and public sectors are well aware of changes in student purchasing power. When student purchasing power is rising (for example, due to increases in federal student financial aid), then increases in tuition charges become very tempting as an alternative to finding areas for spending restraint within their institutions. This dynamic mitigates pressures on institutions to find efficiencies, which makes college less affordable for students and serves to shift more of the costs of higher education from states and institutions to the federal government and students. The explicit federal policy objective of student financial aid—that is, increasing college access and affordability—is thwarted significantly.[18] This is one factor underlying the slippage in the extent to which Pell Grants cover tuition costs at public institutions (see figure 7.2). If increased enrollment and degree attainment are to be national policy priorities—to be achieved largely through educating many more underrepresented students and those of modest means—this perverse dynamic must be addressed.

Modest Annual Increases in Aid Awards

The recent legislation increasing the award amount of Pell Grants—if it survives budget-cutting pressures—represents a large step in the right direction. The law provides a substantial initial boost in the awards, which is unfortu-

FIGURE 7.2   Pell Grants fail to keep pace with escalating tuition

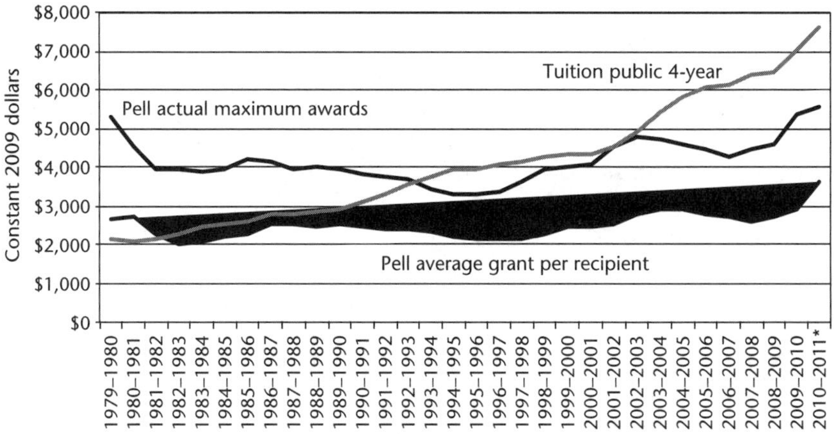

Note: Not adjusted into 2009 dollars.

Source: The College Board, *Trends in Student Aid*, 2010, and *Trends in College Pricing*, 2010. © 2010 The College Board, www.collegeboard.com. Reproduced with permission.

nately at risk from the dynamic described earlier, particularly since the initial jump in the awards coincides with a time of state fiscal stress. The law follows up with modest annual increases in the maximum Pell Grant that, beginning in 2013, are linked to the Consumer Price Index. These steady increases, as compared with big onetime boosts, do not provide the perverse incentives to raise tuition unreasonably, since they are below the increases in tuition that colleges and universities might consider comfortable. In addition, the law provides some reliability for students by connecting grant aid increases to the Consumer Price Index. Unfortunately though, this does not mean that Pell Grants will keep pace with the ever-rising cost of college.[19]

The same logic applies to the borrowing ceilings under the guaranteed college loan programs, which have typically remained flat for long periods, followed by occasional large increases. This pattern facilitates large jumps in tuition when the ceilings are raised. In addition, the long flat periods in the 1990s and the first decade of this century stimulated the emergence and rapid growth of private loans made to students directly by banks and other lenders, without the student protections of the federal program.[20] The Congress and the Department of Education should consider legislation to provide for modest annual growth in borrowing limits that are linked to reasonable targets for annual tuition increases, since tuition must be part of any national strategy to finance increased college attendance and completion. We will offer more specific analysis on tuition in the discussion of state policies later.

A New Incentive Program for State-based Student Financial Aid

In 1972, when the federal government began to provide student financial aid in earnest, it created the Basic Educational Opportunity Grant program (now called Pell Grants) and the State Student Incentive Grant (SSIG) program, which provided incentives for states to establish their own need-based student aid programs. Through SSIG (now called Leveraging Educational Assistance Partnerships, or LEAP), the federal government provided matching funds to states, up to a modest annual limit. Within a few years of its inception, the number of state grant programs jumped from nine in 1974–1975 (the first year of SSIG funding) to twenty-four in 1977–1978.[21] Over the ensuing decades, states became a significant aid provider. As of 2008–2009, they provided some $6 billion in need-based grant aid to undergraduate students and a total of over $10 billion in all for student aid.[22] Meanwhile, the federal government's contribution to the incentive grant program has languished over the years; in 2007–2008, it allotted just $65 million nationwide.[23] Some federal policy makers have thought that this program has done its job, and it has been proposed for elimination by several administrations.

On the contrary, we suggest reviving and substantially expanding this type of federal-state partnership program (with a new name), for several reasons. First, a substantial infusion of funds by the federal government provided on a matching basis could, through its leverage effect, bring to bear many more dollars for student aid from states, which has been the case with other federal matching programs, such as Medicaid).[24] Student aid is generally popular in many states; nationwide, the share of state higher education appropriations for student aid has been increasing steadily (rising from 6.8 percent in 1998–1999 to 10.9 percent in 2008–2009), so a "two for one deal" via federal matching should have a substantial reinforcing effect.[25] Second, if the program were restricted to need-based aid, as SSIG/LEAP has been throughout its history, it would provide an incentive for states to increase appropriations for need-based aid as compared with other student aid, which has been growing faster but targets needy students less effectively.[26]

Further, aid under the federal-state partnership program should be open to students attending any accredited, degree-granting, postsecondary institution. In addition, the program should be liberal, within the bounds of prudent oversight, about how aid recipients are educated—that is, whether online, through appropriate learning assessments and certification, or in traditional college classrooms. As we have argued, these nontraditional methods are needed to broaden access and increase educational capacity efficiently. Ideally, student aid under the federal-state partnership program should be portable across state lines so as to facilitate the use of excess capacity in states with declining youth populations by students from states whose colleges are bursting at the seams. A few states currently have aid portability arrangements, usually with neighboring states. We recognize that for many states, the idea of seeing students "taking tax dollars out of state" might be a hard sell politically, but the incentive of federal dollars, as well as the capacity challenges facing the fastest-growing states, may make this approach sufficiently attractive to win support.

There would also likely be pushback against a federal requirement that students at for-profit institutions be eligible for support in the partnership program. As of 2008–2009, however, thirty-three states provided need-based aid to students enrolled at for-profit institutions, about 5 percent of the total of such aid. The country needs their capacity at this time. Including them in a substantial way could provide impetus for states to work harder to regulate these schools appropriately, whether by delegation of federal authority or by cooperating with federal oversight efforts (as we describe in the following section).

A key component of this new federal incentive program would be to tie its funding to a guarantee by participating states that they link their own student aid support to the scale of tuition increases in their public institutions, as a few already do by statute. If the federal matching funds were substantial enough to be truly attractive to states and induce them to sign on, such a link would provide a bulwark against their permitting unduly large increases in tuition in their public institutions. If the state did allow such increases, it would then be obligated to provide commensurately increased aid appropriations, which could provide a strong deterrent. This shift in incentives could blunt the current perverse dynamic, which can, as described earlier, encourage large tuition hikes.

An alternative approach would be for the federal matching grant program to require participating states to adopt an explicit tuition policy that would, in the interest of college affordability, ensure that tuition increases were regular but moderate, predictable, and linked to students' and families' ability to pay. However, it would be difficult to achieve agreement on the precise criteria for such formulas. In addition, the idea of a direct federal mandate on the setting of tuition, which has always been a policy domain of states or institutions, seems of dubious feasibility or desirability, particularly in light of the variations among states.

Student Loan Reform

Linking student loan repayment to post-college earnings is not a new idea, but implementation has been stymied by the reliance on commercial banks as originators of loan capital, and by a highly decentralized system of repayment. With the recent elimination of the commercial banks in favor of direct federal lending, a key institutional obstacle has been removed. Repayment through the income tax system is also more feasible now than in prior years, as the Internal Revenue Service has demonstrated greater flexibility in cooperating with federal student aid programs, and is the obvious agency to collect loan repayments tied to income. We believe that the concept of income contingent loans is logical and compelling. We endorse the idea, and encourage the further development of implementation strategies.

Oversight of For-profit Higher Education

The for-profit sector has grown at a rapid rate during the past decade, and its growth appears to have accelerated during the recent economic doldrums, as students have sought credentials to give them a leg up in a highly competitive job market. This sector disproportionately serves students of modest means and underrepresented groups, which is very important.[27] For-profit institutions have been innovative in offering efficient, student-friendly programs and services that are responsive to the market. There is little doubt that they will play a significant role in responding to the enrollment demands associated with increasing the nation's college degree output.[28]

At the same time, however, there are legitimate concerns about the for-profit higher education sector, which policy makers need to address. Profit motives in fields such as education and human services call for careful policy oversight, because providers' incentives are not necessarily aligned with those of their clients. Generally, prospective clients are not as well informed as providers concerning the quality or appropriateness of services, yet it is the enrollment of the client that brings opportunities for profits to the provider.[29] There are also serious concerns about program completion rates in this sector.

The U.S. Department of Education has pursued a number of the for-profit institutions, including some well-known national chains, for abuses in the recruiting of students, in particular for violating federal regulations regarding the payment of recruiters per enrollee.[30] A large share of the sector's income derives from tuition paid by students who are receiving federal Pell Grants or student loans. Federal law limits the share to 90 percent, or it might be higher still. Loan default rates tend to be significantly higher than in other sectors, in part because completion rates are low.[31] Beyond this, the Obama administration has questioned whether the programs advertised by for-profits as leading to good jobs for graduates actually result in well-paying positions for those who do graduate. As discussed in chapter 6, the Department of Education has recently issued new regulations regarding the acceptable ratio of student debt load to earnings in a program's targeted occupation, as a way to help students consider potential costs and benefits.[32]

The for-profit higher education industry has, of course, countered criticisms and policy proposals like those discussed, pointing out its service to underserved student groups and working adults and highlighting its innovative approaches. Systematic data on performance of the sector are virtually non-existent and individual schools tend to be resistant to providing information they see as proprietary, but there is broad agreement that institutional performance is highly variable. In our view, since the federal government indirectly supports this industry through its student aid programs and because so many of its students are especially vulnerable to potential abuses, the government has a clear responsibility to gather relevant performance information and provide strong oversight. The other partners in consumer protection and quality assurance, the states and the accrediting bodies, have limited leverage because many of the firms now cross state and even regional lines. Furthermore, the national accrediting organizations overseeing many for-profit schools are creatures of the industry itself.

Perhaps, in the spirit of federalism, states that meet high standards in regulation and enforcement could be delegated regulatory authority from the federal government, if they sought it, similar to delegation of authority to states in occupational health and safety and environmental regulation. It is the federal government, however, that needs to provide a firm floor of standards and the basic regulatory structure. Oversight policies should emphasize the communication of performance information (such as completion rates and job placements and earnings gains in relation to tuition paid) to both prospective students and to federal or state monitors, rather than specifying what should be taught and by whom. More ambitious data collection and oversight would cost the federal government somewhat more than it spends on these functions now, but weak oversight offers only false economy, given the large sums of federal aid involved and the costs in terms of students' debts and unfulfilled hopes. Most importantly, without effective oversight to encourage the expansion of high-quality programs, the federal government's large investments in student aid in the for-profit sector will not likely result in increases in the number of students with quality credentials leading to economically productive careers.

Policies for Allocation of Research Funding

Research accomplishments (including the securing of research funding) are the *sine qua non* of academic prestige and are thought to be a key driver of regional economic development.[33] Since the federal government is by far the largest supporter of academic research in the United States, its research-allocation policies exert significant influence on higher education and, by extension, on economic development. Academic institutions, like other organizations (particularly nonprofit ones), tend to pursue higher levels of prestige and seek to acquire additional resources. In academe, claiming a research mission is one of the primary ways to do this, a process that is often termed

"mission creep." Natural organizational tendencies in this direction are reinforced by local and regional boosters who often seek to influence their legislators to advocate for the addition of a research function, whether officially
or de facto, to the mission of their local state college.

The resulting cost-increasing pressures are difficult for state higher education policy makers to contain. In the last couple of decades, they have been
significantly reinforced by the practice of earmarking substantial sums each
year in federal research funding and research facility support.[34] By this process, funding is provided on the basis of institutions' federal lobbying efforts
rather than through the merit-based peer review process that has historically
been the hallmark of American scientific prowess.[35] Success by one institution, or even the prospect of it, in this earmark-chasing game can change
the political dynamics in a state legislature so that others want to partici-
pate, seek state funding for their efforts, and ultimately try to use any federal support they acquire as leverage to argue for official designation of a new
research mission for their school. This adds prestige to the successful institution and, crucially for our concerns here, raises per student costs sharply, as
faculty seek to lower their teaching loads and to increase their staff and facilities for the pursuit of research.

To be sure, high-quality research universities can produce economic benefits eventually, but research quality is costly and time consuming to develop.
Certainly, not every state needs (nor can afford) a multitude of research institutions. Nor can all the institutions be in the "top forty" to which so many
seem to aspire. With higher education funding so limited, we think it unwise
for federal policies to reinforce tendencies that pull scarce state resources
from established research universities that need adequate support and that
have the effect of raising per student costs at institutions whose primary mission has been to educate undergraduate students. In short, the federal government should take steps to halt or drastically reduce earmarking, at least in
the allocation of research support.[36]

STATE POLICIES

States are the primary shapers of higher education policy since they fund
the public institutions that enroll about three-quarters of the nation's college
students, provide financial aid to students attending private colleges (and
direct support to those institutions in some cases), and are responsible for
licensing all educational institutions. As described, if federal policies were to
reinforce rather than work at cross-purposes with a broadly shared national
agenda to increase degree attainment and productivity, then the state actions
recommended here would be much more effective.

DEGREE ATTAINMENT GOALS

Directed toward national goals along the lines President Obama outlined but based in the realities of state demographics, states should establish statewide goals for increases in bachelor's and associate degrees and postsecondary certificates. These goals should include specific objectives for low- and moderate-income populations and for underrepresented populations. The goals should be ambitious but not so bold that they cannot realistically be achieved or closely approached. Once a truly national conversation is underway and a national framework on this fundamental issue is established (including some federal and philanthropic support), it will become more difficult for reluctant states to avoid joining the party and taking on a share of the national goals.

States' goals should be explicit and incorporate targets for each higher education sector or institution, so that responsibilities are clearly delineated. A state business or financial plan should set out how financial responsibilities are to be allocated, including the role of state appropriations, tuition, and student financial aid, including state, institutional, and federal aid. To better attain their college degree attainment goals, states should set complementary goals throughout the education pipeline for high school graduation rates, college preparedness rates, postsecondary participation, transfers from two-year to four-year institutions, and college completion rates. Progress toward meeting these goals should be assessed annually and linked to the state budget process.

Table 7.3 illustrates one way in which President Obama's national degree attainment goal could be met by the sum of state efforts.[37] Each state is assigned a degree attainment target for 2020 based on its current share of U.S. degree output, modified by its projected young adult population growth and the extent to which it has room to grow its degree output. This "room to grow" metric is based on its current status relative to national norms; states with lower current attainment rates are assumed to have more room to grow. The Obama goal implies an *annual* growth in national degree output of 4.2 percent from 2007--2008 through 2019–2020.[38] Using these parameters, the variation in state increases required is considerable, ranging from 2.4 percent annual growth in the District of Columbia and 3.0 percent in North Dakota up to 5.9 percent in Nevada. States with greater expected population growth and those with lower degree attainment rates at baseline are assigned greater increases. This approach could be modified to reflect state fiscal capacity, poverty rates, or other indicators. As well as introducing greater realism into the state-by-state objectives, such modifications might also clarify the need for federal support for states facing greater challenges. Regardless of the national goals and target dates set, states will need to establish ambitious goals and take serious policy actions if they are to achieve substantive increases in degree output.

TABLE 7.3

How each state should contribute to the goal of producing 8.2 million additional degrees by 2020, adjusting for current levels of educational attainment and population growth by state

A. State	B. Percentage of U.S. associate's and bachelor's produced by state	C. Equal distribution of state contribution to closing the 8.2 million gap between the U.S. and top country by 2020	D. Projected 25- to 34-year-olds in 2020 as a percent of current 25- to 34-year-olds	E. Index value for population growth (higher value, more growth)*	F. Percent of 25- to 34-year-olds with an associate's degree or higher (2008)	G. Index value for educational attainment (higher value, more educational need)**	H. Additional degrees needed by 2020 adjusted for educational attainment and population growth***	I. Additional degrees needed annually to make linear progress toward goal	J. Average annual percentage increase in degree production needed (%)
Alabama	1.4%	115,148	97%	0.89	31.8%	1.19	121,812	1,846	4.4%
Alaska	0.1%	8,928	124%	1.14	30.5%	1.24	12,642	192	5.5%
Arizona	1.9%	159,225	123%	1.14	30.7%	1.23	222,924	3,378	5.4%
Arkansas	0.7%	60,510	97%	0.90	25.9%	1.46	79,098	1,198	5.2%
California	11.1%	902,514	119%	1.10	35.8%	1.05	1,044,231	15,822	4.7%
Colorado	1.8%	146,245	107%	0.99	41.5%	0.91	131,743	1,996	3.9%
Connecticut	1.0%	84,701	110%	1.02	46.3%	0.82	70,157	1,063	3.6%
Delaware	0.3%	23,994	101%	0.93	36.4%	1.04	23,114	350	4.1%
Dist. of Columbia	0.5%	41,595	93%	0.86	63.5%	0.59	21,291	323	2.4%
Florida	6.2%	506,245	121%	1.11	35.3%	1.07	603,724	9,147	4.8%
Georgia	2.3%	186,104	109%	1.00	34.0%	1.11	207,016	3,137	4.6%
Hawaii	0.4%	31,704	112%	1.04	40.9%	0.92	30,430	461	4.1%
Idaho	0.5%	38,252	96%	0.89	34.1%	1.11	37,522	569	4.2%
Illinois	4.5%	365,839	101%	0.93	42.7%	0.88	301,602	4,570	3.6%

A. State	B. Percentage of U.S. associate's and bachelor's produced by state	C. Equal distribution of state contribution to closing the 8.2 million gap between the U.S. and top country by 2020	D. Projected 25- to 34-year-olds in 2020 as a percent of current 25- to 34-year-olds	E. Index value for population growth (higher value, more growth)*	F. Percent of 25- to 34-year-olds with an associate's degree or higher (2008)	G. Index value for educational attainment (higher value, more educational need)**	H. Additional degrees needed by 2020 adjusted for educational attainment and population growth***	I. Additional degrees needed annually to make linear progress toward goal	J. Average annual percentage increase in degree production needed (%)
Indiana	2.3%	189,175	99%	0.92	36.0%	1.05	182,479	2,765	4.1%
Iowa	1.6%	133,445	89%	0.82	45.9%	0.82	90,002	1,364	3.1%
Kansas	1.1%	89,040	96%	0.89	41.5%	0.91	72,091	1,092	3.6%
Kentucky	1.3%	105,151	99%	0.91	32.2%	1.17	112,309	1,702	4.4%
Louisiana	1.1%	92,348	96%	0.89	28.1%	1.35	110,056	1,668	4.8%
Maine	0.4%	34,553	97%	0.90	36.2%	1.04	32,287	489	4.0%
Maryland	1.6%	134,497	119%	1.10	44.6%	0.85	125,214	1,897	4.0%
Massachusetts	2.6%	213,402	111%	1.02	53.4%	0.71	154,319	2,338	3.2%
Michigan	3.5%	284,007	102%	0.95	35.8%	1.06	283,609	4,297	4.2%
Minnesota	2.0%	165,809	104%	0.96	48.3%	0.78	124,574	1,887	3.3%
Mississippi	0.9%	74,160	90%	0.84	31.7%	1.19	73,786	1,118	4.2%
Missouri	2.2%	177,144	102%	0.94	36.6%	1.03	172,616	2,615	4.1%
Montana	0.3%	24,001	90%	0.83	36.1%	1.05	20,840	316	3.8%
Nebraska	0.7%	60,704	93%	0.86	44.1%	0.86	44,911	680	3.3%
Nevada	0.4%	36,272	126%	1.16	28.2%	1.34	56,411	855	5.9%
New Hampshire	0.5%	41,087	109%	1.00	45.6%	0.83	34,151	517	3.6%
New Jersey	2.2%	178,443	107%	0.99	45.9%	0.82	144,993	2,197	3.6%

continued

TABLE 7.3 *continued*

A. State	B. Percentage of U.S. associate's and bachelor's produced by state	C. Equal distribution of state contribution to closing the 8.2 million gap between the U.S. and top country by 2020	D. Projected 25- to 34-year-olds in 2020 as a percent of current 25- to 34-year-olds	E. Index value for population growth (higher value, more growth)*	F. Percent of 25- to 34-year-olds with an associate's degree or higher (2008)	G. Index value for educational attainment (higher value, more educational need)**	H. Additional degrees needed by 2020 adjusted for educational attainment and population growth***	I. Additional degrees needed annually to make linear progress toward goal	J. Average annual percentage increase in degree production needed (%)
New Mexico	0.6%	45,341	98%	0.90	28.5%	1.32	54,257	822	4.8%
New York	7.7%	626,890	106%	0.98	47.7%	0.79	486,171	7,366	3.4%
North Carolina	2.7%	222,658	117%	1.08	36.0%	1.05	251,812	3,815	4.6%
North Dakota	0.3%	27,330	93%	0.85	49.5%	0.76	17,807	270	3.0%
Ohio	3.7%	304,348	99%	0.92	36.4%	1.04	290,111	4,396	4.1%
Oklahoma	1.2%	101,226	97%	0.89	30.3%	1.25	112,917	1,711	4.6%
Oregon	1.1%	91,581	105%	0.97	36.3%	1.04	92,475	1,401	4.3%
Pennsylvania	4.7%	383,747	103%	0.95	42.8%	0.88	322,226	4,882	3.7%
Rhode Island	0.6%	49,270	108%	1.00	43.4%	0.87	42,878	650	3.8%
South Carolina	1.2%	99,549	105%	0.97	34.4%	1.10	106,252	1,610	4.4%
South Dakota	0.3%	24,841	88%	0.81	43.6%	0.87	17,400	264	3.2%
Tennessee	1.6%	131,888	107%	0.99	31.3%	1.21	157,685	2,389	4.8%
Texas	6.2%	508,589	111%	1.02	30.7%	1.23	640,002	9,697	5.0%
Utah	1.3%	108,950	101%	0.94	38.2%	0.99	100,809	1,527	4.0%
Vermont	0.3%	23,225	108%	1.00	43.8%	0.86	19,947	302	3.7%
Virginia	2.5%	207,962	117%	1.08	42.4%	0.89	200,272	3,034	4.1%

A. State	B. Percentage of U.S. associate's and bachelor's produced by state	C. Equal distribution of state contribution to closing the 8.2 million gap between the U.S. and top country by 2020	D. Projected 25- to 34-year-olds in 2020 as a percent of current 25- to 34-year-olds	E. Index value for population growth (higher value, more growth)*	F. Percent of 25- to 34-year-olds with an associate's degree or higher (2008)	G. Index value for educational attainment (higher value, more educational need)**	H. Additional degrees needed by 2020 adjusted for educational attainment and population growth***	I. Additional degrees needed annually to make linear progress toward goal	J. Average annual percentage increase in degree production needed (%)
Washington	2.2%	179,040	118%	1.09	39.4%	0.96	186,719	2,829	4.4%
West Virginia	0.7%	54,124	84%	0.78	28.2%	1.34	56,192	851	4.3%
Wisconsin	1.9%	159,105	97%	0.90	39.7%	0.95	136,210	2,064	3.7%
Wyoming	0.2%	15,903	84%	0.77	34.3%	1.10	13,564	206	3.7%
Nation	100.0%	8,165,954	108%	1.00	37.8%	1.00	8,165,954	123,727	4.2%

Source: National Center for Higher Education Management Systems, "Closing the College Attainment Gap between the U.S. and Most Educated Countries, and the Contributions to be made by the States," April 2010.

*State projected 25- to 34-year-olds as a percent of current 25- to 34-year-olds/U.S. projected 25- to 34-year-olds as a percent of current 25- to 34-year-olds

**U.S. educational attainment/state attainment

***Column C x column E x column G

Student Financial Aid Policy

As we outlined earlier in proposing a new federal/state incentive program similar to the SSIG/LEAP program, we expect that most states would gladly accept substantial federal support to expand their need-based student financial aid. However, state enthusiasm in this area is not a foregone conclusion, given the requirement for a match by the state. States vary widely: in the size of their commitment to student aid relative to enrollments and relative to their spending on institutional support; in the balance they provide between need-based and non-need-based aid; in the eligibility of students at for-profit institutions (students at private, nonprofit colleges and universities are generally eligible); and in numerous program design features.[39]

As we suggested in chapter 5, states that focus their financial policies on providing institutional appropriations and maintaining relatively low tuition may be less inclined to respond to federal incentives to expand student aid than those states with a tradition of providing greater student aid expenditures. (Such reluctance would be less of a concern for affordability and access if these states did indeed maintain low tuition, but this commitment seems to be flagging.) Similarly, states that heavily favor merit-based or other non-need-based aid programs might resist the limitation of the federal-state partnership to need-based aid programs. The need-based criterion is now more necessary than ever, however, because so many of the student groups that the new policies must reach are financially needy. States could still support non-need-based aid on their own, but without a federal match.

Providing need-based student financial aid is a market-based approach to making college more affordable, and it is consistent with recent trends in the states to shift more of their support toward student aid as compared with institutional funding. The following ideas should also be considered by states in regard to student aid program design, to attract students who might not otherwise attend college.

Early commitment programs. Students from financially needy backgrounds and from underrepresented populations who would be the first in their families to attend college tend to overestimate the cost of college and underestimate the financial aid available. They also find it intimidating and difficult to learn about and apply for financial aid.[40] These students also tend to lack knowledge about the academic aspects of preparing for college, which should begin before high school with decisions about course selection. An early guarantee (offered as early as middle school) of substantial financial aid for needy students has been shown to be a significant motivator in preparing more students for college, when that aid is combined with well-designed programs of counseling and academic support, and when it is offered on the condition that the student takes and completes college preparatory courses, makes acceptable grades, and stays out of trouble.[41]

An example of a successful college preparatory program is Indiana's Core 40: a rigorous sequence of high school classes in core academic subjects (English language arts, mathematics, science and social studies, physical education or health and wellness, and electives including world languages, career or technical fields, and the fine arts). The Core 40 became part of the required high school curriculum in Indiana in fall 2007; all students entering high school at that time were expected to complete the Core 40 as a graduation requirement.[42]

An approach such as the Core 40 is especially appropriate if degree output is to be increased in states with stable or declining youth populations, or with large populations that have been traditionally underserved by higher education. The federal-state partnership program for student aid might be designed to support programs like the Core 40, if the challenge of establishing a student's financial need several years in advance of college can be addressed satisfactorily.[43]

Increased utilization of the private higher education sector via student aid. States that have severely constrained public sectors of higher education but that have capacity at accredited private nonprofit colleges should consider structuring parts of their student aid effort to encourage more students to enroll in such colleges. This is particularly the case for those states that have a shortage of physical facilities of public institutions in one or more areas of the state. In these cases, adding a few thousand dollars to a state resident's aid package at a private college is likely to be less expensive for the state than bearing the full cost of adding new capacity in the public sector.[44] Accredited, degree-granting for-profit colleges should also be considered as a potential state resource, subject to the caveats addressed earlier concerning quality assurance and oversight.

Aid for part-time students. Most states do relatively little to provide financial aid to students who can only attend college part time due to family or work commitments. In particular, aid programs need to be made friendlier to adult students beyond the traditional college age, some of whom have already completed college credits. Some states have large numbers of such adults in their work forces and will need to reach out to this group if they are to meet increased targets for degree attainment. According to a recent study, 19.4 percent of adults ages twenty-five to sixty-four have attended college but have not completed a degree. The study finds that the United States is unlikely to meet internationally competitive degree attainment goals without graduating more adult students. Specifically, an estimated thirty-two states will be unable to meet the competitive benchmark by serving traditional college-age students alone, even if those students were to match the completion performance of students in the best-performing states.[45]

Expanding aid to part-time students need not be terribly costly. Often, these students have other means of support for living expenses, and require financial assistance only to pay for tuition, books, and other expenses specific to education. If adult students receive credits for prior course work in colleges and other equivalent venues, the number of additional credits required for a degree may be reduced.[46] Many working adults seek associate degrees, which usually require about half the credits that a bachelor's degree requires.

Tuition Policy

If college is to be more accessible to a wider range of students, then states and public colleges should consider tuition policy commitments that make this goal clear to students and families who are planning ahead.[47] States vary widely, both historically and currently, in the proportion of total public institutional funding that is derived from tuition. There are high tuition-share states and low tuition-share states, and many gradations in between; this variation is not likely to change.[48] Across the board, however, the affordability of public higher education in relation to family income levels has deteriorated badly in recent years.[49] This decline in affordability undercuts the goals of increasing access and degree attainment, and it reduces public confidence in higher education.

In adopting increased attainment goals, states should consider the share of higher education costs they expect student tuition revenue to cover. If tuition revenues, in relation to total higher education costs, are not near the target, then state policy makers should create a published plan to move in this direction at a measured pace over time. In the few cases where tuition revenue constitutes a small percentage of the total, the policy goal might identify the need for a measured increase in tuition's share (for example, in light of fiscal realities, this may be the case for the California community colleges).[50] Such a plan, however, should seek to offset, through need-based aid, projected impacts on access and completion rates, especially for those with low or moderate incomes and those from underrepresented groups. In general, we urge states to establish goals for their tuition and aid policies that build on federal aid opportunities and use federal methodology for identifying student need—such that students in need would not have to borrow heavily or work excessively to attend a public community college or broad-access baccalaureate institution.[51] For low-income and underrepresented students, it is well established that borrowing large sums or working long hours are serious impediments to continuous enrollment and timely completion.[52]

In any case, tuition increases should be gradual, moderate, and predictable over time—unlike the patterns of recent decades—and linked explicitly to students' and families' ability to pay. These criteria are crucial to making college accessible to a broad range of students (even the affluent will appreciate such policies). They will also facilitate program completion and should enhance higher education's eroded standing with the public. In considering the criteria for ability to pay, the most logical benchmark for annual tuition increases is state median family income (MFI). Unlike the Consumer Price Index, which tracks changes in prices throughout the economy, the MFI directly reflects changes in average income, which is what matters to students and families when considering their ability to pay. To reduce volatility, a three-year rolling average of the changes in the MFI index would provide a logical basis for calculating annual changes in tuition. In an economic downturn when state appropriations to colleges and universities might decrease, tuition should not be reduced even if the three-year average change in MFI is negative (a rare event historically). During difficult financial times in the past, good intentions in state tuition policies have often been undermined by expedient actions to close budget gaps. One factor that could serve as a counterbalance to this tendency is the federal government's commitment to degree attainment goals, as manifest in the proposed federal-state student aid partnership described earlier (see section on "Federal Policies"). Under this proposal for federal matching of state-based student aid, the federal government would need to provide sufficient funding to make the partnership attractive for states. The only condition in regard to tuition policy, albeit an important one, would be that states would agree to increase their own funding for need-based aid commensurate with tuition increases, as we described earlier. The requirement that states "pay for" tuition increases in this way provides a powerful incentive for state policy makers to ensure that tuition adjustments are moderate. One way for them to encourage such moderation is to provide sufficient support so that colleges and universities are less pressed to propose large tuition increases.[53]

One of the benefits of tuition moderation in the public sector would be to encourage the same in private institutions, at least among those that are affected by public-sector competition (that is, those that are not in the elite categories). As with public institutions, private colleges enrolling students with state financial aid would get no encouragement for large tuition hikes, since the need determination formula for student aid would increase annually only as much as the three-year state MFI average did, thereby providing a kind of affordability index for tuition and aid increases in both sectors.

We have suggested that the key targets of public policies to increase degree attainment rates should be the community colleges and broad-access baccalaureate institutions. But what about the public research universities? How would they be affected by the tuition and student aid policies we have been discussing? We suggest that they carry forward their higher tuition bases relative to other public institutions, ideally according to explicit state policies. Thus, some students would have to borrow substantially more to attend them, presumably a fair trade for the degree's higher value in the marketplace. Undergraduate students at the public research universities could access need-based aid through the federal-state partnership, but this program would not provide encouragement for these institutions to raise tuition any higher than the MFI-based rate. States could also take actions to discourage larger increases, including by providing adequate budgetary support that is linked to incentives for productivity improvements (see the following section on "Financial Support of Institutions").

In some states, flagship research universities may find that constitutional arrangements regarding institutional autonomy, combined with their appeal in the student market, might lead them to chart their own course with regard to tuition and student aid. This is regrettable but perhaps unavoidable in some places. These universities will most likely take advantage of nonresident tuition premiums by pursuing larger mixes of such students in their undergraduate classes. Up to a point, such geographic diversity can be defended educationally, but pushing beyond that point will most likely lead to greater stratification of student bodies along socioeconomic lines. Those in the upper income brackets will be the most able to pursue unsubsidized higher education out of state at prices that are similar to those at private colleges.

In pursuit of revenue, public research universities will also likely begin charging higher tuition for undergraduate programs that lead graduates into fields with higher incomes—a practice that is already fairly common at the graduate level. Such policies are likely to further stratify opportunities by income (and associated variables), although many universities will try to mitigate these effects through institutionally funded student aid. Over the long run, these kinds of revenue strategies are likely to further undermine public support for research universities, which may, in turn, lead to drops in state budget support and to subsequent decreases in the institutions' attention to state priorities—a downward spiral. As long as state support is substantial, however, the state retains leverage to link its subsidies to these institutions' pursuit of public priorities, if the state chooses.[54]

In quite a different vein, a radical proposal that some states with a preference for low tuition may consider is to support college accessibility strongly by making the first year or two of college free or nominal in price, as has long been the case in the California community colleges. However, the recent California experience, even with efforts to guarantee state budgetary support of these colleges, does not make us sanguine that this approach is workable.[55] Another option would be to subsidize the free tuition years by charging substantially higher rates later. A similar idea has been suggested for Pell Grants, by front-loading the subsidies in the early years to encourage students to begin their higher education. Both of these ideas, though not without some appeal, could discourage transfers from community colleges to baccalaureate institutions and depress baccalaureate completion rates, which are already low by international standards and in need of a substantial boost.

Financial Support of Institutions

States should align appropriations for higher education with their highest priorities, particularly with the goal of raising rates of college completion and attainment. This will require attention to the strategic allocation of state resources available for higher education and the explicit use of finance policy to leverage improvement.

Reemphasizing and reorienting student-linked funding. Although state funding of colleges and universities is an important topic, it is perhaps not as predominantly so as institutional stakeholders might think. Where a state's philosophical orientation permits, we encourage continuation of the general trend in many states toward driving larger proportions of state funding through direct support to students—that is, through more generous need-based student aid policies. In providing financial aid to students, states give them more influence in determining where state funding is distributed, through their decisions to enroll and pay tuition, with broad choice among accredited providers. This approach has the advantage of spurring competition among institutions for enrollments and broadening the base of that competition, which is needed if more students are to be educated. State participation in the federal-state student aid matching program described earlier would reinforce this approach, since it would increase aid spending.

Incentives to enroll more students also need to be provided via direct institutional support. As explained in chapter 6, many states have moved away from enrollment-based funding of their public colleges and universities in recent decades, especially in economic downturns, with state support often being negotiated ad hoc with little reference to enrollments. Funding should once again be closely linked to students, since greater enrollments are needed to produce more degrees. Further, states should consider providing institutional funding through weighted formulas that provide more support for students who are more costly to educate. This is necessary because the student groups whose enrollment rates must be boosted are typically those who have been underrepresented in higher education, and these groups often need additional academic support and guidance to succeed. A logical mechanism would be to provide additional institutional support for enrolling students who are eligible for Pell Grants. Such an arrangement would provide institutions greater incentive to enroll these students when they might otherwise be reluctant to do so, especially in an environment where institutional performance in degree completion is strongly emphasized.

Shifting some funding to emphasize course and degree completion. States should consider increasing incentives for student progress by paying for at least part of student enrollments on the last day of a course (that is, at course completion), rather than early in the term, as is common now. This should discourage course withdrawals and the frequent granting of incomplete grades, practices that are wasteful of capacity and that tend to extend time to degree.

State funding of enrollments and course completions, however, are not sufficient to ensure that more students complete degrees. As some states are beginning to do, states should experiment seriously with adjusting their funding formulas to include incentives for degree completion.[56] Specifically, a portion of enrollment funding should be shifted to reward institutions for students' completion of degrees. This could include a bonus payment for graduating low-income students—for example, those who are Pell Grant eligible. Such incentives might also include payments for student achievement of milestones known along the way to degree completion, as in Washington's Student Achievement Initiative for community colleges.[57]

One obvious milestone to baccalaureate completion is transfer from a community college to a baccalaureate institution. Nearly 40 percent of college students in the United States begin at public community colleges, and the percentage is much higher in some states.[58] Given the size of this population and the low rates of transfer, the improvement of these rates is vital to increasing baccalaureate completion. Many states have tried to improve these rates, but mostly with limited success.[59] We suggest that, with the recent advent of longitudinal data systems that follow students across sectors, explicit financial incentives should reward both the sending and receiving institutions for a successful transfer—perhaps paid in full only after baccalaureate completion. These incentives are necessary to encourage cooperation between two-year and four-year institutions (in areas such as curriculum articulation, assessment, and student guidance), which can increase transfers and improve the success of transfer students. Research shows that institutional expenditures for student services, such as for advising and student support, can improve the persistence and completion of at-risk students.[60] Degree completion incentives should give institutions more motivation to support those services that prove effective. Certainly, state policies should not discourage expenditures on student services, which some policies do in some states.[61]

Adequacy and stability of funding. Higher education needs adequate and stable state support, particularly in light of the discouraging patterns of recent decades that have been exacerbated from 2000 to 2010. Based on these trends and conversations with policy makers over many years, we conclude that higher education's prospects for consistent state support hinge on its ability to rebuild trust—among the public and policy makers—that institutions and those who fund them are pulling in the same direction. We believe that part of the answer is to be found in greater institutional focus on and success in helping more students complete degrees, along the lines suggested. Policy makers, business leaders, parents, and others expect public higher education to produce more citizens who are well educated. They also want to see tuition rates that are moderate and predictable. In addition, the populations that are underrepresented in higher education and that are growing in the United States expect to see more emphasis on need-based student aid and assistance for students in accessing it. We are optimistic that the system can be reoriented to focus on these priorities.

Yet, given the sluggish economy and the pressures on state budgets, higher education in most of the country will have a difficult time for a long while. State funding per student may continue to fall for several years in constant dollar terms. As awareness of this reality increases within higher education, it may set the stage for focusing more attention on improving degree productivity. By providing incentives for degree completion, states can help even more to encourage efficiencies. In addition to promoting degree completion, however, states (with some federal help) should invest in institutional efforts to develop and test ideas to improve educational productivity. These include: offering more online learning; restructuring courses to more efficiently use faculty time as well as technology;[62] using existing facilities more effectively (for example, more intensive evening, weekend, and summer uses); carefully pruning programs and curricula to focus faculty resources on areas that are mission central and in demand; assessing and offering credit for off-campus learning experiences;[63] sharing programs and faculty among nearby campuses (or by electronic means); and examining the cost effectiveness for degree completion of particular types of instructional and student support expenditures.[64] Even though the need for these kinds of efforts is ever more apparent, far too little research and development are being completed in these areas. Unfortunately, institutions have few resources or incentives to investigate these ideas. This needs to change. States can encourage and promote such experimentation directly, and the federal government can and should help.

Regarding stability of funding, business cycles and the resulting periodic constriction of state revenues are probably here to stay. State rainy-day funds can provide some help, but there is no guarantee that they will be used for higher education, especially when recessions generally push up other state costs, such as Medicaid, public assistance, and criminal justice. Also, public institutions have little incentive to create internal rainy-day funds. When times are tough, state budget makers generally raid those agencies that have substantial balances, in order to fund the most urgent state needs. This is unlikely to change.

Recently, federal aid has helped states to weather the fiscal effects of recession. States used $2.3 billion of such aid in fiscal year 2009, and $3.6 billion in fiscal year 2010, to reduce budget cuts to higher education.[65] Federal intervention during recessions, to offset deflationary budget cuts by states, makes sense in terms of macroeconomic policy, particularly since states are not supposed to run budget deficits. However, such actions may or may not be replicated in future downturns, particularly in light of the federal government's own fiscal problems. If the federal government does provide such countercyclical help to higher education in the future, it should leverage its funding by demanding more from states and public institutions than it has to date. Specifically, states receiving federal aid should be precluded from disproportionately reducing higher education funding, as has been their tendency.[66] They should also be provided explicit incentives to maintain enrollments and sustain the types of tuition and student aid policies we suggested earlier. Otherwise, if "nature is allowed to take its course," downturns will lead to serious backsliding on degree-production goals.

Alas, save for countercyclical federal aid, there are no good solutions on the revenue side to the problem of state funding instability. Public institutions of higher education must become more wary of building up large, unsustainable commitments in good times, which in turn create inflexibility in bad times. Expecting students to mitigate the effects of state funding shortfalls through sudden, large tuition hikes (at a time when many can least afford them and when college attendance makes most sense, since labor markets are slack) is not a response that addresses the nation's present challenges. In fact, it is counterproductive and may lead to less state support in the long term, if policy makers think that institutions can always turn to tuition to make up for funding shortfalls, and can do so without political fallout for legislators and governors.

Support for research universities versus broad-access institutions. As we stated earlier, we believe that the community colleges, baccalaureate and comprehensive institutions in both public and private sectors, and for-profit institutions are the primary sources for increased capacity and enthusiasm for the mission of educating many more undergraduate students. Public research universities have other primary missions in knowledge creation and graduate education, and are not the best place to expand undergraduate education greatly. Nonetheless, states should use their financial leverage to provide these elite institutions with incentives to enroll and graduate more low-income and underrepresented students, to improve degree completion rates generally, and to devise and refine new approaches to educating their students more cost effectively.

Controlling mission expansion. If more degree output is to be achieved with little or no increase in real resources per student, states will need to be much more disciplined about containing mission creep—the tendency to add organizational missions, such as research and graduate education—that is perceived to bring higher status and claims to resources. In most cases, such mission accretion in higher education brings higher costs without commensurate benefits to the state as a whole. The calculus is particularly unfavorable at a time when resources are tightly constrained and when the priority should be to educate more students to undergraduate degrees. The federal government can help by not encouraging mission creep through ad hoc earmarking of its research funds to institutions (see earlier section on "Federal Policies"). The primary burden, however, rests with state policy makers. In the absence of compelling evidence of state or national need, expansion of institutional missions in research and advanced graduate education undermines the capacity of higher education to meet critical needs in both research and undergraduate education. It diverts scarce resources from the highest-quality research programs, as well as from college access and attainment.

In market economies, history suggests that business cycles are inevitable. This appears to be no less true now that the world economy is so interconnected. Higher education tends to be disproportionately cut by state budget makers in hard times, followed by efforts to catch up later, if good times last.[67] Well-intended finance policies designed in normal economic circumstances—promises of steady increments in state appropriations and limits on tuition increases at public institutions in particular—have tended to be discarded once state revenues stagnate and recessions produce growing demands for public assistance, Medicaid, and criminal justice expenditures. Thus, we suggest that policy proposals for higher education finance be "stress tested" for the presence of attributes or robust plans that will allow them to survive during downturns, if not to remain entirely unscathed. Conversely, when times are flush, it is crucial that institutions and policies not return to old ways of allocating resources and taking on unsustainable commitments. The challenge in good budgetary times is to invest in the productivity and efficiency of higher education so as to strengthen the capacities of colleges and universities to navigate the inevitable lean years.

Accountability and Data Systems

State policies for accountability and data systems have a complementary role with finance policy in supporting a new agenda for American higher education. If the states are to achieve ambitious goals, then they must monitor performance and effectiveness so that they can apply resources in the most productive ways. Several states have sought to develop statewide longitudinal data systems that span elementary, secondary, and higher education (and the various components within higher education).[68] Florida, Texas, and North Carolina are quite far down this road, and a loosely coordinated national effort supported first by private philanthropy, and more recently by the federal government, appears to be making progress in developing policy-relevant data systems, although not all states have signed on.[69]

In terms of policy, the purpose of these efforts is to facilitate the tracking of students' paths through the various education systems to identify which students are progressing satisfactorily and which are not, and to assess the impact of policy in supporting student success. For example, where appropriate data are in place in an integrated system that spans sectors, the system can do the following: relate high school course-taking patterns to college readiness; track the college readiness and performance of students from particular high schools and identify steps to make improvements; study similar data on transfers and baccalaureate performance of students from specific community colleges; and, ultimately, track graduates from particular majors and specific institutions into the work force to identify their labor market readiness and success. Efforts to improve system accountability for graduation rates can be refined if the many students who transfer laterally across institutions can be tracked. In addition, the system can examine all of these patterns by income and ethnic group to help identify gaps and barriers. If financial and other incentives are provided to build upon most stakeholders' natural desire to improve performance, then these data systems can assist in achieving public goals.

Information systems, however, can be costly to maintain and staff. In order to earn their keep and sustain support, they need to clearly serve public policy goals and be used to improve performance. Ideally, they should be developed through a collaborative process involving the major stakeholders.[70] States may have a range of policy goals for their education accountability and data systems. In most cases, however, we think that the most appropriate goals include preparation for college, college affordability, participation rates, and degree completion rates and related milestones (such as transfers from community colleges to baccalaureate institutions, and indications of the labor market and other benefits associated with college completion). To support pursuit of equity goals, it is necessary that data be disaggregated by income and ethnic group. In addition, the monitoring of trends over time is crucial, as well as the use of the data to identify and correct the causes of unfavorable trends or gaps.

For true accountability to obtain, performance data must influence leadership, policy, and resource decisions so that the system as a whole adjusts and improves its performance over time. One implication for higher education finance is that as soon as data systems can identify gains toward widely shared public goals, then these successes can be publicized and should increase willingness to invest in higher education. In our view, the present stalemate that produces reluctance to invest is born of a widespread sense that precious new resources poured into higher education will not necessarily produce better results on widely held public goals. This needs to change or the unproductive stalemate will persist, to the detriment of the country.

Quality Assurance and Learning Outcomes

One concern that arises in a policy framework that shifts incentives toward output (college degrees, in this case) is that the quality of the product may suffer as ambitious efforts are made to streamline throughput. Professional norms in academe presumably mitigate these risks somewhat, but people in all organizations do respond to sufficiently strong incentives. The best way to address legitimate concerns is to measure more directly the quality of the output: What have graduates learned and what can they do with what they have learned? How do they fare in the labor market, in graduate schools, and on other desired outcomes? How do employers rate their skills?

These issues are the focus of the burgeoning outcomes-assessment movement in higher education. With some federal pressure, accrediting agencies increasingly are requiring that colleges and universities assess program outcomes and student learning. A few state higher education agencies require testing of graduates, or samples thereof, and even of students at the point of transfer from two-year to four-year colleges. Some also require publication of graduate pass rates on state occupational licensure exams (such as in teaching and nursing) and collect data on graduates' job placement and earnings through the state's unemployment insurance records system. Several instruments are in use for student learning assessments, and much work is going on to refine and improve them. The task is daunting because the range of teaching and learning in higher education is diverse. No single test of student learning in college is likely to carry the field, and we doubt that it should.

National associations of public institutions of higher education, albeit feeling some pressure from government agencies, have taken steps recently to disseminate information about assessment instruments and encourage members to select one.[71] Also, many states require periodic peer reviews, which usually include out-of-state experts, of academic programs and units in public colleges and universities. A few states have embarked on what European nations call "tuning," in which explicit efforts are made to examine and "harmonize" the expectations of degree programs in specific fields.[72] We support the development of a culture of assessment and improvement in higher education, and we encourage the U.S. Department of Education, accrediting bodies, and state higher education agencies to both prod and assist institutions in developing this culture. The ultimate test of whether efforts are sufficient lies in the market: what do the public and employers think of the knowledge and skills of the graduates? If the answers are satisfactory, there should be more willingness eventually to invest in increasing the capacity of the higher education system.

Policy Leadership Capacity

Framing a state policy agenda around significant increases in the educational attainment of the population, and aligning the financing of higher education around that agenda, will challenge the leadership capacities of most states. While the specifics will differ, states will require independent, credible entities to develop statewide priorities and play a leadership role in redesigning finance and accountability to support the public agenda. Change of this magnitude is unlikely through the traditional operations of state higher education agencies or the voluntary efforts of institutional leaders, though collaboration of key stakeholders within and outside of government and higher education will be necessary. Whatever the organizational forms, there must be a broad-based public entity with clear responsibilities for increasing the educational attainment of the citizenry and the work force, aligning state funding and policy with this goal, and monitoring progress. What is called for here is not the restoration of outdated regulatory controls over colleges and universities, but new forms of policy capacity for stewardship of a public agenda focused on state needs from higher education.[73]

CONCLUSION

We have sought in this book to make the case for a national focus on the need to better educate our population more successfully if the United States is to remain competitive, prosperous, and reasonably harmonious in a world based increasingly on knowledge and its innovative application. Unlike previous challenges facing higher education, this goal must be achieved with severely constrained resources and through sharp improvements in the educational success rates of population groups that have fared poorly in the past. As a result, policy approaches that met the needs of earlier eras need to be rethought. The nation cannot afford to build large numbers of new campuses, support nascent research missions at institutions that should now focus on expanding their teaching capacity, or allow student aid allocations to reinforce tuition's upward spiral and fail to purchase affordability for needy students. In addition, to educate many more people, new delivery modes and arrangements for certifying knowledge and skills need to be tapped more extensively than they have been, while assuring quality of outcomes.

We know that little will change if the attitudes and incentives embedded in the current higher education system are left unexamined and unchanged. We would like to spur such a reexamination at a level that could have meaningful results and could produce coordinated policy changes focused on system performance and efficiency. We believe this will require high-level attention from the president and the nation's governors, who can then stimulate the participation of others, such as opinion leaders, business, legislators, and both postsecondary and K–12 educators. Public opinion research suggests there is reason to believe the public would be responsive to such efforts. Indeed, the prolonged economic slump, together with the poor fiscal prospects of American governments at all levels, has begun to change perspectives of many stakeholders—even some within higher education. As the saying goes, one should not waste a good crisis.

In short, the stars seem to be well aligned for a serious rethinking of American higher education policy designed to ensure that the nation can meet the demands of the contemporary world within the resources likely to be available. In our view, only such a rethinking and redesign offers any real hope of creating significant new resources to invest. We know well that the payoffs from investing in the higher education of our citizens will be enormous, while the consequences of not doing so will be grave. The better choice is clear.

College Completion Goals by Organization

President Obama

BACKGROUND   American Graduation Initiative. Raise the nation's college attainment rate to 60% (22 million new college degrees) (from 40% currently) in 10 years (by 2020), adding at least 8.2 million new college graduates (based on NCHEMS projections).[1]

Speech at the University of Texas on August 9, 2010. The Georgetown University Center on Education and the Workforce projects that "by 2018, we will need 22 million new college degrees—but will fall short of that number by at least 3 million postsecondary degrees, associate's or better. In addition, we will need at least 4.7 million new workers with postsecondary certificates."

TARGET POPULATION   International comparison target group: 25- to 34-year-olds

WEB SITES   http://www.whitehouse.gov/blog/Investing-in-Education-The-American-Graduation-Initiative/

Complete College America (CCA)

BACKGROUND   Same as American Graduation Initiative. Raise the nation's college graduation rate to 60% in 10 years (by 2020), adding at least 8.2 million graduates.

CCA is a consortium of 20-plus states working toward separate state-adopted "stretch" goals to increase postsecondary completion. The participating states have agreed to use a common set of metrics to measure progress. CCA advocates performance-based funding as a policy tool to provide incentives for institutions to emphasize completion of degrees and certificates.

TARGET POPULATION   International comparison target group: 25- to 34-year-olds

WEB SITES   http://www.completecollege.org/

National Governors Association (NGA)

BACKGROUND   Same goal as the American Graduation Initiative. Raise the nation's college graduation rate to 60% in 10 years (by 2020), adding at least 8.2 million graduates.

NGA has adopted the same metrics as CCA and has created "Complete to Compete," a program focusing on postsecondary completion.

TARGET POPULATION   International comparison target group: 25- to 34-year-olds

WEB SITES   http://www.subnet.nga.org/ci/1011/

Bill & Melinda Gates Foundation

BACKGROUND   "Our goal is to help double the number of low-income adults who earn a college degree or credential with genuine marketplace value by age 26." (Its Web site does not define "credential with genuine marketplace value.")

The Gates Foundation plans to work with "partners large and small, including public and private partners, nonprofits, and other foundations. Three core strategies are to:

• Improve the performance of the postsecondary education system.

• Support young adult success.

• Encourage U.S. leaders to commit to helping students complete their degrees."

TARGET POPULATION   Low-income adults 26 years old and younger

WEB SITES   http://www.gatesfoundation.org/postsecondaryeducation/Pages/default.aspx

http://www.gatesfoundation.org/postsecondaryeducation/Pages/overview.aspx#

Lumina Foundation for Education

BACKGROUND   "Sixty percent of American adults will possess a high quality higher education credential by 2025. This will represent an increase of 23 million graduates above current levels of production," (Lumina Foundation for Education, 2009).

See: http://www.luminafoundation.org/publications/A_stronger_nation_through_higher_education.pdf

"According to the Georgetown University Center on Education and the Workforce, the percentage of the U.S. workforce requiring some level of postsecondary education is up from 28% in 1973 to 59% in 2007 and is expected to increase to 63% by 2018."

"States must increase the number of college degrees awarded each year in the United States, every year, by a total of nearly 280,000 if the nation is to meet the Lumina Foundation for Education's goal of increasing the proportion of American adults with a college degree to 60% by 2025,"(Lumina Foundation for Education, 2009) 2009)

Emphasis is on attainment, defined as completing associate and baccalaureate degrees and credentials. This includes all working-age adults, not just young adults.

WEB SITES   http://www.luminafoundation.org/our_work/

http://www9.georgetown.edu/grad/gppi/hpi/cew/pdfs/ExecutiveSummary-web.pdf

Chronicle of Higher Education, September 21, 2010, http://chronicle.com/article/Lumina-Describes-How-Far/124553/

Lumina Foundation for Education. (2009, February).

A Stronger Nation through Higher Education: How and why Americans must meet a "big goal" for college attainment. Indianapolis, IN: Author.   (Lumina, 2010)

American Association of Community Colleges (AACC)

BACKGROUND   "As organizations representing America's community colleges, we mutually commit and pledge to promote the development and implementation of policies, practices, and institutional cultures that will produce 50% more students with high quality degrees and certificates by 2020, while increasing access and quality. We call for leaders from every sector and constituency of every college to join us in this work."

Association of Community College Trustees, the Center for Community College Student Engagement, the League for Innovation in the Community College, the National Organization for Staff and Organizational Development, and Phi Theta Kappa. *Democracy's colleges: Call to Action.* Washington, DC: Authors. Retrieved 10/18/11 from: Retrieved 10/18/11 from: http://www.league.org/blog/assets/content// callaction_04202010%282%29.pdf

President Obama set a complementary goal in February 2010: "An additional 5 million community college graduates by 2020, including students who earn certificates and associate degrees or who continue on to graduate from four-year colleges and universities."

White House, Office of the Press Secretary (2009, July 14). Excerpts of the President's remarks in Warren, Michigan and fact sheet on the American Graduation Initiative. Washington, DC: Author. Retrieved 10/18/11 from: http://www.whitehouse.gov/the_ press_office/Excerpts-of-the-Presidents-remarks-in-Warren-Michigan-and-fact-sheet-on-the-American-Graduation-Initiative/

Community college leaders respond to this call to action.

In April 2010, the AACC and 5 other community college organizations reaffirmed their commitment to completion while maintaining their commitment to increasing access and quality by issuing a joint statement, *Democracy's Colleges: Call to Action.* The partnering organizations are the Association of Community College Trustees, the Center for Community College Student Engagement, the League for Innovation in the Community College, the National Organization for Staff and Organizational Development, and Phi Theta Kappa.

See link retrieved 10/18/11 from: http://www.league.org/blog/assets/content// callaction_04202010%282%29.pdf

TARGET POPULATION   Adult Americans

WEB SITES   http://www.aacc.nche.edu/Publications/Briefs/Pages/rb06152010.aspx

http://www.aacc.nche.edu/Publications/Briefs/Documents/rebalancing_es.pdf

http://www.aacc.nche.edu/newsevents/News/articles/Documents/callaction_04202010.pdf

http://www.whitehouse.gov/the_press_office/Excerpts-of-the-Presidents-remarks-in-Warren-Michigan-and-fact-sheet-on-the-American-Graduation-Initiative/

(additional 5 million community college graduates by 2020)

http://www.aacc.nche.edu/Publications/Briefs/Documents/rebalancing_06152010.pdf

The College Board Commission on Access, Admissions and Success in Higher Education

BACKGROUND   Fifty-five percent of 25- to 34-year-olds will have an associate degree or higher by the year 2025.

Established a 28-member commission composed of college presidents, university chancellors, admissions and enrollment deans, school counselors, administrators, and other education experts.

In *Coming to Our Senses*, the commission established 10 interdependent recommendations to reach its goal of ensuring that at least 55% of Americans hold a postsecondary degree by 2025. This goal is based on the following: "Many experts say that the United States must establish and reach a goal of ensuring that by the year 2025 fully 55% of young Americans are completing their schooling with a community college degree or higher."[2]

TARGET POPULATION   International comparison target group: 25- to 34-year-olds

WEB SITES   http://advocacy.collegeboard.org/college-admission-completion/access-admissions-success-education-and-american-future

http://advocacy.collegeboard.org/sites/default/files/coming-to-our-senses-college-board-2008.pdf

http://completionagenda.collegeboard.org/

Note: Information gathered as of September 21, 2010.

[1]As cited in Carnevale, Smith, and Strohl, *Help Wanted.*

[2]As cited in State Higher Education Executive Officers (SHEEO), "Second to None in Attainment, Discovery, and Innovation: The National Agenda for Higher Education," *Change* Magazine, September/October, 2008.

State College Completion Goals

Arizona

GOAL   Arizona State University is expected to increase baccalaureate degree production by 50% over the next 10 years (by 2020), in order to meet anticipated work-force needs.

SOURCE   Arizona State University Long Term Strategic Plan 2008–2020, Arizona Board of Regents, https://azregents.asu.edu/rrc/DocumentLibrary/2020-Vision.pdf

Kentucky

GOAL   The Council on Postsecondary Education, the Board of Education, and the Department of Education are mandated by SB 1: (1) to develop a unified strategy to reduce college remediation rates of recent high school graduates by at least 50% by 2014 (from the rates in 2010), and (2) to increase the college completion rates of students enrolled in one or more remedial classes by 3% annually from 2009 to 2014.

SOURCE   SB 1, signed into law in March 2009, refers to the Kentucky Unified Plan for College and Career Readiness. See http://cpe.ky.gov/NR/rdonlyres/704758BF-AE6C-474B-8F73-493AF898F0B0/0/9_SB1UnifiedStrategicPlan.pdf

Mississippi

GOAL The state goal is to increase the educational attainment and skill levels of the state's working-age population to the national average by 2025. It is estimated that this will require 147,144 additional degrees by 2025, or an average increase of 4.7% (962 degrees) annually.

SOURCE   Mississippi Graduation Rate Task Force, http://www.ihl.state.ms.us/graduation/

See 2009 Final Report, http://www.ihl.state.ms.us/graduation/downloads/grtf_report_100120.pdf

Oregon

GOAL   By 2025, Oregon aims to have 40% of its adults with a bachelor's degree or higher; 40% with an associate's degree, professional certificate or equivalent; and the remaining 20% with a high school diploma or equivalent.

Along with these new goals for postsecondary education, the Governor created by executive order the Post Secondary Quality Education Commission (2009) to ensure mandated reporting on education quality throughout the education pipeline.

SOURCE   See Governor's Report on Education: 2009–2011, http://governor.oregon.gov/ Gov/pdf/120208_edreport_2009_2011.pdf

Tennessee

GOAL   The "Tennessee 2025" goal is to produce 20,000 more degrees each year, in order to increase statewide educational attainment levels, by 2025, to the national average of 38% of adults having an associate's degree or higher.

The Complete College Act, enacted in 2010, made several changes designed to enhance cooperation between colleges and universities in the Tennessee Board of Regents (TBR) and University of Tennessee (UT) systems.

SOURCE   Higher Education Working Group memorandum (January 8, 2010) regarding adopting recommendations from Complete College America, http://media.timesfreepress. com/docs/2010/01/TN_College_Completion_Recommendations.pdf

About Tennessee Senate Bill 7005 (January 2010), http://www.state.tn.us/sos/acts/106/ pub/pc0002EOS.pdf

Texas

GOAL   The state goals are: (1) to increase the number of students completing bachelor's degrees, associate degrees, and certificates from 95,000 to 120,000 by 2005; to 140,000 by 2010; and to 163,000 by 2015; and (2) to increase the overall Texas higher education participation rate from 5.0% in 2000 to 5.6% by 2010 and to 5.7% by 2015.

SOURCE   See: Texas Higher Education Coordinating Board Web site, http://www.thecb. state.tx.us/index.cfm?objectid=858D2E7C-F5C8-97E9-0CDEB3037C1C2CA3

Closing the Gaps Goals and Targets Summary (2006-2015), http://www.thecb.state.tx.us/ reports/PDF/1724.PDF?CFID=12811794&CFTOKEN=21981852

Virginia

GOAL   In the Grow by Degrees Campaign, the Virginia Business Higher Education Council joins Governor McDonnell in advocating a 15-year program of investment designed to award a cumulative 100,000 additional undergraduate degrees by 2025. The goal is to maintain the high quality of Virginia's higher education system while increasing the share of working-age Virginians holding college degrees beyond 50%—a key milestone for best-educated states. By Executive Order No. 9, the governor established the Governor's Commission on Higher Education Reform, Innovation, and Investment (July 9, 2010), to establish a plan for achieving this goal.

SOURCE   See Virginia Secretary of Education Web site for Grow by Degrees Campaign, Higher Education Restructuring and Reform: http://www.education.virginia.gov/

http://www.growbydegrees.org/index.phpour_agenda/100000_more_degrees/

http://www.governor.virginia.gov/Issues/ExecutiveOrders/2010/EO-9.cfm

Washington

GOAL   The Strategic Master Plan adopted by the 2008 Legislature calls for increasing annual degree and certificate production by more than 40% by 2018.

In 2009, the Washington State Board for Community and Technical Colleges (SBCTC) launched the Washington State Student Completion Initiative aimed at dramatically increasing community college completion rates. The initiative, one of the most comprehensive completion efforts in the country, will launch new programs and expand successful pilot programs aimed at addressing key barriers to student success. The initiative is supported by the state legislature, the Gates Foundation, and the Ford Foundation.

SOURCE   Washington state Higher Education Coordinating Board 2008 Master Plan, http://www.hecb.wa.gov/news/documents/Opportunities-Implementation-printversion.pdf

Washington State Student Completion Initiative, http://www.gatesfoundation.org/press-releases/Pages/grant-to-launch-washington-state-student-completion-initiative-091014.aspx

Note: Information gathered as of September 21, 2010.

Notes

CHAPTER 1

1. U.S. Department of Education, *Test of Leadership,* ix.
2. The U.S. Department of Education's National Center for Education Statistics Integrated Postsecondary Education Database identified 1,685 two-year institutions in 2007–2008.
3. National Center for Education Statistics Integrated Postsecondary Education Data System, 2007–2008 data.
4. Advisory Committee on Student Financial Assistance, *Access Denied*; National Center for Public Policy and Higher Education, *Responding to the Crisis in College Opportunity.*
5. Zumeta, *Public Funding of Higher Education.*
6. Karoly and Panis, *21st Century at Work,* xvii–xviii.
7. Levy and Murnane, *New Division of Labor*; Karoly and Panis, *21st Century at Work.*
8. For a comprehensive analysis of these trends, see Osterman, *Securing Prosperity.* See also Friedman, *The World is Flat*; Goldin and Katz, *Race Between Education and Technology.*
9. See Carnevale, Smith, and Strohl, *Help Wanted*; Ellwood, "Sputtering Labor Force"; Goldin and Katz, *Race Between Education and Technology*; Hecker, "Occupational Employment Projections"; Karoly and Panis, *21st Century at Work.* Different shadings of this view and some critiques of it are discussed thoroughly in the next chapter.
10. The literature on the individual and societal impacts of individuals' exposure to higher education is vast. See such sources as Bowen, *Costs of Higher Education*; Pascarella and Terenzini, *How College Affects Students*; Institute for Higher Education Policy, *Investment Payoff*; Mortenson, "Why College?"; Moretti "Return to Higher Education"; Sommers and Chance, *Return on Education Investments* and sources cited therein.
11. Organisation for Economic Co-operation and Development, *Education at a Glance 2010.* Education at a Glance. Based on proportion of the relevant population with at least upper secondary education (2008).
12. Tyler, "Economic Benefits of the GED."
13. Heckman and LaFontaine, "Declining American High School Graduation Rate."
14. Organisation for Economic Co-operation and Development, *Education at a Glance 2010,* 26, 42. [Chart A1.1. Average annual growth in the population with tertiary education, tables A1.4 and A1.5]. The average annual increase in the number of individuals in tertiary education due to population growth is about 1.7 percent for the U.S., well above the figures for Sweden and Germany but below those for Poland, Portugal, Italy, and Korea.
15. Mortenson, "College Continuation Rates for Recent High School Graduates."
16. National Center for Public Policy and Higher Education, *Measuring Up 2008,* 6.
17. Ibid., 5.
18. Ibid., 7. These figures apply only to students who begin college enrolled full-time and capture only degrees awarded by their initial institution.

19. This indicator has some flaws, of course. A one-year vocational certificate counts as much as a PhD or medical degree, and it can be distorted by changes in enrollment. Still, it provides some indication of the number of students prepared in some fashion for the labor force.

20. National Center for Public Policy and Higher Education, *Measuring Up 2008*, 6.

21. These are: Australia, Japan, Switzerland, Ireland, the United Kingdom, New Zealand, France, Denmark, Canada, the Czech Republic, and Portugal. Korea and the Netherlands have the same rate as the United States.

22. National Center for Public Policy and Higher Education, *Measuring Up 2008*, 6. International comparative data were provided by Alan Wagner.

23. Organisation for Economic Co-operation and Development, *Education at a Glance 2010*, p. 65, Chart A3.2. Tertiary-type A graduation rates, 1995 to 2008.

24. U.S. Department of Education, *First Look at the Literacy*, 69.

25. Baer, Cook, and Baldi, *Literacy of America's College Students*.

26. Ibid.

27. Ibid.

28. Arum and Roksa, *Academically Adrift*.

29. The CLA is considered to be among the more advanced instruments for measuring such learning but is not without its methodological problems and critics. One problem is that, since the testing is quite demanding of students, there are difficult-to-answer questions about whether representative students are willing to take the test and whether they consistently put forth their best efforts.

30. As reported by Rimer, "Students slog through college, don't gain many critical skills."

31. Gereffi and Wadhwa, "Framing the Engineering Outsourcing Debate." Defined to include computer science and information technology. Note that these figures are considerably less dramatic than those in earlier, less well-documented reports claiming that China produced 600,000 engineers per year and India 350,000, compared to a U.S. output of just 70,000 (covered in Bracey, "600,000 Chinese Engineers"). These earlier reports stimulated Gereffi and Wadhwa to study the issue more thoroughly.

32. Population projections by the U.S. Bureau of the Census are based on historical rates of change for immigration, births, and deaths.

33. Mortenson, "Education attainment and economic welfare: 1940–2008," 6–8.

34. Ibid.

35. National Center for Education Statistics, *The Condition of Education (NCES 2011-033)*.

36. National Center for Education Statistics, Education Attainment, Indicator 19.

37. The group differences are smaller if high school completion (diploma or GED) rates are used rather than diploma rates alone, but GED recipients are less likely than high school graduates to attend higher education (Berktold, Geis, and Kaufman, *Attainment of High School Dropouts*; Murnane, Willett, and Tyler, "Who Benefits from Obtaining a GED?"; Tyler, "Economic Benefits of the GED").

38. National Center for Education Statistics, Education Attainment, Indicator 19. Graduation rates calculated using longitudinal studies that track students through the high school years provide different, usually higher, rates than general population surveys because the former measure actual student performance. Particularly for the Hispanic group, immigration of undereducated workers depresses completion rates calculated on the entire population.

39. Metropolitan Policy Program at Brookings, *Getting Current*.

40. Committee for Economic Development, *Cracks in the Education Pipeline*.

41. National Center for Public Policy and Higher Education, *Income of U.S. Workforce Projected to Decline IF Education Doesn't Improve*.

42. Sommers and Chance, *Return on Education Investments*; O'Mara, *Cities of Knowledge*.

43. Geiger and Sa, "Beyond Technology Transfer."

44. See Feller, "American State Governments"; Geiger and Sa, "Beyond Technology Transfer"; Zumeta, "California."
45. See chapter 6 for our analysis of capacity by sector within the U.S. higher education system.
46. Local appropriations are relevant mainly because in close to half the states, community colleges receive some funds from local property taxes. This 2010 amount includes $4.8 billion in federal American Recovery and Reinvestment Act revenue (State Higher Education Executive Officers, *State Higher Education Finance FY2010*, 7).
47. Zumeta, "Great Recession." Cyclical enrollment demand, which tends to rise in recessions, also plays a role in reducing appropriations per student to the extent institutions accommodate the additional students during these hard times.
48. According to State Higher Education Executive Officers (*SHEEO Annual Finance Report FY2009*, 7), this was the lowest level of per student state support in the past quarter century.
49. Center on Budget and Policy Priorities, *States continue to feel recession's impact*. Federal stimulus funds accounted for $158 billion, leaving about $272 billion that the states had to make up via spending of reserves, budget cuts, and revenue increases over these three years.
50. Ibid.
51. Doyle and Delaney, "Higher Education in State Budgets," 55–76.
52. Boyd, *State Budgets*.
53. Manns and Opp, "Capital Needs for Public Higher Education"; Manns, Katsinas, and Medlin, "Capital Budgeting Practices."
54. See APPA, *Thought Leaders Report 2010*.
55. Rose, *Buildings*, 4. Extrapolated from Kaiser and Davis, *Foundation To Uphold*; and using the Engineering News Record 2006 Building Cost Index, http://enr.com/features/coneco/subs/recentindexes.asp
56. Rose, *Buildings*, 4, citing NCES figures.
57. "Net tuition" revenue subtracts waivers, discounts, medical student tuition and fees, and state-funded student aid from gross tuition and fee revenue (State Higher Education Executive Officers, *SHEEO Annual Finance Report FY2009*, 13).
58. This is the sum of state appropriations and net tuition revenue.
59. State Higher Education Executive Officers, *SHEEO Annual Finance Report FY2009*, figure 4.
60. For the first time, the federal government is taking a serious interest in higher education price containment. As reported by the American Council on Education, "ACE Analysis of the Higher Education Act Reauthorization." Congress reauthorized the Higher Education Act as the Higher Education Opportunity Act, which the president signed into law on August 14, 2008. The reauthorization occurred five years late and after an unprecedented fourteen extensions of the statutory deadline. The act includes various provisions aimed at the rising cost of postsecondary education. While severe tuition price controls floated early in the reauthorization process were not included in the final version, the act's college cost-related disclosure and reporting requirements are extensive. The U.S. Department of Education collects much of the mandated data already, but some items, such as "net price," are new. How effective this consumer information-based strategy will be in moderating tuition growth is debatable, however.
61. Zumeta, "Great Recession."
62. In the private sector, the average increases were 4.5 percent among nonprofits and 5.1 percent among for-profit colleges. The source for these data is the College Board, "Trends in College Pricing 2010," 10, table 1A.
63. National Association of State Student Grant and Aid Programs, *40th Annual Survey Report*, 2.

64. Ibid., 3. Note that these data, the latest available, reflect the effects of the recent recession only in 2008–2009. In that year, there was essentially no change in the inflation-adjusted total of aid available to undergraduates. Tuition growth, of course, far exceeded the general rate of inflation.

65. Ibid., 8.

66. College Board, "Trends in College Pricing 2010," 10. The data are preliminary.

67. Ibid., 2. Nearly $7 billion in federal tax benefits were claimed in 2009. Yet, it is not at all clear that this sizable "tax expenditure" yields much in terms of increased enrollment.

68. Ibid., 14.

69. H.R. 4137: Higher Education Opportunity Act, Congressional Research Service Summary.

70. College Board, "Trends in College Pricing, 2010," 10.

71. Ibid., 22.

72. Ibid.

73. Calculated from ibid., 10.

74. This compares to a total of $41.3 billion in federal grant aid in 2009–2010.

75. Ibid., 13.

76. Ibid., 18–19.

77. Ibid., 13

78. See Wright, "Direct Lending"; Field, "House Bill"; Field, "Student-Loan Companies"; Basken, "Consumer Protections"; Nelson "Compromise Budget Bill."

79. See Madzelan, "Title IV Student Loans."

80. Burdman, *Student Debt Dilemma*; King, *Missed Opportunities*; Clinedinst, Cunningham, and Merisotis, *Characteristics of Undergraduate Borrowers*.

81. Wei et al., *Decade of Undergraduate Student Aid*. Community college students in particular tend to work long hours at low paying jobs rather than borrow (King, *Missed Opportunities*; Zumeta and Frankle, *California Community Colleges*).

82. Bowen, *Costs of Higher Education*; see also Clotfelter, *Buying the Best*.

83. Externally funded student aid, for all its benefits, has the perverse effect of reducing institutions' incentive to worry about the effect of price increases on student enrollments. Institutionally funded aid, which has increased markedly in recent years, particularly in the private sector, is in part a mechanism for schools to compete on price for "market segments" of students whose enrollment decisions are thought to be price sensitive (Bowen and Breneman, "Student Aid"). Even students who are strictly locally oriented in their choice set pay attention to the comparative reputations of the nearby schools, whether community colleges, public four-year colleges, or private, religiously oriented institutions. Advertised prices among schools competing within a given category, including the Ivy League, are usually quite similar.

84. This is due in part to the tendency of consumers to define quality in terms of elements such as faculty available per student (or the size of the orchestra if the industry under study is symphonies), which makes productivity improvements almost impossible by definition as long as these perspectives prevail (Baumol and Bowen, *Performing Arts*).

85. Upward pressures on salaries are especially strong in disciplines with strong nonacademic labor markets such as business, engineering, many health fields, as well as for nonfaculty IT professionals.

86. Zumeta, "Great Recession."

87. To this list might be added the usually futile search for more effective ways of lobbying the state government for more money. The effort is very seductive on campuses but mostly futile because states face serious structural and political pressures regarding spending (and taxation) of their own.

88. On the effects of increases in part-time faculty on various indicators of quality, see Ehrenberg and Zhang, "Tenured and Tenure-Track Faculty"; Bettinger and Long, "Adjunct Instructors."

89. According to a nationally representative poll of high school students by the College Board, "Student Poll-Effects of the Recession on College Plans," on the effects of the recession on college plans, two-thirds reported an effect and 16 percent reported a change in their college plans due to the economic downturn. Lower-income families reported a stronger impact: 29 percent of students from lower-income families ($40,000 or less) reported that their college plans had changed, compared to 16 percent of middle-income ($40,001 to $100,000) students and 10 percent of high-income ($100,001-plus) respondents.

90. Mortenson, "College Continuation Rates for Recent High School Graduates."

91. Ibid.

92. Ibid.

93. Ehrenberg, introduction to *What's Happening?*; Morphew and Eckel, *Privatizing the Public University.*

94. The Western Interstate Commission on Higher Education projects that by 2021–2022, there will be "explosive growth" (greater than 20 percent) in high school graduates in six states: Arizona, Florida, Georgia, Nevada, Texas, and Utah; rapid expansion in four states (more than 10percent–20 percent growth): Arkansas, Idaho, Indiana, and North Carolina; and manageable expansion in five states and the District of Columbia (increases between 5 percent and 10 percent)—Alabama, Colorado, Delaware, New Jersey, and Virginia. There are seventeen states that will remain relatively stable, and eighteen states that are projected to have reductions in high school graduates (2008). Projections are based upon the U.S. Department of Education's Common Core of Data for the 2005–2006 academic year. (Phan and Glander, *Documentation to the NCES Common Core of Data Local Education Agency Locale Code File.*)

95. There are just two states, Delaware and Michigan, which have neither type of agency but only advisory and voluntary planning bodies.

CHAPTER 2

1. If good labor market information is available and absent impediments to students enrolling and completing appropriate study programs (such as capacity constraints), the supply side of the market should respond to the positive signals by producing more of the graduates who are in demand. If such impediments are present, then public policies should be enacted to remove them, assuming the demand is not judged to be evanescent.

2. Brown, Hamilton, and Medoff, *Employers Large and Small*; Collins, "The New Rags to Riches"; Hopkins, "4 That Forged Ahead."

3. Van Praag and Cramer, "Roots of Entrepreneurship."

4. Osterman, *Securing Prosperity.*

5. Livingstone, "Lifelong Learning."

6. See Freeman, *Market for College-Trained Manpower,* for the classic treatment.

7. Collins, *The Credential Society*; Thurow, *The Zero-Sum Society.*

8. Cohn and Geske, *Economics of Education.*

9. It is possible that the benefits that additional education brings in such cases are not sufficient to offset the social costs of providing this level of education. This trade-off, however, should not be assessed statically, as is usually done, but rather only after the long-run effects of having more educated workers in jobs that did not formerly require their credentials can be evaluated. In general, the historical evidence from the U.S. economy's successful use of increasingly educated labor over time to innovate and enhance productivity suggests strongly that the payoffs exceed the costs (see Denison, *Trends in American Economic Growth*; Marshall and Tucker, *Thinking for a Living*; Goldin and Katz, *Race Between Education and Technology*).

10. National Center for Education Statistics, *Projections of Education Statistics to 2016* (see Hussar and Bailey).

11. Cohn and Geske, *Economics of Education.*
12. Baum, *Education Pays?*
13. Immerwahr and Johnson, *Squeeze Play 2010.*
14. Card, "Estimating the Return to Schooling," cited in Psacharopoulos and Patrinos, "Returns to Investment in Education: A Further Update," 116.
15. Ibid. These findings are based on studies that take costs into account, including the opportunity cost of time that students take away from paid work.
16. Psacharopoulos and Patrinos, "Returns to Investment in Education: A Further Update," 114.
17. Psacharopoulos, "Returns to Investment in Education: A Global Update," cited in Psacharopoulos and Patrinos, "Returns to Investment in Education: A Further Update," 125. The data used in this study are outdated however, covering the year 1987.
18. Psacharopoulos and Patrinos, "Returns to Investment in Education: A Further Update," 111–114. These are not, strictly speaking, return-on-investment studies since they do not estimate lifetime earnings. Rather, they estimate the effect on annual earnings of an incremental year of schooling.
19. Kling, "Instrumental Variable Estimates"; Psacharopoulos, "Costs of Child Labor."
20. America's competitor nations appear to understand the value of increasing the level of education in their populations. For example, see the large gains in the college degree attainment rates of many OECD nations referred to in chapter 1 and depicted in Wagner, "Measuring Up Internationally."
21. One factor at work is that differences in individual earnings by education level tend to be magnified in family incomes by the tendency of family members to have similar educational backgrounds. Economists call this affinity among spouses "assortative mating."
22. Of course, differences in education are not the only factor behind widening income inequality. Other analysts have pointed to the role of declining unionization, the decreasing real value of the minimum wage, increased immigration of less-skilled workers, and less progressive taxation as additional influences (Mishel and Rothstein, "Response to Marc Tucker").
23. Mortenson, "Spreadsheet: Bachelor's Degree Attainment by Age 24" These changes are calculated as three-year averages to smooth out single-year fluctuations.
24. Haskins, "Education and Economic Mobility," 3–5, citing data from Panel Study of Income Dynamics.
25. Ibid.
26. Ibid., 6.
27. Data and analysis presented in this section do not reflect the deep recession that began in December 2007. At this writing, the impact of that lengthy downturn remains to be thoroughly assessed by the Bureau of Labor Statistics and other analysts.
28. Aggregate economic growth is expected to slow somewhat to an annual rate of 2.4 percent, compared with 2.5 percent over 1998–2008 and 3.0 percent in the decade prior to that (Wyatt and Byun, "Employment Outlook," 15, 16). BLS also studies the mix of educational credentials held by incumbents in each occupational category. It classifies occupations by predominant educational credentials according to recent census data. There are eleven categories ranging from "short term on-the-job training" through "postsecondary vocational award" up to "doctoral degree" and "first professional degree" (Lacey and Wright, "Employment Projections," 88). In the BLS projections of numbers with particular credentials that are expected to be employed in the future, shifts in the mix of occupations in the economy are carefully estimated but, importantly, shifts in the typical credentials held by employees within job categories are not taken into account.
29. Lacey and Wright, "Employment Projections," 82.

30. Among all BLS occupational groupings, the largest projected growth is within the health practitioners group that includes registered nurses. This category is expected to add 581,500 net new jobs, or 22 percent of its 2008 employment. U.S. Bureau of Labor Statistics, "Tomorrow's Jobs," 107.

31. Observe that the ratio of the gains in jobs for these two broad categories of credentials is far closer than the ratio of total jobs for each, reflecting the much more rapid rate at which the "college jobs" are growing.

32. This is the "equimarginal" returns implication of microeconomic investment theory.

33. National Center for Public Policy and Higher Education, *Measuring Up 2008*.

34. The U.S. Department of Education's National Center for Education Statistics (NCES), in its *Projections of Education Statistics to 2016*, foresees (in its "middle alternative" projections) increases of 9 percent in associate degrees and 26 percent in bachelor's degrees over the twelve-year projection period from 2004–2005 to 2016–2017 (Hussar and Bailey, *Projections of Education Statistics*, iii). The growth projection for bachelor's degrees is several times the expected growth in the young population over this period. The NCES enrollment projection methodology takes into account the population size of each major racial and ethnic group and their respective enrollment (that is, participation) rates. As a result, the projections should reflect the effects of the demographic shift in the youth population toward underrepresented minority groups (ibid., 87–90). However, NCES's methodology does not take into account the expected shift toward more lower-income youth or the likely continued real price increases in higher education. Thus, its enrollment projections may be biased upward. Since the degree projections are based upon the enrollment projections, this effect carries forward to forecasts concerning degrees. Moreover, the NCES degree-projection equations make no allowance for the likely depressing effects on degree-completion rates of having more students from either underrepresented minorities or low-income groups (ibid., 110–112) and thus are more likely to be upwardly biased (that is, the projections of degrees awarded are likely to be higher than the actual numbers, given past success rates of these students). NCES has calculated that, over its past nine series of projections, the mean absolute percentage errors at ten years from the baseline have been 14.8 percent for associate degree projections and 11.2 percent for bachelor's degree projections (ibid., 110).

35. Alpert and Auyer, "Employment Projections," 13–37; Stekler and Thomas, "Economic Projections," 45–56.

36. Alpert and Auyer, "Employment Projections," 13, 14. BLS has an ongoing program to better understand the economy and improve its projection methodology, but some limitations in forecasting the future accurately are inevitable (Franklin, "Employment Outlook").

37. Carnevale, Smith, and Strohl, *Help Wanted*, Appendix 4.

38. Carnevale, "College For All?," 27.

39. Carnevale, Smith, and Strohl, *Help Wanted*, Appendix 4.

40. Ibid., 17–18.

41. Blinder, "Offshoring," 113–128; Uhalde and Strohl, *America in the Global Economy*.

42. Blinder, "Offshoring"; Uhalde and Strohl, *America in the Global Economy*. Prominent examples include the movement of computer programming jobs and the reading of radiology scans and legal work to India (Lakshimi, "India's Law Graduates").

43. Moncarz, Wolf, and Wright, "Service-Providing Occupations." BLS accounts for offshoring by assessing particular job characteristics thought to affect the likelihood that past relationships between U.S. economic activity and employment will be negatively affected. These judgments are reflected in the BLS projections for 2008–2018 described, and thus they are also built into the Carnevale et al. projections for the same period.

44. Given the dependence of projections of its future pace on a host of hard-to-predict technological advances, competitive conditions, and possible policy responses around

the globe, it is quite difficult to forecast how many "college jobs" may migrate abroad and how fast. One largely uncontrollable factor is that if developing economies, notably China and India, continue to grow at a rapid pace, then U.S.-based firms will inevitably offshore some jobs connected to these markets in order to better serve them and to meet pressures from those governments. On the other hand, "the spread of build-to-order and just-in-time strategies, such as lean retailing, are likely to keep many jobs in the U.S" (Troppe and Carlson, *Market and Skill Changes*, 13).

45. McCarthy, "3.3 Million U.S. Service Jobs."

46. Bardhan and Kroll, "New Wave of Outsourcing." Farrell and Rosenfeld write, "Contrary to popular opinion, only 11 percent of U.S. jobs could be feasibly offshored and only a small fraction of these actually will be" ("U.S. Offshoring," 123).

47. Blinder, "Offshoring," 122.

48. Uhalde and Strohl, *America in the Global Economy*.

49. Uhalde and Strohl, "America in the Global Economy," 38.

50. Moncarz, Wolf, and Wright, "Service-Providing Occupations," 71–86.

51. Ibid., 77.

52. Ibid., 78.

53. Farrell and Rosenfeld, "U.S. Offshoring," 128. That many of these factors—in addition to having many highly skilled workers—favor the United States is suggested by this country's performance in attracting investments by foreign companies, a measure on which it leads the world.

54. Ibid.

55. Ibid., 123.

56. The authors note that U.S. employment in the computer and data-processing sector has grown far faster than overall employment and that, across the economy, both employment growth and wages are higher in tradable than nontradable services (ibid., 128, 129). This sort of pattern may help account for the findings by BLS analysts (noted earlier) that recent domestic employment and wage growth have been highest in offshorable service occupations requiring high levels of education.

57. The OECD reports that the re-employment rate of displaced workers in the U.S. economy is the highest in the world by almost a factor of two (cited in Farrell and Rosenfeld, "U.S. Offshoring," 133). Nonetheless, more can be done to make transitions less painful and more likely to lead to new jobs with a promising future.

58. As noted earlier, the well educated have advantages in the face of job loss; they are generally more employable and are more likely to profit from additional education or training.

59. Blinder, "Offshoring," 113–128.

60. Barton, "How Many College Graduates?"; Handel, *Worker Skills*; Mishel and Rothstein, "Response to Marc Tucker"; Grubb and Lazerson, *Education Gospel*.

61. National Center on Education and the Economy, *Tough Choices*.

62. Income trends for well-educated men turned upward again after 2003. This was also the case for women, and their dip was shallower. Mishel and Rothstein, "Response to Marc Tucker."

63. Grubb and Lazerson, *The Education Gospel*, chapter 8.

64. Spence, *Market Signaling*. Michael Spence did the classic theoretical work on signaling theory in a labor market context. The relative contribution within the value created by educational credentials of human capital development versus signaling has proven difficult to pinpoint empirically, however.

65. Collins, *The Credential Society*.

66. Heckman and LaFontaine, "American High School Graduation Rate."

67. The Bill & Melinda Gates Foundation estimates this percentage to be about one-third (Khadaroo, "Push to Boost College Graduation Rates").

68. The Heritage Foundation, "Education."
69. Leef, "Overselling of Higher Education."
70. Herrnstein and Murray, *The Bell Curve*.

CHAPTER 3

1. Smiley, "Unemployment Rate Estimates," 487–493.
2. Harris, *Statistical Portrait*, 412; Ottinger, *Fact Book on Higher Education*, 57.
3. See Bennett, *When Dreams Came True*, or any of numerous other accounts of this historic legislation.
4. Harris, *Statistical Portrait*, 412; Ottinger, *Fact Book on Higher Education*, 57.
5. President's Commission on Higher Education, *Establishing the Goals*.
6. President's Commission on Higher Education, *Establishing the Goals*; Wilkinson, *Financial Aid in America*.
7. Ottinger, *Fact Book on Higher Education*, 57.
8. Harris, *Statistical Portrait*, 412.
9. Gladieux and Wolanin, *Congress and the Colleges*, 5.
10. U.S. Department of Education, National Center for Education Statistics, *The Condition of Education 2000*, 5. Current fund revenues are money received during the current fiscal year from revenue that can be used to pay obligations currently due, and surpluses reappropriated for the current fiscal year. Categories included under current fund revenues include funding from: student tuition and fees, federal government, state government, local government, endowment earnings, private gifts and grants, sales and service of educational activities, auxiliary enterprises, hospitals, and other current income.
11. Snyder and Dillow, *Digest of Education Statistics 2009*, table 351; Bureau of Labor Statistics, Consumer Price Index. Between 1930 and 1940, prices, as reflected in the consumer price index (CPI), declined by 16 percent, whereas between 1940 and 1950 prices increased by 72 percent.
12. Ottinger, *Fact Book on Higher Education*, 4.
13. Ibid., 57.
14. Lingenfelter, "Financing of Public Colleges and Universities," 653.
15. Snyder and Dillow, *Digest of Education Statistics 2009*, table 265.
16. Ibid. The data are for public two-year institutions.
17. Snyder and Dillow, *Digest of Education Statistics 2009*, table 351; Bureau of Labor Statistics, Consumer Price Index. Over the same time period, the increase in prices (CPI) was only 31 percent.
18. Lingenfelter, "Financing of Public Colleges and Universities," 654. These amounts are not adjusted for inflation.
19. See Becker, *Human Capital*. The first edition was published by the National Bureau of Economic Research, in Cambridge, MA, in 1964. The third edition was published by the University of Chicago Press in 1994.
20. Denison, *Sources of Economic Growth*; Denison, *Why Growth Rates Differ*.
21. Denison, *United States Economic Growth*, 345.
22. See Carnegie Commission, *Priorities for Action*, for a summary of the commission's recommendations, and Carnegie Commission, *Sponsored Research*, for a summary of authored volumes.
23. Perhaps the best-known case was the 1967 firing of Clark Kerr, president of the University of California, by the newly elected governor, Ronald Reagan, who promised during his campaign to "clean up the mess at Berkeley."
24. Hansen and Weisbrod, *Benefits, Costs, and Finance*.
25. The Hansen and Weisbrod analysis was completed before major revisions of the California tax code were enacted in 1967. The effect of these changes was to make the state income tax more progressive by raising tax rates on middle- and high-income Californians.

26. Cheit, *New Depression*, 139.
27. See the discussion in Cartter, *The Ph.D. and the Academic Labor Market.*
28. Freeman, *The Overeducated American.*
29. See Denison, *Slower Economic Growth;* Levy, *Dollars and Dreams.*
30. Bureau of Labor Statistics, Consumer Price Index.
31. Ottinger, *Fact Book on Higher Education,* 4–5.
32. Snyder and Dillow, *Digest of Education Statistics 2009,* table 189.
33. Ottinger, *Fact Book on Higher Education,* 5.
34. Snyder and Dillow, *Digest of Education* Statistics 2009, table 351. Over the same time period, prices (CPI) rose by 112 percent (Bureau of Labor Statistics, Consumer Price Index).
35. Carnegie Commission, *Higher Education,* 16.
36. Committee for Economic Development, *Management and Financing of Colleges,* 25.
37. Carnegie Commission, *Tuition,* 5.
38. Ibid., 13.
39. Keynes, *Employment, Interest and Money.*
40. Breneman, Finn, and Nelson, *Public Policy and Private Higher Education.*
41. A news release from the American Association of State Colleges and Universities dated April 12, 1978, in Thackery, "Brookings," 542–543.
42. Thackery, "Brookings," 542–543.
43. Wikipedia, "Sallie Mae." The Student Loan Marketing Association was originally created in 1972 as a government-sponsored enterprise (GSE) and began privatizing its operations in 1997, a process it completed at the end of 2004 when Congress terminated its federal charter, ending its ties to the government.
44. Thelin, "Coming of Age in America"; Breneman, Leslie, and Anderson, *ASHE Reader;* Hearn, "Growing Loan Orientation."
45. Breneman, "Education."
46. Ibid., 117.
47. See Hearn, "Paradox of Growth," 283; Arthur M. Hauptman and Cathy Krop, "Federal Student Aid and the Growth in College Costs and Tuitions: Examining the Relationship."
48. The College Board, *Trends in Student Aid 2010,* tables 1 and 2. Federal expenditures for grants and loans increased by 56 percent in current dollars. Federal expenditures for grants, loans, tax credits, and work-study increased by 60 percent in current dollars.

CHAPTER 4

1. See Friedman, *Capitalism and Freedom.* Supply-side theory, popularized by journalist Jude Wanniski, is attributed to economist Arthur Laffer's drawing of the so-called Laffer Curve on a cocktail napkin.
2. Bureau of Labor Statistics, Consumer Price Index.
3. Andersen, *Fact Book for Academic Administrators,* 5.
4. Data are from Palmer, "Grapevine: An Annual Compilation of Data on State Fiscal Support for Higher Education." Over the same decade, inflation increased by 59 percent (Bureau of Labor Statistics, Consumer Price Index).
5. Kane, Orzag, and Gunter, *State Fiscal Constraints and Higher Education Spending.*
6. Palmer, "Grapevine: An Annual Compilation of Data on State Fiscal Support for Higher Education"; Bureau of Economic Analysis, "National Income and Product Accounts."
7. Bureau of Economic Analysis, "National Income and Product Accounts," table 3.16; Kane, Orzag, and Gunter, *State Fiscal Constraints and Higher Education Spending,* 30–31.
8. State support includes state appropriations and state funds for grants and contracts. National Center for Education Statistics, Integrated Postsecondary Data Analysis System, 2008 Revenue file.
9. McPherson and Schapiro, *Student Aid Game,* 28.

10. Ibid.
11. Ibid. Data are in 1994 dollars.
12. Ibid., 29.
13. For a discussion of the economics of this practice, see Breneman, *8 Liberal Arts Colleges*, 36–65.
14. Baum, "The Student Aid System," 710.
15. Snyder and Dillow, *Digest of Education Statistics 2009*, table 189.
16. Murphy and Welch, "Wage Premiums."
17. Breneman, *Higher Education*, 1.
18. HOPE was an acronym for "Helping Outstanding Pupils Educationally."
19. Cornwell and Mustard, "Evaluating HOPE-Style Merit Scholarships."
20. Cornwell, Lee, and Mustard, "Student Responses," 895–917.
21. College Board, *Trends in Student Aid 2010*, table 6.
22. Ibid., table 1.
23. Sallie Mae is the former Student Loan Marketing Association, now a private firm; First Marblehead is a new investment bank specializing in private student loans.
24. Baum, "The Student Aid System," 710.
25. Winston and Zimmerman, "Peer Effects in Higher Education."
26. McPherson and Schapiro, *The Student Aid Game*.
27. Archibald, *Redesigning the Financial Aid System*, 10–11.
28. Ibid.
29. Ibid., 11.
30. National Center for Public Policy and Higher Education, *Measuring Up 2008*, 12.
31. Western Interstate Commission for Higher Education, *Knocking at the College Door*, 4.
32. Snyder and Dillow, *Digest of Education Statistics 2009*, table 190.
33. Ibid.
34. Ibid.
35. National data compiled at Palmer, Grapevine data, Center for the Study of Education Policy, Illinois State University, http://grapevine.illinoisstate.edu/.
36. Hovey, *State Spending for Higher Education*. See also Doyle and Delaney, "Higher Education Funding."
37. Kane, Orzag, and Gunter, *State Fiscal Constraints and Higher Education Spending*, 3.
38. A structural deficit means that, over a business cycle, revenue sources under existing tax policies are estimated to raise less revenue than required to meet current services needs under existing laws. See Hovey, *State Spending for Higher Education*, 6–10; National Center for Public Policy and Higher Education, "State Shortfalls," *Policy Alert* (Feb. 2000);Dennis Jones, "State Shortfalls Projected to Continue," *Policy Alert* (Feb. 2006).
39. Breneman, "Privatization of Public Universities."
40. U.S. Congress, *Public Law 105-18*, (Title IV, Cost of Higher Education Review, 1997).
41. The report called primarily for more transparency about costs and pricing decisions. National Commission on the Cost of Higher Education, *Straight Talk*; Doyle and Conklin, "Tuition Inflation"; Conklin and Trombley, "Short History"; Conklin and Trombley, "Straight Talk?"
42. Baumol and Blackman, "Rising College Costs."
43. Dow Jones Indexes, "The Dow 1999–2009."
44. Palmer, *Grapevine*, table 5.
45. College Board, *Trends in College Pricing 2010*, table 4a ("Average Published Tuition and Fees in Current Dollars").
46. Western Interstate Commission for Higher Education, *Knocking at the College Door*, 6.
47. Snyder and Dillow, *Digest of Education Statistics 2009*, table 189.
48. Immerwahr and Johnson, *Squeeze Play 2009*; Immerwahr and Johnson, *Squeeze Play 2010*.

49. Friedman, *The World is Flat*.

50. Organisation for Economic Co-operation and Development, *Education at a Glance 2010*.

51. The U.S. is ranked tenth in the educational attainment of adults ages 25 to 34. National Center for Public Policy and Higher Education, *Measuring Up 2008*, 6; Organisation for Economic Co-operation and Development, *Education at a Glance 2010*, table A1.3A ("Population with Tertiary Education").

52. Bowen, Kurzweil, and Tobin, *Equity and Excellence in American Higher Education*, 95–136.

53. U.S. Congress, *College Opportunity and Affordability Act of 2008*, HR 4137, Sections 111 and 116.

54. Grassley, "Wealthy Colleges," A36.

55. Ewell, *Making the Grade*, vii–ix.

56. National Center for Public Policy and Higher Education, *Measuring Up 2008*, 12.

57. Miller and Ewell, *Measuring Up on College-Level Learning*.

58. Spellings Commission Report, *A Test of Leadership*, 24.

59. Association of Public and Land-Grant Universities, *Voluntary System*.

60. The story is best told in Lewis, *The Big Short*.

61. Paul E. Lingenfelter, "Financing of Public Colleges and Universities," 666.

62. National Bureau of Economic Research, "Business Cycle Dating Committee."

63. National Conference of State Legislatures, *Update on State Budget Gaps*; Doughterty and Troianovski, "States Slammed by Tax Shortfalls"; U.S. Energy Information Administration, "Cushing, OK."

64. National Conference of State Legislatures, *State Budget Update*.

65. College Board, *Trends in Student Aid 2009*, table 1.

66. Kelly, *Closing the College Attainment Gap*, 4.

67. The State Fiscal Stabilization Fund targeted $5.9 billion for educational operations through its "Stabilization Fund." The State Fiscal Stabilization Fund also included a separate fund called the "Government Services Fund," which included spending on educational capital projects. The total spent on higher educational operations and capital expenditures for 2009 and 2010 was $6.6 billion. National data compiled at Palmer, "Grapevine: An Annual Compilation of Data on State Fiscal Support for Higher Education"

68. Lederman, "Student Loan Overhaul Advances"; U.S. Congress, *Health Care and Education Reconciliation Act of 2010*, HR 4872, Sections 1501 and 2102.

69. For additional information, see chapter 7.

70. For additional information, see chapter 7.

71. National Center for Public Policy and Higher Education, *Presidential Leadership for Public Purpose*.

CHAPTER 5

1. Snyder, Dillow, and Hoffman, *Digest of Education Statistics 2008*; Baum, Payea, and Steele, *Trends in Student Aid*.

2. National Association of State Student Grant & Aid Programs, *40th Annual Survey Report*.

3. Zumeta, "Accountability and the Private Sector"; Zumeta, "Meeting the Demand," 364–425.

4. State Higher Education Executive Officers, *State Higher Education Finance FY 2010*. Federal stabilization funds under the American Recovery and Reinvestment Act provided another 4 percent of the total, and local public funding provided 6 percent.

5. State Higher Education Executive Officers defines *educational revenues* as the sum of public appropriations for operations plus tuition and fee revenues less state-provided student aid. (*State Higher Education Finance FY2010*, 33.) Thus, a substantial part of institutions' operations (especially those of research universities) such as student housing and food services, research, and hospitals are excluded from this calculation entirely. This exclusion is appropriate for our purposes.

6. Zumeta, "Accountability and the Private Sector," 25–64.

7. Boyd, *What Will Happen?* Based on prerecession data.

8. National Governors Association and National Association of State Budget Officers, *Fiscal Survey of States*, vii–viii. This source reports that the proportion of state spending represented by federal funds was nearly 35 percent in fiscal 2010, up sharply from 26 percent two years earlier.

9. Snyder, Dillow, and Hoffman, *Digest of Education Statistics 2008*.

10. There is considerable variation among states in the percentage of students enrolled in private institutions who are state residents, as well as in the share of students enrolled in traditional nonprofit colleges versus for-profit schools.

11. Bradburn, Hurst, and Peng, *Community College Transfer Rates*; Doyle, "Community College Transfers"; Desrochers, Lenihan, and Wellman, *Trends in College Spending*.

12. Richardson et al., *Designing State Higher Education Systems*; Desrochers, Lenihan, and Wellman, *Trends in College Spending*.

13. National Center for Public Policy and Higher Education, *Measuring Up 2008*.

14. Ibid.

15. Western Interstate Commission for Higher Education, *Knocking on the College Door*.

16. Ibid.

17. Soares, *Working Learners*.

18. U.S. Bureau of Economic Analysis, "Regional Economic Accounts."

19. Beyle, "Governor's Formal Powers"; McLendon, "Politics of Higher Education."

20. Monear, "Stability and Upheaval."

21. Elazar, *American Federalism*.

22. Zumeta, "Meeting the Demand."

23. Glenny, *Autonomy of Public Colleges*. At the time Glenny was writing, there were a significant number of states that fell into a third category, that of "planning boards." Only two states, Delaware and Michigan, could be so classified now. This is the most minimal level of statewide governance.

24. For a detailed categorization of the many subtypes and combinations, see the Education Commission of the States' online Postsecondary Structures Database, Education Commission of the States, "Postsecondary Governance Structures Database," at http://www. ecs.org/html/educationIssues/Governance/GovPSDB_intro.asp.

25. Even those states with coordinating boards, however, have done relatively little to incorporate private, for-profit institutions into their policy approach. Zumeta, "State Policies and Private Higher Education."

26. Richardson and Martinez, *Policy and Performance*.

27. As noted in the study by Richardson and Martinez, a key such mechanism includes effective statewide controls over mission creep. See Clark, *Creating Entrepreneurial Universities*; Skolnik, "Design, Deregulation or Just Drifting." Leadership can be as important as structure here, though.

28. Kelly and Jones, *New Look*; Richardson and Martinez, *Policy and Performance*.

29. Kelly and Jones, *New Look*.

30. Dynarski, "Lowering the Cost of College"; Leslie and Brinkman, "Student Price Response"; and Heller, "Update to Leslie and Brinkman."

31. McPherson and Schapiro, *Keeping College Affordable*; St. John, *Refinancing the College Dream*.

32. Heller, "Public College Enrollment"; Thompson and Zumeta, "Effects of Key State Policies."

33. National Association of State Student Grant & Aid Programs, *40th Annual Survey Report*. These programs are typically funded, at least primarily, with state lottery revenues.

34. Dynarski, "Lowering the Cost of College"; Henry, Rubenstein, and Bugler, "Is HOPE Enough?"; Cornwell, Mustard, and Sridhar, "Enrollment Effects of Merit-Based Financial Aid."

35. Lumina Foundation for Education, *Results and Reflections*.
36. Jones, *Financing in Sync*; Richardson and Martinez, *Policy and Performance*.
37. National Center for Public Policy and Higher Education, *Measuring Up 2008*.
38. Burke, *Funding Public Colleges and Universities for Performance*, 21.
39. Banta et al., "Performance Funding"; Burke, "Reinventing Accountability"; Dougherty and Natow, "Popular but Unstable."
40. Zumeta and Kinne, "Potential and Reality of Performance Agreements."
41. Zumeta, "New Accountability," 12–13.
42. Kirst and Venezia, *From High School to College*.
43. Only about a third of community college students who begin in remedial courses ever reach college-level courses, according to the Bill & Melinda Gates Foundation, as reported in Khadaroo, "Push to Boost College Graduation Rates." This weak linkage between secondary and postsecondary systems is a major problem for the overall performance of the education system.
44. Kirst and Venezia, *From High School to College*.
45. The Common Core Standards project emerged in 2010 to establish common high school graduation and college preparedness standards across states. This promising project includes participation of the American Diploma Project, Achieve Inc., Education Trust, the Fordham Foundation, the National Alliance of Business, the Council of Chief State School Officers, the National Association of System Heads, and the National Governors Association.
46. Hoachlander, Sikora, and Horn, *Community College Students*.
47. Ibid.
48. Doyle, "Community College Transfers."
49. National Center for Public Policy and Higher Education, *Affordability and Transfer*, 15.
50. The University of Washington currently commits that 30 percent of its new enrollees each year will be transfers from the state's community colleges.
51. Ewell and Kelly, *State-Level Completion and Transfer Rates*.
52. Ibid.
53. Floyd, Skolnik, and Walker, *Community College Baccalaureate*.
54. Allen and Seaman, *Class Differences*.
55. Means, *Evidence-Based Practices in Online Learning*.
56. Bramble and Panda, *Economics of Distance and Online Learning*.
57. Some states have more issues with remotely located populations than others, but the problem applies to most states in some degree. Online opportunities can also help improve access in densely populated areas by limiting the need to commute to campus.
58. Zumeta, "State Policies and Private Higher Education"; Zumeta, "Meeting the Demand."
59. Zumeta, "Meeting the Demand."
60. Zumeta, "Utilizing Private Higher Education." States can contract with private institutions to pay for *increases* in targeted types of enrollments (such as teachers and nurses or simply state resident undergraduates). This is difficult to do with state aid to students since it is not practical to provide more attractive aid grants only to *additional* students. Students who would have attended a private institution anyway thus receive a windfall, which can seriously dilute cost effectiveness
61. Zumeta, "State Policies and Private Higher Education"; Zumeta, "Meeting the Demand."
62. National Association of State Student Grant & Aid Programs, *40th Annual Survey Report*.
63. Federal policy has an important role to play here too, since many of the for-profit providers cross state lines and most students at for-profit institutions receive federal student aid. We have more to say about this in chapter 7.
64. Ewell and Boeke, *Critical Connections*, 4.
65. See www.dataqualitycampaign.org/. State Higher Education Executive Officers are also active in this field.

66. Bound and Turner, *Cohort Crowding*. The historical supply of higher education has been highly inelastic, meaning that states have historically not increased capacity to match increased levels of demand. Instead, in most states, the capacity of higher education has changed only slowly in response to increasing demand. Consequently, attainment rates relative to the population have suffered.

67. Wagner, *Measuring Up Internationally*.

68. National Center for Public Policy and Higher Education, *Measuring Up 2008*.

69. Western Interstate Commission for Higher Education, *Knocking on the College Door*.

70. National Center for Public Policy and Higher Education, *Measuring Up 2008*.

71. Goldin and Katz, *Race Between Education and Technology*. Some states with depressed economies are plagued by this problem, however, as opportunities for college graduates may be limited.

72. "On-time" high school completion rates are variously estimated at 70 percent to 75 percent nationally, as per Heckman and LaFontaine, "American High School Graduation Rate," 242–262. Unfortunately, later completion does not improve graduates' earnings or chances for postsecondary completion very much, according to Tyler, "Economic Benefits of the GED."

73. Cataldi, Laird, and Kewal Ramani, *High School Dropout and Completion Rates*.

74. Bozick, Lauff, and Wirth, *Education Longitudinal Study of 2002*.

75. This is not to say that stronger K–16 linkages can correct all the complex problems of the nation's elementary and secondary schools.

76. Indiana's 21st Century Scholars Program provides a good model of how to do this.

77. Vandal, *Revving the Economic Engine*.

78. The enrollment of students from low-income families, compared with students from high-income families, tends to be more responsive to financial assistance. Difficulties may arise, however, if state politics nudge subsidies away from the most needy and toward the middle and upper economic classes, or if economic dislocations lead to cuts in aid at the same time that tuitions jump most sharply.

79. National Center for Public Policy and Higher Education, *Measuring Up 2008*.

80. Ibid.

81. Snyder, Dillow, and Hoffman, *Digest of Education Statistics 2010*.

82. Long and Kurlaender, "Viable Pathway."

83. Venezia and Kirst, "Inequitable Opportunities."

84. ACT, *Ready for College and Ready for Work*.

85. Horn and Nevill, *Profile of Undergraduates*.

86. Doyle, "Interactive Instructional Technology."

87. Horn and Berger, *College Persistence on the Rise?*

88. Note that this measure, based on the federal definition of the graduation rate, leaves out the many students who transfer between institutions and all part-time students. Thus, it is both seriously narrow and certainly overstates the aggregate on-time graduation rate.

89. Wagner, *Measuring Up Internationally*.

90. Kuh, Kinzie, and Schuh, *Student Success in College*; Braxton, *Reworking the Student Departure Puzzle*.

91. Shulock and Moore, *Rules of the Game*.

92. Zumeta, "State Policies and Private Higher Education."

CHAPTER 6

1. In 2010, the federal government stopped insuring loans made by private banks and began supplying the loan capital directly through the Federal Direct Loan Program.

2. Lumina Foundation, *Lumina's Big Goal*.

3. Snyder and Dillow, *Digest of Education Statistics 2010*, table 275.

4. Ibid., table 197.

5. Bound and Turner, *Cohort Crowding*, 877–899.

6. Breneman, Finn, and Nelson, *Financing Community Colleges*.

7. Zumeta and Frankle, *California Community Colleges*.

8. Rivera, "California Community Colleges."

9. Ahumada, "Analysis of State Formula Budgeting," 331–354.

10. American Association of State Colleges and Universities, "Members by States and Territories."

11. Many of these issues are discussed in detail, with considerable empirical findings, in Bowen, Chingos, and McPherson, *Crossing the Finish Line*.

12. For a list of member institutions, see Association of American Universities, "AAU Members"; Association of Public and Land-Grant Universities, "APLU Members."

13. Leading institutions, however, may be innovators in devising new forms of educational pedagogy that may have a substantial impact on behavior in less selective institutions.

14. For an explanation of tuition discounting, see Breneman, *Liberal Arts Colleges*.

15. Zumeta and LaSota, "Recent Patterns."

16. For more detailed discussion, see Zumeta and LaSota, "Recent Patterns," and also the discussion of this issue in chapter 5, this volume.

17. U.S. Government Accountability Office, *For-Profit Schools*. The "90–10 rule" prohibits them from earning more than 90 percent of total revenues from federal student aid; most are at or near that level.

18. In addition, a majority of states allow some part of their financial aid to students to be used at for-profit colleges.

19. For further discussion, see Breneman, Pusser, and Turner, *Earnings from Learning*.

20. Dias, "Educators or Predators?"; Hechinger, "For-Profit Colleges Need More Oversight"; Abramson, "Senate Panel Scrutinizes For-Profit Colleges."

21. Lewis, *The Big Short*; MarketFolly.com, "Subprime Goes to College."

22. U.S. Senate Health, Education, Labor & Pensions Committee, "Federal Education Dollars at For-Profit Colleges."

23. MarketFolly.com, "Subprime Goes to College."

24. U.S. Government Accountability Office, *For-Profit Colleges*.

25. According to Kantrowitz ("What is Gainful Employment?"), "The Higher Education Act of 1965 requires for-profit colleges to provide 'an eligible program of training to prepare students for gainful employment in a recognized occupation' but does not currently define gainful employment."

26. Nelson, "For-Profit Debate Redux"; Nelson, "Concessions or a Cave-In?" The new rules on gainful employment issued in June 2011 require vocational schools to show that at least 35 percent of their students are repaying their loans or that the annual loan payment does not exceed 30 percent of a typical graduate's discretionary income or 12 percent of total income.

27. Means et al., *Evidence-Based Practices in Online Learning*. This meta-study limited its search to Web-based instruction, which eliminated studies of video- and audio-based courses or stand-alone, computer-based instruction. It included only studies with random-assignment or controlled quasi-experimental designs. And it examined objective measures of student learning, rather than student/teacher perceptions of quality or other nonobjective measures.

28. Means et al., *Evidence-Based Practices in Online Learning*, ix.

29. Ibid., xv.

30. Ibid., xvi.

31. Allen and Seaman, *Class Differences*, 8, 22. The 2010 findings were based on a sample of 2,583 colleges and universities that represented about 80 percent of all higher education enrollments, including public, private nonprofit, and private for-profit institutions as

well as research universities, master's and baccalaureate institutions, and associate's and specialized institutions.

32. Allen and Seaman, *Class Differences*, 5. The Sloan report focuses on online education only and defines it as 80 percent of the course content being delivered online. The report defines face-to-face instruction to include courses in which 0 percent to 29 percent of the content is delivered online; this category includes both traditional and Web-facilitated courses. Blended or hybrid education is defined as having between 30 percent and 80 percent of the course content delivered online.

33. Allen and Seaman, *Learning on Demand*; Allen and Seaman, *Class Differences*, 4, 14.

34. Allen and Seaman, *Class Differences*, 9.

35. Ibid., 11.

36. Ibid., 14.

37. Allen and Seaman, *Learning on Demand*.

38. Carnegie Mellon, *Open Learning Initiative*.

39. Carnegie Mellon, "Community College—Open Learning Initiative."

40. National Center for Academic Transformation (NCAT), "Program in Course Redesign, Lessons Learned," http://www.thencat.org/PCR/R1Lessons.html.

41. NCAT, "The NCAT Course Redesign Program: Improving Student Learning While Reducing Instructional Costs," http://www.thencat.org/States/State-based%20Redesign%20Program%20Desc%20woBudget.pdf

42. Ibid.

43. NCAT, "Program in Course Redesign," Virginia Tech, Linear Algebra, http://www.thencat.org/PCR/R1/VT/VT_Overview.htm.

44. NCAT, "Tennessee Board of Regents: Developmental Studies Redesign Initiative," Cleveland State Community College, http://www.thencat.org/States/TN/Abstracts/CSCC%20Algebra_Abstract.htm.

45. NCAT, "Five Principles of Successful Course Redesign," http://www.thencat.org/PlanRes/R2R_PrinCR.htm.

46. Witkowsky, "Indiana's 'Eighth University.'"

47. Ibid., 4.

48. Ibid., 4.

49. Ibid., 4.

50. Legislative Analyst's Office, *Master Plan*.

51. Witkowsky, "Indiana's 'Eighth University.'"

52. As of mid-2011, two more states had established similar arrangements with WGU: Washington and Texas. (Legislative Analyst's Office, *Master Plan*.)

53. Daniel, *Mega Universities and Knowledge Media*.

CHAPTER 7

1. Johnson and Lichter, *Changing Faces of America's Children and Youth*, 2.

2. Mortenson, "Family Income and Educational Attainment."

3. See chapter 2 for a summary of Haskins, "Education and Economic Mobility," demonstrating the importance of higher education for income mobility in the United States.

4. Heckman and LaFontaine, "American High School Graduation Rate," 242–262.

5. See Kirst, *Enhancing College Completion*; Bozick, Lauff, and Wirt, *Education Longitudinal Study*; Ingels and Dalton, *Trends Among High School Seniors*.

6. Mortenson, "Family Income and Educational Attainment"; Organisation for Economic Co-operation and Development, *Education at a Glance 2010*; National Center for Public Policy and Higher Education, *Measuring Up 2008*.

7. Kerr, *Preserving the Master Plan*.

8. The Institute for College Access and Success, "Quick Facts About Student Debt."

9. Congressional Budget Office, Projection of Medicaid Costs."

10. Calculation based on data from Kelly, *Closing the College Attainment Gap.*
11. See, for example, Brenneman et al., *Good Policy, Good Practice II.*
12. Immerwahr and Johnson, *Squeeze Play 2010*, 10.
13. The recent increases in Pell Grants notwithstanding, as will be explained presently. In addition to the underwhelming responses of states and institutions to reach the president's goal, the administration's own decision to focus the goal entirely on younger workers ignores undereducated workers over thirty-four. As discussed later in this chapter, this latter group must be reached in many states if they are to achieve the attainment levels that have been established for their work forces as a whole.
14. Association of American Universities, "AAU Summary of the Education Provisions," 2.
15. Ibid.
16. These changes were made by President Bush in May 2008 when he signed legislation that increased loan limits for individual borrowers by $2,000 (Institute for College Access and Success, *Project on Student Debt*).
17. For example, according to the Associated Press ("Coast to Coast Double Digit Tuition Hikes"), "Florida college students could face yearly 15% tuition increases for years, and University of Illinois students will pay at least 9% more. The University of Washington will charge 14% more at its flagship campus. And in California, tuition increases of more than 30% have sparked protests reminiscent of the 1960s."
18. McPherson and Schapiro (*Student Aid Game*), using financial data from institutions spanning 1978–1979 to 1985–1986, found that "public four-year institutions tended to raise tuition by $50 for every $100 increase in federal student aid" during that period (ibid., 84). Based on a panel of 1,554 colleges and universities from 1989 to 1996, Singell and Stone ("For Whom the Pell Tolls") found "little evidence of the Bennett hypothesis [that institutions raise tuition in response to federal student aid increases] for in-state tuition for public universities. For private universities though, increases in Pell grants appear to be matched nearly one for one by increases in list (and net) tuition. Results for out-of-state tuition for public universities are similar to those for private universities, suggesting that they behave more like private ones in setting out-of-state tuition. Institutional responses in these latter cases appear at odds with federal grants-in-aid policy."
19. Increases in tuition and fees have greatly outpaced inflation in the last thirty years. See National Center for Public Policy and Higher Education, *Measuring Up 2008*, figure 5.
20. According to the American Council on Education ("College Graduation Rates"), "Total borrowing through private student loan programs grew by more than 900%, in inflation-adjusted terms, between 1995-96 and 2005-06."
21. National Association of State Scholarship and Grant Programs, *9th Annual Survey Report*; Lee, *State Student Incentive Grant Program.*
22. National Association of State Student Grant & Aid Programs, *40th Annual Survey Report.*
23. U.S. Department of Education, Federal Financial Aid, "2007–2008 Award Year."
24. That is, a much larger state expenditure for student aid would be matched than is currently the case under SSIG/LEAP. To avoid having states offer, as their match, funds that they would have provided anyway, the federal government should consider matching *increases* in state support above a recent baseline year.
25. National Association of State Student Grant & Aid Programs, *30th Annual Survey Report*; National Association of State Student Grant & Aid Programs, *40th Annual Survey Report*. An even richer match might be considered initially, perhaps two federal dollars for each additional state dollar provided for need-based aid up to a limit, in order to jumpstart efforts in states that have historically done little in this area.
26. From 1999 to 2009, non-need-based aid grew by 158 percent in constant dollars, while need-based aid grew 51 percent over the same period (National Association of State Student Grant & Aid Programs, *40th Annual Survey Report*).

27. Hentschke, Lechuga, and Tierney, *For-Profit Colleges and Universities*; Knapp, Kelly-Reid, and Whitmore, *Enrollment in Postsecondary Institutions*.

28. According to Levy ("Global Growth in Private Higher Education"), private higher education institutions around the world, many resembling the for-profits in the U.S., have been burgeoning in recent years as demand for higher education soars while governments are unable to respond with large investments in public-sector capacity.

29. Theoretically, this is a problem of "information asymmetry" (Weimer and Vining, "Policy Analysis," 105). Standard policy remedies include better consumer information, enforcement of regulations about approved and disapproved practices, and, ideally, the development of professional norms among providers that better align their behavior with clients' interests.

30. This practice is thought to encourage enrollment—and even misleading—of unqualified students.

31. U.S. Government Accountability Office, "For-Profit Colleges" (GAO 10-948T); Lewin, "Lower Loan Repayment."

32. Nelson, "For-Profit Debate Redux"; Nelson, "Concessions or a Cave-In?" The new rules on gainful employment issued in June 2011 require vocational schools to show that at least 35 percent of their students are repaying their loans or that the annual loan payment does not exceed 30 percent of a typical graduate's discretionary income or 12 percent of total income.

33. Kantor and Whalley, *Regional Economic Development*; Trani and Holzworth, *Indispensable University*.

34. Feller, "Academic Greed"; Field, "Congressional Earmarks." The practice, however, is by no means limited to research and development.

35. Wolfle, *Home of Science*.

36. There has been considerable discussion in Congress recently about earmark reform, but little legislative progress had been made.

37. This analysis was developed by the National Center for Higher Education Management Systems (Kelly, *Closing the College Attainment Gap*).

38. This is an ambitious target for annual output increases, particularly in light of recent trends that show annual growth of well under 0.5 percent. Such large increases imply substantial growth of entering students, increases in enrollments of students with prior credits, and strong gains in degree completion rates of both groups. (Kelly, *Closing the Attainment Gap*.)

39. In 2008–2009, state student aid contributions per undergraduate enrollment ranged from $7 in Wyoming to $1,916 in South Carolina (National Association of State Student Grant & Aid Programs, *40th Annual Survey Report*, 23). The average state student aid commitment was $660 per FTE undergraduate, and only fifteen states exceeded this amount. The proportion of state support for higher education going to student aid ranged from less than 1 percent in Alaska, Hawaii, and Wyoming to nearly one-third in South Carolina (ibid., 25). Non-need-based aid constituted 28 percent of all state grant aid in 2008–2009. Forty states supported non-need-based aid programs. The following states allocated most of their grant funding to non-need-based aid: Georgia (99.8 percent), South Dakota (95 percent), Mississippi (87 percent), Louisiana (82 percent), and New Mexico (69 percent) (ibid., 8). About two-thirds of the states (thirty-three) provided aid to students at proprietary institutions in 2008–2009. In eight of these states, less than 1 percent of total state student aid dollars went to students in for-profit institutions. At the upper end of the scale, five states provided more than 10 percent of total state aid to students in the for-profit sector. Ohio, at 25 percent, reported the greatest share of its statewide support for student aid going to students at for-profit institutions (ibid.).

40. College Board, *2010 Progress Report;* College Board, *State Policy Guide.*
41. Zachry and Schneider, *Building Foundations for Student Readiness;* Wimberly and Noeth, *College Readiness Begins in Middle School.*
42. See http://www.doe.in.gov/core40/ (Brenneman et al., *Good Policy, Good Practice II*).
43. College Board, "Student Poll."
44. In expensive fields like the health sciences, several states pay private nonprofit colleges directly per state resident student enrolled or, in a few cases, per degree granted (Zumeta, "State Policies and Private Higher Education").
45. Council for Adult and Experiential Learning, *Adult Learning in Focus.*
46. States and the federal government could provide research and development support and incentives to improve capabilities for assessing prior learning.
47. We recognize that these commitments would need to be accompanied by steps to ensure adequate funding and provide for better cost containment. These matters are addressed later.
48. According to the State Higher Education Executive Officers (*SHEEO Annual Finance Report FY2009*), the range in the share of public institutions' educational revenue derived from net tuition runs from Wyoming's 12 percent all the way to Vermont's 84 percent. Twenty-nine states are above the national average of 37.3 percent of educational revenues derived from tuition sources.
49. See National Center for Public Policy and Higher Education, *Measuring Up 2008.*
50. See Zumeta and Frankl, *California Community Colleges.*
51. For student-held jobs, excessive work is commonly defined as more than twenty hours per week at typical wage rates.
52. King, *Crucial Choices;* Tuttle, McKinney, and Rago, *College Students Working;* Kim, "Effects of Loans."
53. As part of the federal-state student aid partnership, the federal government could go further to mandate an explicit state tuition policy as a condition for participation, but this would likely be perceived as heavy-handed. Moreover, during economic downturns when tuition levels might be raised beyond the agreed-upon policy limits, the federal government would find it difficult to cut off states from federal student aid. Furthermore, dropping students from financial aid at a time when tuition has increased penalizes students for the state's inability to maintain consistent funding.
54. Suppose a public university were to receive only $100 million annually from the state, after having received substantially higher levels of support previously. To replace this influx of general-fund dollars that can be used for core expenses, the university would need to *add* more than $2 billion to its endowment. Only a few public campuses now have *total* endowments of this size.
55. Zumeta and Frankle, *California Community Colleges.*
56. See Zumeta and Kinne, "Accountability Policies in Higher Education," for recent actions in Tennessee, Ohio, and Indiana.
57. Washington's Student Achievement Initiative uses four categories of student achievement milestones. Research has shown the first three to be associated with program completion. These are: (1) building toward college-level skills (basic skills gains and passing precollege writing or math); (2) first-year retention while earning at least fifteen college-level credits; (3) completing a college-level math course; and (4) completing an apprenticeship, certificate, or associate's degree (Jenkins, Zeidenberg, and Keinzl, "Educational Outcomes of I-BEST").
58. Among all first-time freshmen in degree-granting institutions in fall 2008 (Snyder and Dillow, *Digest of Educational Statistics 2010,* table 198).
59. Horn and Weko, *On Track to Complete?;* Herzel Associates, "Best Practices in Statewide Articulation and Transfer Systems"; Herzel Associates, "Promising Practices in Statewide Articulation and Transfer Systems."

60. Shulock and Moore, *Rules of the Game*; Webber and Ehrenberg, *Expenditures Other Than Instructional Expenditures*.
61. Shulock and Moore, *Rules of the Game*.
62. See the discussion of this topic in chapter 6.
63. One method of gaining credit for off-campus work is through the College-Level Examination Program (CLEP), which is a series of examinations that provide credit for knowledge acquired through alternative means (see College Board http://www.collegeboard.com/student/testing/clep/exams.html). In addition, many institutions now have programs that allow students to count knowledge acquired outside of the classroom through prior learning assessment. A recent study found that 56 percent of students who earned prior learning assessment credit went on to earn a degree (see Lederman, "Prior Learning").
64. See, for example, Bettinger and Long, "Adjunct Instructors"; Webber and Ehrenberg, *Expenditures Other Than Instructional Expenditures*; Jenkins, Zeidenberg, and Keinzl, "Educational Outcomes of I-BEST."
65. Palmer, "*Annual Compilation of Data.*"
66. Doyle and Delaney. "Higher Education in State Budgets"; The College Opportunity and Affordability Act of 2007 (H.R. 4137) contained, as a condition of federal aid, a maintenance-of-effort mandate on state higher education funding. This mandate required that state funding for higher education not fall below the average of such spending for the previous five years. The American Recovery and Reinvestment Act (ARRA) of 2009 mandated that states not reduce higher education funding below 2005–2006 levels, but this still allowed for substantial reductions and did not preclude states from increasing tuition.
67. Delaney and Doyle, "Higher Education in State Budgets."
68. Ewell and Boeke, *Critical Connections*.
69. Data Quality Campaign, *The Next Step*; Ewell and Boeke, *Critical Connections*.
70. Zumeta, "New Accountability."
71. See Association of Public and Land-Grant Universities and the Association of State Colleges and Universities, *Voluntary System*.
72. Adelman, *Higher Education Reforms in Other Countries*.
73. See National Center for Public Policy and Higher Education, *State Capacity for Higher Education Policy*.

Bibliography

Abramson, Larry. "Senate Panel Scrutinizes For-Profit Colleges." NPR, March 25, 2011. http://www.npr.org/templates/story/story.php?storyId=128099980.

"Accounting for Offshoring in Occupational Projections." *Occupational Projections and Training Data*, 2006–2007 ed. Bulletin 2602. Washington, DC: U.S. Department of Labor, February 2006.

ACT. *Ready for College and Ready for Work: Same or Different?* Iowa City, IA: ACT, 2006. http://www.act.org/research/policymakers/pdf/ReadinessBrief.pdf.

Adelman, C. *What state leaders can learn from higher education reforms in other countries.* Session presented at the 2010 National Forum on Education Policy of the Education Commission of the States, Portland, OR, August 19, 2010.

Advisory Committee on Student Financial Assistance. *Access Denied: Restoring the Nation's Commitment to Equal Educational Opportunity.* Washington, DC: Advisory Committee on Student Financial Assistance, 2001.

Ahumada, Martin M. "An Analysis of State Formula Budgeting in Higher Education." In *ASHE Reader on Finance in Higher Education*, rev. ed., eds. David W. Breneman, Larry L. Leslie, and Richard E. Anderson, 331–354. Needham Heights, MA: Ginn Press, 1993.

Allen, I. Elaine, and J. Seaman. *Class Differences: Online Education in the United States, 2010.* Newburyport, MA: Babson Survey Research Group and Sloan Consortium, November 2010. http://sloanconsortium.org/publications/survey/class_differences.

———. *Learning on Demand: Online Education in the United States, 2009.* Newburyport, MA: Sloan Consortium, 2010.

———, *Staying the Course: Online Education in the United States, 2008.* The Sloan Consortium, November 2008. Research sponsored by the Alfred P. Sloan Foundation.

Alpert, Andrew, and Jill Auyer. "Evaluating the BLS 1988–2000 Employment Projections." *Monthly Labor Review* 126 (2003): 13–37.

America's Student Loan Providers."Loan limits." *America's Student Loan Providers*, 2010. http://www.studentloanfacts.org/loanfacts/overview/Loan+Limits.htm.

American Association of State Colleges and Universities. "Members by States and Territories." http://www.aascu.org/members/by-state-and-territory/ correct link to "Members"

American Association of State Colleges and Universities, news release, April 12, 1978.

American Council on Education. "College Graduation Rates: Behind the Numbers." http://www.acenet.edu/links/pdfs/cpa/2010_09_30_collegegraduationrates.html.

American Council on Education. "Who Borrows Private Loans?" *American Council on Education Issue Brief*, August 2007, November 11, 2010, citing 2007 College Board's *Trends in Student Aid.* http://www.acenet.edu/AM/Template.cfm?Template=/CM/ContentDisplay.cfm&ContentID=23410.

American Council on Education. "ACE Analysis of the Higher Education Act Reauthorization." August 2008. http://www.acenet.edu/AM/Template.cfm?Section=Government_Relations_and_Public_Policy&Template=/CM/ContentDisplay.cfm&ContentID=29218

Andersen, Charles J. *Fact Book for Academic Administrators: 1981–82*. Phoenix, AZ: American Council on Education/Oryx Press, 1981.

APPA. *Thought Leaders Report 2010: Assessing and Forecasting Facilities in Higher Education*. Alexandria, VA: Association of Higher Education Facilities Officers, 2010.

Archibald, Robert B. *Redesigning the Financial Aid System: Why Colleges and Universities Should Switch Roles with the Federal Government*. Baltimore: The Johns Hopkins University Press, 2002.

Arum, Richard, and Josipa Roska. *Academically Adrift: Limited Learning on College Campuses*. Chicago: University of Chicago Press, 2011.

Associated Press. "Coast to coast double digit tuition hikes: State budget deficits contribute to higher education costs," February 1, 2010. Retrieved from http://www.msnbc.msn.com/id/35185920/.

Association for Institutional Research. "College Costs and Prices: Report of the National Commission on the Cost of Higher Education," July 1998. http://www.airweb.org/page.asp?page=114.

Association of American Universities. AAU Summary of the Education Provisions of the Health Care and Education Reconciliation Act of 2010, April 9, 2010. http://www.aau.edu/policy/student_aid_reconciliation.aspx?id=8410.

Association of American Universities. "AAU Members." http://www.aau.edu/about/default.aspx?id=4020.

Association of Public and Land-Grant Universities. "APLU Members." http://www.aplu.org/page.aspx?pid=249.

Association of Public and Land-Grant Universities and the Association of State Colleges and Universities. *APLU/AASCU Voluntary System of AccountabilityProgram*. 2010. http://www.voluntarysystem.org/index.cfm?page=about_vsa.

Baer, Justin D., Andrea L. Cook, and Stéphane Baldi. *The Literacy of America's College Students*. Washington, DC: American Institutes for Research, 2006.

Bailey, Thomas R., Norena Badway, and Patricia J. Gumport. *For-profit Higher Education and Community Colleges*. Stanford, CA: National Center for Postsecondary Improvement, 2001.

Banta, Trudy W., L. B. Rudolph, J. Van Dyke, and H. S. Fisher. "Performance Funding Comes of Age in Tennessee." *The Journal of Higher Education* (1996): 23–45.

Bardhan, Ashok Deo, and Cynthia Kroll. "The New Wave of Outsourcing." Washington DC: Fisher Center for Real Estate & Urban Economics. Fisher Center Research Reports: Report #1103, 2003. Cited in Uhalde, Ray, and Jeff Strohl. *America in the Global Economy: A Background Paper for the New Commission on the Skills of the American Workforce*. Washington, DC: National Center on Education and the Economy.

Barton, Paul E. "How Many College Graduates Does the U.S. Labor Force Really Need?" *Change: The Magazine of Higher Learning* 40, no.1 (2008):16–21.

Bartsch, Kristina. "The Employment Projections for 2008–18." *Monthly Labor Review* 132, no. 11 (2009): 9.

Basken, Paul. "Congress Mulls Consumer Protections as Colleges Increasingly Lend to Their Own Students." *Chronicle of Higher Education*, December 2, 2009.

Baum, Sandy. *Education Pays: 2007 the Benefits of Higher Education for Individuals and Society*. Washington, DC: College Board, 2007.

———. "The Student Aid System: An Overview." In *Handbook of Research in Education Finance and Policy*, eds. Helen F. Ladd and Edward B. Fiske. New York: Routledge, 2007.

Baum, S., K. Payea, and P. Steele. *Trends in Student Aid*. New York: College Board, 2009.

Baumol, William J., and Sue Anne Batey Blackman. "How to Think About RisingCollege Costs." *Planning for Higher Education* 23 (Summer 1995): 1–7.

Baumol, William J., and William G. Bowen. *Performing Arts—the Economic Dilemma: A Study of Problems Common to Theater, Opera, Music and Dance*. Cambridge, MA: The MIT Press, 1966.

Becker, Gary S. *Human Capital: A Theoretical and Empirical Analysis, with Special Reference to Education*, 3rd ed. Chicago: University of Chicago, 1994.

Bennett, Michael J. *When Dreams Came True: The G.I. Bill and the Making of Modern America*. New York: Brassey's, 1996.

Berdahl, Robert Oliver, Jane Graham, and Don R. Piper. *Statewide Coordination of Higher Education*. Washington, DC: American Council on Education, 1971.

Berktold, Jennifer, Sonya Geis, and Philip Kaufman. *Subsequent Educational Attainment of High School Dropouts*. Washington, DC: National Center for Education Statistics, 1998.

Besley, T., and A. Case. "Political Institutions and Policy Choices: Evidence from the United States." *American Economic Review* 41, no.1 (2003): 7–73.

Bettinger, Eric P., and Bridget Terry Long. "The Increasing Use of Adjunct Instructors at Public Universities: Are We Hurting Students?" In *What's Happening to Public Higher Education?*, ed. Ronald G. Ehrenberg, 51–70. Westport, CT: Praeger, 2006.

Beyle, T. L. "The Governor's Formal Powers: A View from the Governor's Chair." *Public Administration Review* 28, no. 6 (1968): 540–45.

Blinder, Alan S. "Offshoring: The Next Industrial Revolution?" *Foreign Affairs* 85, no. 2 (March-April 2006): 113–28.

Bound, John, and Sara Turner. *Cohort Crowding: How Resources Affect College Attainment*. National Bureau of Economic Research, working paper 12424, August 2006.

Bowen, Howard Rothmann. *The Costs of Higher Education: How Much Do Colleges and Universities Spend per Student and How Much Should They Spend?* San Francisco: Jossey-Bass, 1980.

Bowen, W. G., and David W. Breneman. "Student Aid: Price Discount or Educational Investment?" *The Brookings Review* 11 (Winter 1993): 28–31.

Bowen, W. G., Matthey M. Chingos, and Michael McPherson. *Crossing the Finish Line: Completing College at America's Public Universities*. Princeton, NJ: Princeton University Press, 2009.

Bowne, W. G., Martin A. Kurzweil, and Eugene M. Tobin. *Equity and Excellence in American Higher Education* (Thomas Jefferson Foundation Distinguished Lecture). Charlottesville: University of Virginia Press, 2006.

Boyd, Donald. *State Fiscal Outlooks from 2005–2013: Implications for Higher Education*. Boulder, CO: National Center for Higher Education Management Systems, 2005. http://www.higheredinfo.org/analyses/Boyd%20Article%20June2005.pdf.

Boyd, D. *What Will Happen to State Budgets When the Money Runs Out?* Boulder, CO: National Center for Higher Education Management Systems, 2009.

Bozick, Robert, Erich Lauff, and John Wirt. *Education Longitudinal Study of 2002 (ELS: 2002): A First Look at the Initial Postsecondary Experiences of the High School Sophomore Class of 2002*. Washington, DC: U.S. Dept. of Education, Institute of Education Sciences, National Center for Education Statistics, 2007.

Bracey, Gerald W. "Heard the One about 600,000 Chinese Engineers?" *Washington Post*, May 21, 2006, B3.

Bradburn, E. M., D. G. Hurst, and S. E. Peng (Project Officer). *Community College Transfer Rates to 4-Year Institutions Using Alternative Definitions of Transfer*, NCES 2001-197.Washington, DC: U.S. Department of Education, National Center for Education Statistics, 2001.

Bramble, W. J., and S. Panda. *Economics of Distance and Online Learning*. New York and London: Routledge, 2008.

Braxton, John M. *Reworking the Student Departure Puzzle*. Nashville, TN: Vanderbilt University Press, 2000.

Breneman, David W. "Education." In *Setting National Priorities: the 1979 Budget*, ed. Joseph A. Pechman, 117–25. Washington, DC: Brookings Institution, 1978.

———. *Higher education: On a collision course with new realities* (AGB Occasional paper). Washington, DC: Association of Governing Boards of Universities and Colleges, 1994.

——. *Liberal Arts Colleges: Thriving, Surviving, or Endangered?* Washington, DC: Brookings Institution, 1994.

——. "The Privatization of Public Universities: Mistake or Model?" *The Chronicle of Higher Education*, March 7, 1997, B4.

——, Chester E. Finn, and Susan C. Nelson. *Financing Community Colleges: An Economic Perspective.* Washington, DC: Brookings Institution, 1981.

——, Chester E. Finn, and Susan C. Nelson. *Public Policy and Private Higher Education.* Washington, DC: Brookings Institution, 1978.

——, Larry L. Leslie, and Richard E. Anderson, editors. *ASHE Reader on Finance in Higher Education.* Needham Heights, MA: Ginn, 1993.

Breneman, David W., Brian Pusser, and Sarah E. Turner, eds., *Earnings from Learning: The Rise of For-Profit Universities.* Albany, NY: SUNY Press, 2006.

Brenneman, Meghan Wilson, Patrick M. Callan, Peter T. Ewell, Joni E. Finney, Dennis P. Jones, and Stacey Zis. *Good Policy, Good Practice II: Improving Outcomes and Productivity in Higher Education: A Guide for Policymakers.* San Jose, CA: National Center for Public Policy and Higher Education, 2010.

Brown, Charles, James Hamilton, and James Medoff. *Employers Large and Small.* Cambridge, MA: Harvard University Press, 1990.

Burdman, Pamela. *The Student Debt Dilemma: Debt Aversion as a Barrier to College Access*, CSHE 12.05. Berkeley: University of California, Center for Studies in Higher Education, 2005.

Bureau of Economic Analysis. "National Income and Product Accounts." http://www.bea.gov/index.htm.

Bureau of Labor Statistics. Consumer Price Index, All Urban Consumers. http://nces.ed.gov/programs/digest/d09/tables/dt09_351.asp.

Burke, Joseph C. *Funding Public Colleges and Universities for Performance: Popularity, Problems, and Prospects.* Albany, NY: Rockefeller Institute, 2002.

——. "Reinventing Accountability: From Bureaucratic Rules to Performance Results." In *Achieving Accountability in Higher Education: Balancing Public, Academic, and Market Demands*, ed. Joseph C. Burke, 216–245. San Francisco: Jossey-Bass, 2005.

Callan, Patrick M. "Modest Improvements, Persistent Disparities, Eroding Global Competitiveness." In *Measuring Up 2008*. National Center for Public Policy and Higher Education. http://measuringup2008.highereducation.org/commentary/callan.php.

——, Peter Ewell, Joni E. Finney, and Dennis Jones. *Good policy, good practice: Improving outcomes and reducing costs in higher education: A guide for policymakers.* San Jose, CA: National Center for Public Policy and Higher Education, 2007. http://www.highereducation.org/reports/Policy_Practice/index.shtml.

Card, David. "Estimating the Return to Schooling: Progress on Some Persistent Econometric Problems." *Econometrica* 69, no. 5 (2001): 1127–60.Cited in George Psacharopoulos and Harry A. Patrinos. "Returns to Investment in Education: A Further Update." *Education Economics* 12 (2004): 111–34.

Carnegie Commission. *Higher Education: Who Pays? Who Benefits? Who Should Pay?* New York: McGraw-Hill, 1973.

——. *Priorities for Action: Final Report of the Carnegie Commission on Higher Education.* New York: McGraw-Hill, 1973.

——. *Sponsored Research of the Carnegie Commission on Higher Education.* New York: McGraw-Hill, 1975.

——. *Tuition: A Supplemental Statement to the Report of the Carnegie Commission on Higher Education on "Who Pays? Who Benefits? Who Should Pay?"* New York: McGraw-Hill, 1974.

Carnegie Mellon. "Community College–Open Learning Initiative," *Open Learning Initiative.* http://oli.web.cmu.edu/openlearning/initiative/research/158.

Carnegie Mellon. *Open Learning Initiative.* http://oli.web.cmu.edu/openlearning/initiative.

Carnevale, Anthony P. "College For All?" *Change: The Magazine of Higher Learning* 40, no. 1 (2008): 22–31.

———, Jeff Strohl, and Michelle Melton. *What's It Worth?* Washington, DC: Georgetown University Center on Education and the Workforce, 2011.

———, and Donna M. Desrochers. *Standards for What? The Economic Roots of K–16 Reform.* Washington, DC: Educational Testing Service, 2003.

———, Nicole Smith, and Jeff Strohl. *Help Wanted, Projections of Jobs and Education Requirements Through 2018.* Center on Education and the Workforce, Georgetown University, Appendix 4, 2010.

Cartter, Allan Murray. *The Ph. D. and the Academic Labor Market*, a Carnegie Commission sponsored report. New York: McGraw-Hill, 1976.

Cataldi, E. F., J. Laird, and A. Kewal Ramani. *High School Dropout and Completion Rates in the United States: 2007* (NCES 2009-064). Washington, DC: National Center for Education Statistics, Institute of Education Sciences, 2009.

Center on Budget and Policy Priorities. *States continue to feel recession's impact.* http://www.cbpp.org/cms/index.cfm?fa=view&id=711.

Center on Budget and Policy Priorities. "Recession Continues to Batter State Budgets." Center on Budget and Policy Priorities, October 20, 2009. http://www.cbpp.org.

Center on Budget and Policy Priorities. *States continue to feel recession's impact.* http://www.cbpp.org/cms/index.cfm?fa=view&id=711.

Cheit, Earl Frank. *The New Depression in Higher Education: A Study of Financial Conditions at 41 Colleges and Universities.* New York: McGraw-Hill, 1971.

Clark, Burton R. *Creating Entrepreneurial Universities: Organizational Pathways of Transformation.* Oxford, England: Published for the IAU by Pergamon, 1998.

Clinedinst, Melissa E., Alisa F. Cunningham, and Jamie P. Merisotis. *Characteristics of Undergraduate Borrowers, 1999–2000.* Washington, DC: U.S. Department of Education, Institute of Education Sciences, National Center for Education Statistics, 2002.

Clotfelter, Charles T. *Buying the Best: Cost Escalation in Elite Higher Education.* Princeton, NJ: Princeton University Press, 1996.

Cohn, Elchanan, and Terry Geske. *The Economics of Education,* 3rd ed. Oxford, England: Pergamon Press, 1990.

The College Board. *The College Completion Agenda: 2010 Progress Report.* Washington, DC: College Board, 2010. http://completionagenda.collegeboard.org/.

The College Board. *The College Completion Agenda: State Policy Guide.* Washington, DC: College Board, 2010. http://completionagenda.collegeboard.org/.

———. *Fulfilling the Commitment: Recommendations for Reforming Student Aid.* A Report from the Rethinking Student Aid Study Group. New York: College Board, 2008.

———. "Student Poll-Effects of the Recession on College Plans." In *Educators: Education Professionals-Test Dates to Annual Forum-College Board.* College Board and Art and Science Group, 2009. http://professionals.collegeboard.com/data-reports-research/trends/studentpoll/recession.

———. *Trends in College Pricing 2010.* Washington, DC: The College Board, 2010. http://trends.collegeboard.org/college_pricing.

———. "Trends in Student Aid." In *Trends in Higher Education* 2009. http://trends.collegeboard.org/downloads/archives/SA_2009.pdf.

———. *Trends in Student Aid 2009.* Washington, DC: The College Board, 2009.

———. *Trends in Student Aid 2010.* Washington, DC: The College Board, 2010.

The College Opportunity and Affordability Act of 2007 (H.R. 4137). GovTrack.us. http://www.govtrack.us/congress/bill.xpd?bill=h110-4137.

Collins, Clayton. "The New Rags to Riches: Entrepreneurs Still Pursue the American Dream. Only Many Are Pushed into It by a Sour Economy." *Christian Science Monitor*, November 1, 2004, 13.

Collins, Randall. *The Credential Society: An Historical Sociology of Education and Stratification.* New York: Academic, 1979.

Committee for Economic Development. *Cracks in the Education Pipeline: A Business Leader's Guide to Higher Education Reform.* Washington, DC: Committee for Economic Development, 2005.

———. *The Management and Financing of Colleges.* New York: Committee for Economic Development, 1973, 25.

"Compromise Budget Bill Would Increase Pell Grants and Funds for NIH and NSF." *Chronicle of Higher Education,* December 9, 2009.

"Congress Mulls Consumer Protections as Colleges Increasingly Lend to Their Own Students." *Chronicle of Higher Education,* December 2, 2009.

Congressional Budget Office. *The budget and economic outlook: Fiscal years 2010 to 2020,* January 2010. Retrieved 1/7/2011 from: http://www.cbo.gov/ftpdocs/108xx/doc10871/01-26-Outlook.pdf.

Congressional Budget Office. "Projection of Medicaid Costs: The Long-Term Outlook for Medicare, Medicaid, and Total Healthcare Spending." 2010. http://www.cbo.gov/ftpdocs/102xx/doc10297/chapter2.5.1.shtml.

Conklin, Kristin, and William Trombley, "A Short History of the Cost Commission." *National CrossTalk,* Spring 1998. http://www.highereducation.org/crosstalk/ct0598/voices0598-history.shtml.

Conklin, Kristin, and William Trombley, "Straight Talk About College Costs and Prices." *National CrossTalk,* Spring 1998. http://www.highereducation.org/crosstalk/ct0598/voices0598-chart.shtml.

Cornwell, Christopher, and David Mustard, "Evaluating HOPE-Style Merit Scholarships." In *Innovation in Education: A Federal Reserve Bank of Cleveland Research Conference; Proceedings of a Conference Held in Cleveland, Ohio, November 17–18, 2005.*Cleveland, OH: Federal Reserve Bank of Cleveland, 2006. http://www.clevelandfed.org/research/Conferences/2005/november/Papers/Innovation%20in%20Education%20Proceedings.pdf.

Cornwell, Christopher C., Kyung Hee Lee, and David B. Mustard. "Student Responses to Merit Scholarship Retention Rules," *Journal of Human Resources* 40 (2005): 895–917. http://www.terry.uga.edu/hope/hope.academic_choices.pdf.

Cornwell, C., D. B. Mustard, and D. J. Sridhar, "The Enrollment Effects of Merit-Based Financial Aid: Evidence from Georgia's HOPE Scholarship." *Journal of Labor Economics* (2006): 761–86.

Council for Adult and Experiential Learning. *Fueling the race to postsecondary success: A 48-institution study of prior learning assessment and adult student outcomes.* Chicago: CAEL, March 2010.

——— with National Center for Higher Education Management Systems (NCHEMS). *Adult Learning in Focus: National and State-by-State Data.* Chicago: CAEL, 2008. http://www.cael.org/pdf/State_Indicators_Monograph.pdf.

Daniel, John S. *Mega Universities and Knowledge Media.* London: Kogan Page Limited, 1999.

Data Quality Campaign. *The next step: Using longitudinal data systems to improve student success.* Washington, DC: Data Quality Campaign, 2009. http://www.dataqualitycampaign.org/resources/details/384.

Delaney, J. A., and W. R. Doyle. "The role of higher education in state budgets." In *The Challenges of Comparative State-Level Higher Education Policy Research,* eds. K. Shaw and D. Heller, 55–76. Stirling, VA: Stylus, 2007.

Denison, Edward Fulton. *Accounting for Slower Economic Growth: The United States in the 1970's.* Washington, DC: Brookings Institution, 1979.

Denison, Edward F. *Accounting for United States Economic Growth, 1929–1969* (Washington, DC: Brookings Institution, 1974).

———. *The Sources of Economic Growth in the United States and the Alternatives Before Us.* New York: Committee for Economic Development, 1962.

———. *Trends in American Economic Growth, 1929–1982.* Washington, DC: Brookings Institution, 1985.

———. *Why Growth Rates Differ: Postwar Experience in Nine Western Countries.* Washington, DC: Brookings, 1967.

"Department Prepares for Switch to 100% Direct Lending." *Chronicle of Higher Education,* July 9, 2009.

Desrochers, D. M., C. M. Lenihan, and J. V. Wellman. *Trends in College Spending 1998–2008.* Washington, DC: Delta Project on Postsecondary Costs, Productivity and Accountability, 2010.

Dias, Elizabeth. "For-Profit Colleges: Educators or Predators?" *Time.* http://www.time.com/time/business/article/0,8599,2000160,00.html.

Dougherty, Amy Marie, and Anton Troianovski. "States Slammed by Tax Shortfalls." *Wall Street Journal,* July 24, 2008, 1.

Dougherty, K. J., and R. S. Natow. "Popular but Unstable: Explaining Why State Performance Funding Systems Do Not Persist." Paper presented at American Educational Research Association Annual Conference, San Diego, CA, April 15, 2009.

Dow Jones Indexes. "The Dow 1999–2009." *Dow Jones Industrial Average Learning Center.* Accessed April 4, 2011. http://www.djindexes.com.

Doyle, W. R. "Interactive instructional technology: Northern Arizona University offers new long-distance teaching strategies." *National CrossTalk* 5, no. 2 (1997): 1–4.

———."Community college transfers and college graduation: Whose choices matter most?" *Change: the Magazine of Higher Education* 38, no. 3 (May-June 2006): 42–44.

——— and Kristin Conklin. "Tuition Inflation" *National CrossTalk,* Fall 1997. http://www.highereducation.org/crosstalk/ct1097/news1097-inflation.shtml.

———, and J. Delaney. "Higher education funding: The new normal." *Change: the Magazine of Higher Education* 44, no. 4 (July-August 2009): 60–62.

———, and J. Delaney. "The role of higher education in state budgets." In *The Challenges of State-Level Higher Education Policy Research*, eds. K. M. Shaw and D. E. Heller, 55–76. Sterling, VA: Stylus, 2007.

Dynarski, S. "The consequences of lowering the cost of college—the behavioral and distributional implications of aid for college." *The American Economic Review* 92, no. 2 (2002): 279–86.

Education Commission of the States. "Governance Postsecondary Governance Structures Database." http://www.ecs.org/html/educationIssues/Governance/GovPSDB_intro.asp.

Ehrenberg, Ronald G. "Introduction." In *What's Happening to Public Higher Education?,* ed. Ronald G. Ehrenberg, xiii. Westport, CT: Praeger, 2006.

———.and Liang Zhang. "Do Tenured and Tenure-Track Faculty Matter?" In *What's Happening to Public Higher Education?,* ed. Ronald G. Ehrenberg, 37–50. Westport, CT: Praeger, 2006.

———. and Douglas A. Webber. *Do expenditures other than instructional expenditures affect graduation and persistence rates in higher education?* NBER Working Paper w15216, August 2009.

Eisman, Steven. "Subprime Goes to College." June 24, 2010. http://help.senate.gov/imo/media/doc/Eisman.pdf.

Elazar, Daniel Judah. *American Federalism: A View from the States.* New York: Harper and Row, 1966.

Ellwood, David T. "The Sputtering Labor Force of the Twenty-first Century: Can Social Policy Help?" In *The Roaring Nineties: Can Full Employment Be Sustained?,* eds. Alan B. Krueger and Robert M. Solow. New York: Russell Sage Foundation, 2001.

Erikson, Robert S., Gerald C. Wright, and John P. McIver, "State Political Culture and Public Opinion." *American Political Science Review* 81, no. 3 (1984): 494–814.

Ewell, Peter. *Assessing Student Learning Outcomes: A Supplement to Measuring Up 2000.* San Jose, CA: National Center for Public Policy and Higher Education, 2000.

———. *Making the Grade: How Boards Can Enhance Academic Quality.* Washington, DC: Association of Governing Boards of University, 2006, vii–ix.

———, and Marianne Boeke. *Critical Connections: Linking States' Unit Record Systems to Track Student Progress.* Boulder, CO: National Center for Higher Education Management Systems, 2007.

———, and Patrick Kelly. *State-Level Completion and Transfer Rates: Harnessing a New National Resource.* San Jose, CA: National Center for Public Policy and Higher Education, 2009.

———, Patrick J. Kelly, and Rebecca Klein-Collins. *Adult Learning in Focus: National and State-by-State Data.* Boulder, CO: National Center for Higher Education Management Systems, 2008.

Farrell, Diana. *Offshoring: Understanding the Emerging Global Labor Market.* McKinsey Global Institute Series. Boston, MA: Harvard Business School Press, 2006.

———, and Jaeson Rosenfeld. "U.S. Offshoring: Rethinking the Response." In *Offshoring: Understanding the Emerging Global Labor Market*, ed. Diana Farrell. McKinsey Global Institute Series. Boston, MA: Harvard Business School Press, 2006.

Felderer, Bernhard, and André Drost. "Cyclical Occupational Choice in a Model with Rational Wage Expectations and Perfect Occupational Mobility." Institute for Advanced Studies, Vienna, Economic Series No. 81, 2000.

Feller, Irwin. "American State Governments as Models for National Science Policy." *Journal of Policy Analysis and Management* 11, no. 2, (Spring 1992): 288–309.

———. "Research Subverted by Academic Greed." *The Chronicle of Higher Education*, January 16, 2004.

Field, Kelly. "Congressional Earmarks Crowd out Merit-based Grants for Innovation in Higher Education." *The Chronicle of Higher Education*, December 14, 2004.

_____. "House Bill Would End Guaranteed Student Loans and Overhaul Perkins Program." *Chronicle of Higher Education*, July 15, 2009.

_____. "Student-Loan Companies Spend Millions on Lobbying and Campaign Contributions." *Chronicle of Higher Education*, September 28, 2009.

Floyd, Deborah L., Michael L. Skolnik, and Kenneth P. Walker. *The Community College Baccalaureate: Emerging Trends and Policy Issues.* Sterling, VA: Stylus Publishing, 2005.

Franklin, James. "Employment Outlook: 2006–16—An Overview of BLS Projections to 2016—The U.S. Economy Is Projected to Grow at a Moderate Pace over the Next 10 Years." *Monthly Labor Review* 130, no. 11 (2007): 3–12.

Freeman, Richard B. *The Market for College-Trained Manpower: A Study in the Economics of Career Choice.* Cambridge, MA: Harvard University Press, 1971.

———. *The Overeducated American.* New York: Academic, 1976.

Frey, William H., Alan Berube, Audrey Singer, and Jill H. Wilson. *Getting Current Recent Demographic Trends in Metropolitan America.* Washington, DC: Metropolitan Policy Program, Brookings Institution, 2009. htte://www.brookings.edu/~/media/Files/rc/reports/2009/03_metro_demographic_trends/03_metro_demographic_trends.pdf. http://www.brookings.edu/search.aspx?doQuery=1&q=Getting%20Current%20Recent%20Demographic%20Trends%20in%20Metropolitan%20America.

Friedman, Milton. *Capitalism and Freedom.* Chicago: University of Chicago Press, 1962.

Friedman, Thomas L. *The World is Flat.* New York: Farrar, Straus, and Giroux, 2005.

Fry, R. "College Enrollment Hits All Time High, Funded by Community College Surge." *A Social and Demographic Trends Report.* Washington, DC: Pew Research Center, October 2009.

Geiger, Roger L., and Sa Cresco. "Beyond Technology Transfer: U.S. State Policies to Harness Research for Economic Development." *Minerva* 43 (2005): 1–21.

Gereffi, Gary, and Viveck Wadhwa. "Framing the Engineering Outsourcing Debate: Placing the United States on a Level Playing Field with China and India." Duke University, 2005.

Gladieux, Lawrence E., and Thomas R. Wolanin. *Congress and the Colleges: The National Politics of Higher Education.* Lexington, MA: Lexington, 1976.

Glenny, Lyman A. *Autonomy of Public Colleges; the Challenge of Coordination.* New York: McGraw-Hill, 1959.

Goldin, Claudia Dale, and Lawrence F. Katz. *The Race Between Education and Technology.* Cambridge, MA: Belknap of Harvard University Press, 2008.

Grassley, Charles E. "Wealthy colleges must make themselves more affordable." *Chronicle of Higher Education,* May 30, 2008.

Grubb, W. Norton, and Marvin Lazerson. *The Education Gospel: The Economic Power of Schooling.* Cambridge, MA: Harvard University Press, 2004.

"H.R. 4137 [110th]: Higher Education Opportunity Act (GovTrack.us)." *GovTrack.us: Tracking the U.S. Congress.* http://www.govtrack.us/congress/bill.xpd?bill=h110-4137.

Handel, Michael J. *Worker Skills and Job Requirements: Is There a Mismatch?* Washington, DC: Economic Policy Institute, 2005.

Hansen, W. Lee., and Burton Allen Weisbrod. *Benefits, Costs, and Finance of Public Higher Education.* Chicago: Markham Publishers, 1969.

Harris, Seymour E. *A Statistical Portrait of Higher Education. A Report for the Carnegie Commission on Higher Education.* New York: McGraw-Hill, 1972.

Harvey, James. *Straight Talk about College Costs and Prices: Report of the National Commission on the Cost of Higher Education.* Phoenix, AZ: Published at the Request of the National Commission on the Cost of Higher Education by the American Council on Education and the Oryx Press, 1998.

Haskins, R. "Education and Economic Mobility." In *Getting Ahead or Losing Ground: Economic Mobility in America,* eds. J. Isaacs, I. Sawhill, and R. Haskins, 91–105. Washington, DC: Brookings Institution, 2008.

Hauptman, Arthur M., and Cathy S. Krop. *Federal Student Aid and Tuition Growth: Examining the Relationship.* New York: Council for Aid to Education, 1998.

Hearn, James C. "The Paradox of Federal Aid to College Students, 1965–1990." In *The Finance of Higher Education: Theory, Research, Policy, and Practice,* eds. Michael B. Paulsen and John C. Smart, 267–315. New York: Agathon, 2001.

———. "The growing loan orientation in federal financial aid policy: A historical perspective," In *ASHE Reader on Finance in Higher Education,* ed. John L. Yeager. Boston, MA: Pearson Custom Publishing, 2001.

———, and Carolyn P. Griswold. "State-Level Centralization and Policy Innovation in U.S. Postsecondary Education." *Educational Evaluation and Policy Analysis* 16, no. 2 (1994): 161–90.

———, Carolyn P. Griswold, and Ginger M. Marine. "Region, Resources, and Reason: A Contextual Analysis of State Tuition and Student Aid Policies." *Research in Higher Education* 37, no. 3 (1996): 241–78.

Hechinger, John. "For-Profit Colleges Need More Oversight, Senator Says." *Business Week.* http://www.businessweek.com/news/2010-06-24/for-profit-colleges-need-more-oversight-senator-says.html.

Hecker, Daniel E. "Occupational Employment Projections to 2014."*Monthly Labor Review* 128, no. 11 (2005).

Heckman, James J., and Paul A LaFontaine. "The American High School Graduation Rate: Trends and Levels." *The Review of Economics and Statistics.* 92, no.2. Cambridge, MA: MIT Press (2010): 244–262, 01.

———, and Paul A. LaFontaine, 2008. "The Declining American High School Graduation Rate: Evidence, Sources, and Consequences." *NBER Reporter: Research Summary,* no. 1. http://www.nber.org/reporter/2008number1/heckman.html.

Heller, D. E. "Student price response in higher education: An update to Leslie and Brinkman."*Journal of Higher Education* 68, no. 6 (1997): 624–59.

_____. "The effects of tuition and state financial aid on public college enrollment." *Review of Higher Education* 23, no. 1 (1999): 65–89.

Henry, G. T., R. Rubenstein, and D. T. Bugler. "Is HOPE Enough? Impacts of Receiving and Losing Merit-Based Financial Aid." *Educational Policy* 18, no. 5 (2004): 686–709.

Hentschke, Guilbert C., Vicente M. Lechuga, and William G. Tierney. *For-profit Colleges and Universities: Their Markets, Regulation, Performance, and Place in Higher Education.* Sterling, VA: Stylus Publishers, 2010.

The Heritage Foundation. "Education." 2010. http://www.heritage.org/Issues/Education. Accessed October 7, 2011.

Herrnstein, Richard J., and Charles Murray. *The Bell Curve: Intelligence and Class Structure in American Life.* New York: Free Press Paperbacks, 1994.

Herzel Associates. "Best Practices in Statewide Articulation and Transfer Systems: Research Literature Review." Boulder, CO: Western Interstate Commission on Higher Education, February 2009.

———. "Promising Practices in Statewide Articulation and Transfer Systems." Boulder, CO: Western Interstate Commission on Higher Education, June 2010.

Hoachlander, E. Gareth, Anna C. Sikora, and Laura Horn, *Community College Students: Goals, Academic Preparation, and Outcomes.* Washington, DC: National Center for Education Statistics, U.S. Dept. of Education, Institute of Education Sciences, 2003.

Hopkins, Jim. "4 That Forged Ahead and Beat the Odds." *USA Today,* September 1, 2004, B3.

Horn, Laura, and Rachael Berger. *College Persistence on the Rise? Changes in 5-year Degree Completion and Postsecondary Persistence Rates between 1994 and 2000.* Washington, DC: U.S. Department of Education, Institute of Education Sciences, National Center for Education Statistics, 2004.

_____, and S. Nevill. *Profile of Undergraduates in U.S. Postsecondary Education Institutions: 2003–04: With a Special Analysis of Community College Students.* NCES 2006-184. Washington, DC: U.S. Department of Education, 2006.

_____, and Thomas Weko. *On Track to Complete? A Taxonomy of Beginning Community College Students and Their Outcomes 3 Years after Enrolling: 2003–04 through 2006.* Washington, DC: U.S. Dept. of Education, National Center for Education Statistics, Institute of Education Sciences, 2009.

"House Bill End Guaranteed Student Loans and Overhaul Perkins Program." *Chronicle of Higher Education,* July 15, 2009.

Hovey, Harold A. *State Spending for Higher Education in the Next Decade: The Battle to Sustain Current Support.* San Jose, CA: The National Center for Public Policy and Higher Education, 1999.

Hussar, William, and Tabitha Bailey. *Projections of Education Statistics to 2016.* Washington, DC: National Center for Education Statistics, Institute of Education Sciences, U.S. Dept. of Education, 2007. http://nces.ed.gov/pubs2008/2008060.pdf.

Imagine America Foundation. "Graduating At-risk Students: A Cross-sector Analysis." Virginia Beach, VA: Imagine America Foundation, 2009.

Immerwahr, John, and Jean Johnson, with Amber Ott and Jonathan Rochkind. *Squeeze Play 2010: Continued Public Anxiety on Cost, Harsher Judgments on How Colleges Are Run.* San Jose, CA: National Center for Public Policy and Higher Education, 2010. http://www.highereducation.org/reports/squeeze_play_10/squeeze_play_10.pdf.

_____, with Paul Gasbarra, Amber Ott, and Jonathan Rochkind. *Squeeze Play 2009: The Public's Views on College Costs Today.* San Jose, CA: National Center for Public Policy and Higher Education, 2009. http://www.highereducation.org/reports/squeeze_play_09/squeeze_play_09.pdf.

Indiana Department of Education. "Indiana Core 40." http://www.doe.in.gov/core40/.

Ingels, S. J., and B. W. Dalton. *Trends Among High School Seniors, 1972–2004* (NCES 2008-320). Washington, DC: National Center for Education Statistics, Institute for Education Sciences, U.S. Department of Education, 2008.

Institute for College Access and Success. "Quick Facts About Student Debt." *The Project on Student Debt.* January 2010. http://projectonstudentdebt.org/files/File/Debt_Facts_and_Sources.pdf.

Institute for College Access and Success. *Project on Student Debt.* June 2010. http://www.projectonstudentdebt.org.Institute for Higher Education Policy. *The Investment Payoff: A 50-state Analysis of the Public and Private Benefits of Higher Education.* Washington, DC: Institute for Higher Education Policy, 2005.

Isaacs, Julia, Isabel V. Sawhill, and Ron Haskins. *Getting Ahead or Losing Ground: Economic Mobility in America.* Washington, DC: Brookings Institution, 2008.

Jenkins, D., M. Zeidenberg, and G. Keinzl. "Educational Outcomes of I-BEST. Washington State Community and Technical College System's Integrated Basic Education and Skills Training Program: Findings from a Multivariate Analysis." CCRC Working Paper No. 16. New York: Columbia University Teachers College, May 2009. http://www.sbctc.ctc.edu/college/abepds/multivariateanalysis_workingpaper16_may2009.pdf.

Johnson, K. M., and D. T. Lichter. *The changing faces of America's children and youth.* Issue Brief No. 15. Durham, NH: Carsey Institute, University of New Hampshire, Spring 2010. Accessed 10/12/2010 at: http://www.carseyinstitute.unh.edu/publications/IB_Johnson_ChangingFaces.pdf.

Jones, Dennis P. *Financing in Sync: Aligning Fiscal Policy with State Objectives.* Boulder, CO: Western Interstate Commission for Higher Education, 2003.

_____. *State Shortfalls Projected to Continue Despite Economic Gains.* San Jose, CA: National Center for Public Policy and Higher Education, 2006.

Kaiser, Harvey H., and Jerry S. Davis. *A Foundation To Uphold: A Study of Facilities Conditions at U.S. Colleges and Universities.* Alexandria, VA: APPA, 1996.

Kane, Thomas J., Peter R. Orzag, and David L. Gunther. *State fiscal constraints and higher education spending: The role of Medicaid and the business cycle.* Washington, DC: Urban Institute. Discussion Paper No. 11, Urban-Brookings Tax Policy Center, 2003.

Kantor, S., and A. Whalley. *Do public subsidies for higher education affect regional economic development?* TIAA-CREF Institute Research Dialogue, Issue No. 91, 2008. http://www.tiaa-crefinstitute.org/pdf/research/research_dialogue/91.pdf.

Kantrowitz, Mark. *Characteristics of students enrolling at for-profit colleges. Student Aid Policy Analysis.* Washington, DC: National Association of Student Financial Aid Administrators, December 22, 2009. http://www.nasfaa.org/publications/2010/rforprofit010810.html.

Kantrowitz, Mark. "What is Gainful Employment? What is Affordable Debt?" *Finaid.org,* March 11, 2010. http://www.finaid.org/educators/20100301gainfulemployment.pdf.

Karoly, Lynn A., and Constantijn W. A. Panis. *The 21st Century at Work: Forces Shaping the Future Workforce and Workplace in the United States.* Santa Monica, CA: RAND, 2004.

Kelly, Patrick. *Closing the College Attainment Gap Between the U.S. and Most Educated Countries, and the Contributions to Be Made by the States.* Boulder, CO: National Center for Higher Education Management Systems, 2010. http://www.nchems.org/pubs/docs/Closing%20the%20U%20S%20%20Degree%20Gap%20NCHEMS%20Final.pdf.

_____, and Dennis P. Jones. *A New Look at the Institutional Component of Higher Education Finance.* Boulder, CO: National Center for Higher Education Management System, 2005.

Kerr, Clark. *Higher education cannot escape history: Issues for the twenty–first century.* Albany, NY: State University of New York Press, 1994.

_____. *Preserving the Master Plan.* An Occasional Paper. San Jose, CA: The California Higher Education Policy Center, 1994.

Keynes, John Maynard. *The General Theory of Employment, Interest and Money.* London: Macmillan, 1936.

Khadaroo, Stacy Teicher. "A push to boost college graduation rates." *Christian Science Monitor*, December 4, 2008. http://www.csmonitor.com/USA/Society/2008/1204/p02s01-ussc.html.

Kim, D. "The effects of loans on students' degree attainment: Differences by student and institutional characteristics." *Harvard Educational Review* 77, no. 1 (2007): 64–100.

King, Jacqueline E., *Crucial Choices: How Students' Financial Decisions Affect Their Academic Success.* Washington, DC: American Council on Education, Center for Policy Analysis, 2002.

———. *Missed Opportunities: Students Who Do Not Apply for Financial Aid.* Washington, DC: American Council on Education, 2004.

Kirst, Michael. *Enhancing college completion: Secondary schools and colleges must work together.* Paper prepared for the Penn State University conference, "Revisioning the American High School for an Engaged Citizenry," June 7, 2007. http://www.stanford.edu/group/bridge-project/Enhancing%20College%20Completion22.pdf.

———, and AndreaVenezia. *From High School to College: Improving Opportunities for Success in Postsecondary Education.* San Francisco: Jossey-Bass Publishers, 2004.

Kling, Jeffrey. "Interpreting Instrumental Variable Estimates of the Returns of Schooling." Working Paper No. 415. Princeton, NJ: Industrial Relations Section, Princeton University, 1999.

Knapp, Laura G., Janice E. Kelly-Reid, and Roy W. Whitmore. *Enrollment in Postsecondary Institutions, Fall 2005; Graduation Rates, 1999 and 2002 Cohorts; and Financial Statistics, Fiscal Year 2005* (NCES2007-154). Washington, DC: U.S. Department of Education, National Center for Education Statistics, 2007. http://nces.ed.gov/pubsearch/pubsinfo.asp?pubid=2007154.

Kuh, George D., J. Kinzie, and J. H. Schuh. *Student Success in College: Creating Conditions That Matter.* San Francisco: Jossey-Bass, 2005.

Lacey, T. Alan, and Benjamin Wright. "Occupational Employment Projections to 2018." *Monthly Labor Review* 132, no. 11 (2009): 82–123.

Lakshimi, Rama. "Plenty of Outsourced Work for India's Law Graduates." *Seattle Times*, May 11, 2008, A12.

Lav, I. J., and E. McNichol. "State Budget Troubles Worsen." Center on Budget and Policy Priorities. June 29, 2009. http://www.cbpp.org/cms/index.cfm?fa=archivePage&id=9-8-08sfp.htm.

Lav, Iris J., and Elizabeth McNichol. "New Fiscal Year Brings No Relief from Unprecedented State Budget Problems." Center on Budget and Policy Priorities, September 3, 2009. http://www.cbpp.org/cms/?fa=view&id=711.http://governor.mt.gov/news/docs/Center_on_Budget_Policy.pdf.

Lederman, Doug. "The 'Prior Learning' Edge." *Inside Higher Ed*, March 1, 2010. http://www.insidehighered.com/news/2010/03/01/prior.

———. "Student Loan Overhaul Advances." *Inside Higher Ed*, March 22, 2010. http://www.insidehighered.com/news/2010/03/22/safra.

Lee, John. *State Student Incentive Grant Program: Issues in Partnership.* ERIC Document 187248. Denver, CO: Education Commission of the States, 1980.

Leef, George. 2006. "The Overselling of Higher Education." Inquiry Paper No. 25. The William Pope Center for Higher Education Policy. http://www.popecenter.org/inquiry_papers/article.html?id=1725.

Legislative Analyst's Office. *The Master Plan at 50: Using Distance Education to Increase College Access and Efficiency.* Sacramento, CA: Legislative Analyst's Office, October 25, 2010.

Lenth, Charles S. *The Tuition Dilemma: State Policies and Practices in Pricing Public Higher Education.* Denver, CO: State Higher Education Executive Officers, 1993.

Leslie, L. L., and P. T. Brinkman. "Student price response in higher education: The student demand studies." *Journal of Higher Education* 58, no. 2 (1987): 181–204.

_____. "The Economic Value of Higher Education." American Council on Education/Macmillan Series on Higher Education. New York: Macmillan Publishing, 1988.

Leslie, L. L., and G. Ramey. "State Appropriations and Enrollments: Does Enrollment Growth Still Pay?" *The Journal of Higher Education* 57, no. 1 (1986): 1–9.

Levy, Daniel J. "The Global Growth in Private Higher Education." In *The Global Growth of Private Higher Education.* eds. Kevin Kinser and others, 121–33. San Francisco: Jossey-Bass, 2010. ASHE Higher Education Report 36:3.

Levy, Frank. *Dollars and Dreams: The Changing American Income Distribution.* New York: Norton, 1988.

_____, and Richard J. Murnane. *The New Division of Labor: How Computers Are Creating the Next Job Market.* Princeton, NJ: Princeton University Press for the Russell Sage Foundation, 2004.

Lewin, T., "Low Loan Repayment Is Seen at For-Profit Schools." *New York Times*, August 13, 2010. http://www.nytimes.com/2010/08/14/education/14college.html?scp=6&sq=for%20 profit%20colleges&st=cse.

Lewis, Michael. *The Big Short: Inside the Doomsday Machine.* New York: W.W. Norton & Co., 2009.

Lingenfelter, Paul E. "The Financing of Public Colleges and Universities in the United States." In *Handbook of Research in Education Finance and Policy,* eds. Helen F. Ladd and Edward B. Fiske, 653. New York: Routledge, 2008.

Livingstone, D. W. "Lifelong Learning and Underemployment in the Knowledge Society: A North American Perspective." *Comparative Education* 35, no. 2 (1999): 163–86.

Long, B. T., and M. Kurlaender. "Do community colleges provide a viable pathway to the baccalaureate degree?" *Educational Evaluation and Policy Analysis* 31, no. 1 (2009): 30–53.

Long, Katherine. "Rising tuition a threat to GET." *Seattle Times*, February 2, 2011, A1.

Lumina Foundation. "Lumina's big goal: To increase the proportion of Americans with high-quality degrees and credentials to 60 percent by the year 2025." http://www.luminafoundation.org/goal_2025/goal3.html.

———. *A Stronger Nation Through Higher Education.* Indianapolis, IN: Lumina Foundation, 2010. http://www.luminafoundation.org/publications/A_stronger_nation.pdf

———. *Results and Reflections: An Evaluation Brief.* Indianapolis, IN: Lumina Foundation, 2008. http://www.luminafoundation.org/grants/ResultsAndReflections_Apr21.pdf.

Madzelan, D. "Title IV Student Loans Update: FFEL, Direct Loans, and Perkins." Proceedings of NASFAA National Conference, Washington, DC, accessed December 29, 2009. http://www.nasfaa.org/subhomes/annualconference2009/ /TitleIVLoansUpdate.ppt.

Manns, Derrick, Stephen Katsinas, and E. Lander Medlin. "Capital Budgeting Practices for Higher Education: Capital Needs. Project of SHEEO Professional Development Conference, Philadelphia, August 13, 2004.

Manns, Derrick, and Ron Opp. "A Fifty State Assessment of Capital Needs for Public Higher Education: Policy Objectives." *Facilities Manager* 17, no. 4 (July/August 2001).

MarketFolly.com. "Steve Eisman & FrontPoint Partners Ira Sohn Presentation: Subprime Goes to College." *MarketFolly.com*, May 27, 2010. http://www.marketfolly.com/2010/05/steve-eisman-frontpoint-partners-ira.html.

Marshall, Ray, and Marc Tucker. *Thinking for a Living: Education and the Wealth of Nations.* New York: Basic Books, 1992.

McCarthy, John C. "3.3 Million U.S. Service Jobs to Go Offshore." Forrester Research, Inc. In Uhalde and Strohl, op. cit., 2006.

McGuinness, Aims C., R. Epper, and S. Arredondo. *State Postsecondary Education Structures Handbook.* Denver, CO: Education Commission of the States, 1994.

McLendon, M. K. "The Politics of Higher Education: Toward an Expanded Research Agenda." *Educational Policy* 17, no. 1 (2003): 165–91.

_____, J. C. Hearn, and R. Deaton. "Called to Account: Analyzing the Origins and Spread of State Performance-Accountability Policies for Higher Education." *Educational Evaluation and Policy Analysis* 28, no. 1 (2006): 1–24.

McPherson, Michael S., and Morton Owen Schapiro. *Keeping College Affordable: Government and Educational Opportunity*. Washington, DC: Brookings Institution, 1991.

_____. *The Student Aid Game: Meeting Need and Rewarding Talent in American Higher Education*. Princeton, NJ: Princeton University Press, 1998.

Means, B., Y. Toyama, R. Murphy, M. Bakia, and K. Jones. *Evaluation of Evidence-Based Practices in Online Learning: A Meta-Analysis and Review of Online Learning Studies*. Washington, DC: U.S. Department of Education, Office of Planning, Evaluation, and Policy Development and Program Studies Services, 2010. http://www2.ed.gov/rschstat/eval/tech/evidence-based-practices/finalreport.pdf.

Metropolitan Policy Program at Brookings, 2009. *Getting Current: Recent Demographic Trends in Metropolitan America*. Accessed September 13, 2009 from: http://www.brookings.edu/~/media/Files/rc/reports/2009/03_metro_demographic_trends/03_metro_demographic_trends.pdf.

Miller, Ben. "The Truth About CC vs. For-Profit Graduation Rates." *The Quick and the Ed*, Education Sectorblog post, October 7, 2010. http://www.quickanded.com/2010/10/the-truth-about-cc-vs-for-profit-graduation-rates.html.

Miller, Margaret A., and Peter Ewell. *Measuring Up on College-Level Learning*. San Jose, CA: National Center for Public Policy and Higher Education, 2005.

Mishel, Lawrence. "Future Jobs Much Like Current Jobs." *Economic Snapshots*. Washington, DC: Economic Policy Institute, December 19, 2007.

_____, Jared Bernstein, and Sylvia Allegretto. *The State of Working America 2006/2007*. Washington, DC: Economic Policy Institute, 2007.

_____, and Richard Rothstein. "Response to Marc Tucker." Washington, DC: Economic Policy Institute, June 1, 2007.

Moncarz, Roger J., Michael G. Wolf, and Benjamin Wright. "Service-Providing Occupations, Offshoring, and the Labor Market." *Monthly Labor Review* 131, no.12 (2008): 71–86.

Monear, D. A. "Explaining Stability and Upheaval in State-level Education Governance: A Multiple-case Study Analysis Using Advocacy Coalition Theory and Punctuated Equilibrium Theory." PhD dissertation, University of Washington, 2008.

Moretti, Enrico. "Estimating the Social Return to Higher Education: Evidence from Longitudinal and Repeated Cross-sectional Data." *Journal of Econometrics* 121 (2004): 175–212.

Morphew, Christopher C., and Peter D. Eckel. *Privatizing the Public University: Perspectives from Across the Academy*. Baltimore: Johns Hopkins University Press, 2009.

Mortenson, Thomas G. "College Continuation Rates for Recent High School Graduates." *Postsecondary Education OPPORTUNITY*, 215 (May 2010), www.postsecondary.org.

_____. "Family income and educational attainment: 1970 to 2008." *Postsecondary Education OPPORTUNITY*, no. 209 (November 2009).

_____. "Family income and educational attainment 1970 to 2009." *Postsecondary Education OPPORTUNITY*, no. 221 (November 2010): 1.

_____. "Why College? Private Correlates of Educational Attainment." *Postsecondary Education OPPORTUNITY* 81 (1999). http://www.postsecondary.org.

_____. 2009. *Postsecondary Education OPPORTUNITY*, Spreadsheet: Bachelor's Degree Attainment by Age 24, retrieved October 15, 2009, from www.postsecondary.org.

Mortenson, T. Education attainment and economic welfare: 1940-2008, *Postsecondary Education Opportunity, Number 196* (October 2008). Retrieved September 12, 2009, from http://www.postsecondary.org.

Murnane, Richard J., John B. Willett, and John H. Tyler. "Who Benefits from Obtaininga GED? Evidence from High School and Beyond." *The Review of Economics and Statistics* 82, no. 1. (2000): 23–37.

Murphy, Kevin, and Finis Welch. "Wage Premiums for College Graduates: Recent Growth and Possible Explanations." *Educational Researcher* 18, no. 4 (1989): 17–26.

National Association of State Student Grant &Aid Programs. *40th Annual Survey Report on State-Sponsored Student Financial Aid, 2008–2009 Academic Year.* Washington, DC: National Association of State Student Grant & Aid Programs, 2010. http://www.nassgap. org/viewrepository.aspx?categoryID=3.

_____. *39th Annual Survey Report on State-sponsored Student Financial Aid, 2007–2008 Academic Year.* Washington, DC: National Association of State Student Grant & Aid Programs, 2009.

_____. *31st Annual Survey Report on State-Sponsored Student Financial Aid, 1999–2000 Academic Year,* 2001. http://www.nassgap.org/viewrepository.aspx?categoryID=3.

_____. *30th Annual Survey Report on State-Sponsored Student Financial Aid, 1998–1999 Academic Year,* 2000. http://www.nassgap.org/viewrepository.aspx?categoryID=3.

National Association of State Scholarship and Grant Programs. *9th Annual Survey Report of the 1977-1978 Academic Year,* 1979. http://www.nassgap.org/viewrepository.aspx?category ID=3.

National Bureau of Economic Research. "Business Cycle Dating Committee, National Bureau of Economic Research." Revised December 11, 2008. http://www.nber.org/cycles/ dec2008.html.

National Center for Academic Transformation. *Program in Course Redesign, Lessons Learned.* National Center for Academic Transformation. http://www.thencat.org/PCR/R1Lessons. html.

National Center for Academic Transformation, "The NCAT Course Redesign Program: Improving Student Learning While Reducing Instructional Costs," http://www.thencat. org/States/State-based%20Redesign%20Program%20Desc%20woBudget.pdf.

National Center for Academic Transformation, "Program in Course Redesign," Virginia Tech, Linear Algebra, http://www.thencat.org/PCR/R1/VT/VT_Overview.htm.

National Center for Academic Transformation, "Tennessee Board of Regents: Developmental Studies Redesign Initiative," Cleveland State Community College, http://www.thencat. org/States/TN/Abstracts/CSCC%20Algebra_Abstract.htm.

National Center for Academic Transformation, "Five Principles of Successful Course Redesign," http://www.thencat.org/PlanRes/R2R_PrinCR.htm.

National Center for Education Statistics. Integrated Postsecondary Education Data System. Peer Analysis System. Electronic Resource, 2009. Available: http://nces.ed.gov/ipeds/ datacenter/.

_____. "Table 198. Total first-time freshmen fall enrollment in degree-granting institutions, by attendance status, sex of student, and type and control of institution: 1955 through 2008." 2010. http://nces.ed.gov/programs/digest/d09/tables/dt09_198.asp.

National Center for Education Statistics. Integrated Postsecondary Education Data Systems (IPEDS). http://nces.ed.gov/ipeds/.

National Center for Education Statistics. *The Condition of Education* (NCES 2011-033), indicator 24. National Center for Education Statistics (NCES), U.S. Department of Education, 2011.

National Center for Education Statistics. *2007–08 National Postsecondary Student Aid Study (NPSAS:08).* Washington, DC: Author, 2009. http://nces.ed.gov/pubs2009/2009166.pdf.

National Center for Education Statistics. *The Condition of Education 2009 Fast Facts.* http:// nces.ed.gov/search/?output=xml_no_dtd&client=nces&site=nces&q=condition+of+edu cation+2009.

National Center for Education Statistics. *A First Look at the Literacy of America's Adults in the 21st Century.* Washington, DC: U.S Department of Education, National Center for Education Statistics, 2006.

National Center for Public Policy and Higher Education. *Affordability and Transfer: Critical to Increasing Baccalaureate Degree Completion.* San Jose, CA: National Center for Public Policy and Higher Education, 2011.

National Center for Public Policy and Higher Education. *Presidential Leadership for Public Purposes*. San Jose, CA: National Center for Public Policy and Higher Education, May 2011. http://www.highereducation.org/crosstalk/ct0511/CrossTalk-online-Insert.pdf.

———. *Beyond the Rhetoric: Improving College Readiness Through Coherent State Policy*. Atlanta, GA: Southern Regional Education Board and the National Center for Public Policy and Higher Education, June 2010. http://www.highereducation.org/reports/college_readiness/CollegeReadiness.pdf.

———. *Income of U.S. Workforce Projected to Decline IF Education Doesn't Improve*. San Jose, CA: National Center for Public Policy and Higher Education, 2005.

———. *Measuring Up 2008: The State-by-State Report Card on Higher Education*. San Jose, CA: National Center for Public Policy and Higher Education, 2008. http://measuringup2008.highereducation.org/.

———. *Responding to the Crisis in College Opportunity*. San Jose, CA: National Center for Public Policy and Higher Education, 2004.

———. *State capacity for higher education policy—A special supplement to National Crosstalk*. San Jose, CA: National Center for Public Policy and Higher Education, 2005. http://www.highereducation.org/crosstalk/ct0305/news0305-insert.pdf.

National Commission on the Cost of Higher Education. *Straight Talk about College Costs and Prices: The Final Report and Supplemental Material from the National Commission on The Cost Of Higher Education*. American Oryx Press Series on Higher Education. Phoenix, AZ: American Council on Education/Oryx Press, 1998.

National Center on Education and the Economy. *Tough Choices or Tough Times: The Report of the New Commission on the Skills of the American Workforce*. San Francisco, CA: Jossey-Bass, 2007.

National Conference of State Legislatures. *State Budget Update*. Denver, CO, and Washington, DC: National Conference of State Legislatures, 2010. http://www.ncsl.org/documents/fiscal/november2010sbu_free.pdf.

———. *Update on State Budget Gaps: FY 2009 & FY 2010*. Denver, CO, and Washington, DC: Fiscal Affairs Program, National Conference of State Legislatures, 2009. http://www.ncsl.org/Portals/1/documents/pubs/statebudgetgaps.pdf.

National Governors Association and National Association of State Budget Officers. *Fiscal Survey of States*. Washington, DC: National Governors Association, December 2010.

Nelson, Glenn M., Eugenie A. Potter, John C. Weidman, and Thomas G. Zullo, eds. "The Growing Loan Orientation in Federal Financial Aid Policy." In *ASHE Reader on Finance in Higher Education*, ed. John L. Yeager. Boston, MA: Pearson Custom Publishing, 2001.

Nelson, Libby. "Compromise Budget Bill Would Increase Pell Grants and Funds for NIH and NSF." *Chronicle of Higher Education*, December 9, 2009.

Nelson, Libby. "Concessions or a Cave-In?" *Inside Higher Ed*, June 2, 2011. http://www.insidehighered.com/news/2011/06/02/new_gainful_employment_rules.

Nelson, Libby. "For-Profit Debate Redux." *Inside Higher Ed*, July 22, 2011. http://www.insidehighered.com/news/2011/07/22/harkin_hosts_roundtable_on_for_profit_colleges.

Obama, Barack. "Remarks of President Barack Obama—As Prepared for Delivery Address to Joint Session of Congress," Tuesday, February 24, 2009. http://www.whitehouse.gov/the_press_office/Remarks-of-President-Barack-Obama-Address-to-Joint-Session-of-Congress/.

O'Mara, Margaret. *Cities of Knowledge: Cold War Science and the Next Silicon Valley*. Princeton, NJ: Princeton University Press, 2005.

Organisation for Economic Co-Operation and Development. *OECD: Annual Report: 2002*. Paris: Organisation for Economic Co-Operation and Development, 2002.

Organisation for Economic Co-operation and Development. *Education at a Glance 2007: OECD Indicators*. Paris: OECD, 2007.

Organisation for Economic Cooperation and Development. *Education at a Glance 2007*. (Tech rep). Paris, OECD, 2007.

Organisation for Economic Co-operation and Development. *Education at a Glance 2009.* Organisation for Economic Co-operation and Development. http://www.oecd.org/docu ment/24/0,3746,en_2649_39263238_43586328_1_1_1_1,00.html.

Organisation for Economic Co-operation and Development. *Education at a Glance 2010: OECD Indicators.* Paris: Organisation for Economic Co-operation and Development, 2010. http:// www.oecd.org/document/52/0,3343,en_2649_39263238_45897844_1_1_1_1,00.html.

Osterman, Paul. *Securing Prosperity: The American Labor Market—How It Has Changed and What to Do About It.* Princeton, NJ: Princeton University Press for the Century Foundation, 1999.

Ottinger, Cecilia A. *Fact Book on Higher Education: 1986–87.* New York: American Council on Education, 1987.

Palmer, Jim. *Grapevine.* Illinois State University. http://www.grapevine.ilstu.edu.

Palmer, James, ed. "Grapevine: An annual compilation of data on state fiscal support for higher education." Normal, IL: Center for Higher Education and Educational Finance, Illinois State University, 2010. http://www.grapevine.ilstu.edu/tables/index.htm.

Palmer, James C., ed. *Grapevine Survey of State Higher Education Tax Appropriations for Fiscal Year 2005.* Normal, IL: Center for the Study of Education Policy, Illinois State University.

Pascarella, Ernest T., and Patrick T. Terenzini. *How College Affects Students, Vol.2: A Third Decade of Research.* San Francisco: Jossey-Bass/Wiley, 2005.

Phan, T., and M. Glander, M. *Documentation to the NCES Common Core of Data Local Education Agency Locale Code File: School Year 2005-06* (NCES 2007-388). Washington, DC: National Center for Education Statistics, Institute of Education Sciences, U.S. Department of Education, 2007.

Planty, M., W. Hussar, T. Snyder, G. Kena, A. Kewal Ramani, J. Kemp, K. Bianco, and R. Dinkes. *The Condition of Education 2009* (NCES 2009-081). Washington, DC: National Center for Education Statistics, Institute of Education Sciences, U.S. Department of Education, 2009. http://nces.ed.giv/programs/coe/2009/pdf/19_2009.pdf.

Planty, M., W. Hussar, T. Snyder, G. Kena, A. Kewal Ramani, J. Kemp, K. Bianco, and R. Dinkes. *The Condition of Education 2009 Fast Facts* (NCES 2009-081). Washington, DC: National Center for Education Statistics, Institute of Education Sciences, U.S. Department of Education, 2009. http://nces.ed.gov/fastFacts/display.asp?id=27.

Planty, M., W. Hussar, T. Snyder, G. Kena, A. Kewal Ramani, J. Kemp, K. Bianco, and R. Dinkes, *The Condition of Education 2009* (NCES 2009-081). Washington, DC: National Center for Education Statistics, Institute of Education Sciences, U.S. Department of Education, 2009. Indicator 23, Educational Attainment, 56, based on Table A-23-1. http:// nces.ed.gov/pubs20009/2009081.pdf.

President's Commission on Higher Education. *Establishing the Goals.* vol. 1. *Higher Education for American Democracy: A Report of the President's Commission on Higher Education.* Washington, DC: Government Printing Office, 1947.

Project on Student Debt, Institute for College Access and Success. "Quick Facts About Student Debt," January 2010. http://projectonstudentdebt.org/files/File/Debt_Facts_and_ Sources.pdf.

Project on Student Debt. "Federal student loan amounts and terms for 2010-2011," June 2010. http://projectonstudentdebt.org/files/pub/2010-11_loan_terms.pdf.

Psacharopoulos, George, and Harry Anthony Patrinos. "Returns to Investment in Education: A Further Update." *Education Economics* 12 (2004): 111–134.

Psacharopoulos, George. 1994. "Returns to Investment in Education: A Global Update." *World Development* 22, no. 9 (1994): 1325–1343.

Psacharopoulos, George. "The Economic Costs of Child Labor." *The Sweat and Toil of Children.* Washington, DC: U.S. Department of Labor, 2000.

Richardson, R., K. R. Bracco, P. Callan, and J. Finney. *Designing State Higher Education Systems for a New Century.* Phoenix, AZ: ACE/Oryx Press, 1999.

Richardson, R., and M. Martinez. *Policy and Performance in American Higher Education.* Baltimore: Johns Hopkins University Press, 2009.

Rimer, Sara. "Students slog through college, don't gain many critical skills." *The Seattle Times,* January 19, 2011, A3.

Rivera, Carlos. "California community colleges to slash enrollment, classes." *Los Angeles Times,* March 31, 2011. http://www.latimes.com/news/local/la-me-0331-community-colleges-20110331,0,7036490.story.

Rose, R., with D. A. Cain, J. J. Dempsey, and R. Schneider. *Buildings . . . the gifts that keep on taking.* Alexandria, VA: APPA, Center for Facilities Research, 2007.

Rosenbaum, James. *Beyond College for All: Career Paths for the Forgotten Half.* New York: Russell Sage Foundation, 2001.

Rusk, J. J., and L. L. Leslie. "The Setting of Tuition in Public Higher Education."*Journal of Higher Education* 49, no. 6 (1978): 531–47.

Shulock, Nancy, and Colleen Moore. *Rules of the Game: How State Policy Creates Barriers to Degree Completion and Impedes Student Success in the California Community Colleges.* Sacramento, CA: California State University Sacramento, Institute for Higher Education Leadership & Policy, 2007.

Singell, Larry D., Jr., and Joe A. Stone. "For whom the Pell tolls: The response of university tuition to federal grants-in-aid." *Economics of Education Review* 26, no. 3 (June 2007): 285–295.

Skolnik, M. L. "Design, Deregulation or Just Drifting: Ontario Universities Need Firmer Direction." *The University of Toronto Bulletin* 12 (December 9, 1996).

Smiley, Gene. "Recent Unemployment Rate Estimates for the 1920s and 1930s." *The Journal of Economic History* 43, no. 2 (1983): 487–93.

Snyder, T. D., and S. A. Dillow. *Digest of Education Statistics 2009.* NCES 2010-013. Washington, DC: National Center for Education Statistics, Institute of Education Sciences, U.S. Department of Education, 2010. http://nces.ed.gov/pubs2010/2010013_0.pdf.

_____, and C. M. Hoffman. *Digest of Education Statistics 2008.* NCES 2009-020. Washington, DC: National Center for Education Statistics, Institute of Education Sciences, U.S. Department of Education, 2009.

_____. *Digest of Education Statistics 2010.* NCES 2011-015. Washington, DC: National Center for Education Statistics, Institute of Education Sciences, U.S. Department of Education, 2011.

Soares, Louis. *Working Learners: Educating Our Entire Workforce for Success in the 21st Century.* Washington, DC: Center for American Progress, 2009.

Sommers, Paul, and William Chance. *The Return on Education Investments.* Rep. Olympia, WA.: Report from NORED, to Washington Office of Financial Management, 2006.

Southern Regional Education Board. *Promoting a culture of student success: How colleges and universities are improving degree completion.* Atlanta, GA: Southern Regional Education Board, 2010a.

Southern Regional Education Board and the National Center for Public Policy and Higher Education. *Beyond the rhetoric: Improving college readiness through coherent state policy,* June 2010. http://www.highereducation.org/reports/college_readiness/CollegeReadiness.pdf.

Spence, Michael. *Market Signaling: Informational Transfer in Hiring and Related Screening Processes.* Cambridge, MA: Harvard University Press, 1974.

Spellings Commission Report, *A Test of Leadership.* Washington, DC: U.S. Department of Education, 2006.

St. John, E. P. *Refinancing the College Dream: Access, Equal Opportunity, and Justice for Taxpayers.* Baltimore: Johns Hopkins University Press, 2003.

St. John, E. P. S., S. Hu, and J. Weber. "State Policy and the Affordability of Public Higher Education: The Influence of State Grants on Persistence in Indiana." *Research in Higher Education* 42, no. 4 (2001): 401–438.

State Higher Education Executive Officers. *State Higher Education Finance FY2010.* Boulder, CO: State Higher Education Executive Officers, 2011.

State Higher Education Executive Officers. *SHEEO Annual Finance Report FY2009*. Boulder, CO: State Higher Education Executive Officers, 2010.

State Higher Education Executive Officers. *State Higher Education Finance FY2008*. Boulder, CO: State Higher Education Executive Officers, 2008.

State Higher Education Executive Officers. "Second to None in Attainment, Discovery, and Innovation: The National Agenda for Higher Education." *Change: The Magazine of Higher Education*, September/October 2008. http://www.changemag.org/Archives/Back%20Issues/September-October%202008/full-second-to-none.html.

Stekler, H. O., and R. Thomas. "Evaluating BLS Economic Projections for 2000." *Monthly Labor Review*128, no. 7 (2005): 46–56.

"Student Lenders, Fighting to Survive, Spend Millions to Lobby Congress." *Chronicle of Higher Education*, September 28, 2009.

Swail, Watson Scott. *Graduating At-risk Students: A Cross-sector Analysis*. Washington, DC: Imagine America Foundation, 2009.

Thackery, Russell I. "Did Brookings Miss an Important Opportunity" *Phi Delta Kappan*, 1979, 542–43.

Thelin, John R. "Coming of Age in America: Higher Education as a Troubled Giant." In *A History of American Higher Education*. Baltimore: Johns Hopkins University Press, 2004.

Thompson, F., and W. Zumeta. "Effects of Key State Policies on Private Colleges and Universities: Sustaining Private-sector Capacity in the Face of the Higher Education Access Challenge." *Economics of Education Review* 20, no. 6 (2001): 517–531.

Thurow, Lester. *The Zero-Sum Society: Distribution and the Possibilities for Economic Change*. New York: Basic Books, 1980.

Trani, Eugene P., and Robert D. Holzworth. *The Indispensable University: Higher Education, Economic Development, and the Knowledge Economy*. Lanham, MD: Rowan and Littlefield, 2010.

Troppe, Mark, and Pete Carlson. *An Analysis of Market and Skill Changes: the Impact of Globalization on American Jobs in Selected Industries*. A Report of the New Commission on the Skills of the American Workforce. National Center on Education and the Economy. San Francisco: John Wiley & Sons, 2006.

Tuttle, Tina, Jeff McKinney, and Melanie Rago. *College students working: The choice nexus. A review of research literature on college students and work*. Bloomington, IN: Indiana Project on Academic Success, 2005. http://www.indiana.edu/~ipas1/workingstudentbrief.pdf.

Tyler, John H. "Economic Benefits of the GED: Lessons from Recent Research." *Review of Educational Research* 73, no. 3 (Fall 2003): 369–403.

Uhalde, Ray, and Jeff Strohl. *America in the Global Economy: A Background Paper for the New Commission on the Skills of the American Workforce*. Washington, DC: National Center on Education and the Economy, 2006.

U.S. Bureau of Economic Analysis. *Regional Economic Accounts*, 2009. http://www.bea.gov/regional/index.htm.

U.S. Bureau of Labor Statistics, 2010. "Labor Force Statistics and the Current Population Survey." http://data.bls.gov:8080/PDQ/outside.jsp?survey=ln.

U.S. Bureau of Labor Statistics. "Consumer Price Index (CPI): All Urban Consumers." http://www.bls.gov/cpi/#tables.

U.S. Bureau of Labor Statistics. "The employment situation, July 2010." Washington, DC: U.S. Department of Commerce, Economics and Statistics Administration, 2010. Summary Table A. http://www.bls.gov/news.release/archives/empsit_08062010.pdf.

U.S. Bureau of Labor Statistics. *Historical Occupational Data*. Washington, DC: U.S. Department of Labor, Office of Occupational Employment Statistics, 2008.

U.S. Bureau of Labor Statistics. "Tomorrow's Jobs." *Occupational Outlook Handbook*. Washington, DC: U.S. Department of Labor, Office of Occupational Statistics and Employment Projections, 2007.

U.S. Census Bureau. *Current Population Survey: Income.* Historical Tables P-16, P-18, F-1 and A-2. Washington, DC: U.S. Department of Commerce, Economics and Statistics Administration, August 2010.

U.S. Census Bureau. *U.S. Interim Projections by Age, Sex, Race, and Hispanic Origin: 2000-2050.* Washington, DC: U.S. Dept. of Commerce, Economics and Statistics Administration, U.S. Census Bureau, January 2000.

U.S. Census Bureau. *Current Population Survey: Annual Social and Economic Supplements.* Tables P-15 and P-16. Washington, DC: U.S. Department of Commerce, Economics and Statistics Administration, January 2007.

U.S. Census Bureau. *Current Population Survey: Educational Attainment.* Table A-2. Washington, DC: U.S. Department of Commerce, Economics and Statistics Administration, April 2009.

U.S. Census Bureau. *American Community Survey: Percent of Population 18–24 Enrolled in Higher Education,* 2009. http://www.census.gov/acs/www/data_documentation/public_ use_microdata_sample/.

U.S. Congress. *H.R. 4972: Health Care and Education Reconciliation Act of 2010.* http://www. govtrack.us/congress/billtext.xpd?bill=h111-4872.U.S. Department of Education. *A Test of Leadership: Charting the Future of U.S. Higher Education.* Secretary of Education's Commission on the Future of Higher Education. Washington, D.C.: U.S. Department of Education, 2006. http://www.ed.gov/about/bdscomm/list/hiedfuture/reports/final-report.pdf.

_____. "Proposed Rule Links Federal Student Aid to Loan Repayment Rates and Debt-to-Earnings Levels for Career College Graduates," July 23, 2010. http://www.ed.gov/news/press-releases/ proposed-rule-links-federal-student-aid-loan-repayment-rates-and-debt-earnings.

_____, Federal Financial Aid. "2007–2008 Award Year Federal Allotments to States," 2007. http://www.fp.ed.gov/fp/attachments/misc/0708Awards.pdf.

_____, *H.R. 4137: An Act to amend and extend the Higher Education Act of 1965.* http://www.gpo. gov/fdsys/pkg/BILLS-110hr4137eh/pdf/BILLS-110hr4137eh.pdf.

U.S. Department of Education. "Cost of Higher Education Review (Public Law 105-18) http://frwebgate.access.gpo.gov/cgi-bin/getdoc.cgi?dbname=105_cong_public_laws& docid=f:publ18.105.

U.S. Department of Education, National Center for Education Statistics. *The Condition of Education 2000,* NCES 2000–062. Washington, DC: U.S. Government Printing Office, 2000.

_____. *The Condition of Education 2009.* Washington, DC: U.S. Department of Education, National Center for Education Statistics.

_____. *Digest of Education Statistics, 2007.* Washington, DC: U.S. Department of Education, 2008.

_____. *A First Look at the Literacy of American's Adults in the 21st Century.* Washington, DC: National Center for Education Statistics, 2006.

U.S. Department of Labor. "Accounting for Offshoring in Occupational Projections." *Occupational Projections and Training Data 2006-2007.* Bulletin 2602, February 2006. Washington, DC: Department of Labor.

U.S. Energy Information Administration, "Cushing, OK WTI Spot Price FOB (Dollars per Barrel)." http://www.eia.gov/dnav/pet/hist/LeafHandler.ashx?n=PET&s=RWTC&f=M.

U.S. Government Accountability Office. *For-Profit Colleges: Undercover Testing Finds Colleges Encourages Fraud and Engaged in Deceptive and Questionable Marketing Practices.* Washington, DC: U.S. Government Accountability Office, August 4, 2010. http://www.gao.gov/ products/GAO-10-948T.

U.S. Government Accountability Office. *For-Profit Schools: Large Schools and Schools that Specialize in Healthcare Are More Likely to Rely Heavily on Federal Student Aid.* Washington, DC: U.S. Government Accountability Office, October 4, 2010. http://www.gao.gov/products/ GAO-11-4.

U.S. Government Accountability Office. *Higher education: Tuition continues to rise, but patterns vary by institution type, enrollment, and educational expenditures.* GAO-08-245. A Report to the Chairman, Committee on Education and Labor, House of Representatives. Washington, DC: Author, November 2007. Retrieved 10/17/11 from: http://www.gao.gov/new. items/d08245.pdf.

U.S. News and World Report. "Rankings." http://www.usnews.com/rankings.

U.S. Senate Health, Education, Labor and Pensions Committee. "Emerging risk?: An overview of growth, spending, student debt, and unanswered questions in for-profit higher education," June 24, 2010. http://harkin.senate.gov/documents/pdf/4c23515814dca.pdf.

U.S. Senate Health, Education, Labor and Pensions Committee. "HELP Committee to Hold First Hearing on Oversight of Federal Education Dollars at For-Profit Colleges." press release, June 21, 2010. http://help.senate.gov/newsroom/press/release/ ?id=ed74fbe4-3583-4aad-8f2e-270cc0b134f2&groups=Chair.

Van Praag, C. M., and J. S. Cramer. "The Roots of Entrepreneurship and Labour Demand: Individual Ability and Low Risk Aversion." *Economica* 68, no. 269 (2001): 45–62.

Vandal, B. *Revving the Economic Engine: Effectively Aligning Education, Workforce and Economic Development Policy.* Denver, CO: Education Commission of the States, 2009.

Venezia, A., and M. Kirst. "Inequitable opportunities: How current education systems and policies undermine the chances for student persistence and success in college." *Educational Policy* 19 (2005): 283–307.

Wadhwa, Vivek, and Gereffi, Gary. "Framing the Engineering Outsourcing Debate." 2005. http://ssrn.com/abstract=1015831.

Wagner, Alan P. *Measuring Up Internationally: Developing Skills and Knowledge for the Global Knowledge Economy.* San Jose, CA: National Center for Public Policy and Higher Education, 2006.

Webber, Douglas A., and Ronald G. Ehrenberg. *Do Expenditures Other than Instructional Expenditures Affect Graduation and Persistence Rates in American Higher Education.* Cambridge, MA: National Bureau of Economic Research, Working Paper W15216, 2009.

Wei, C. C., L. Berkner, S. He, S. Lew, M. Cominole, and P. Siegel. *2007–08 National Postsecondary Student Aid Study (NPSAS:08): Student Financial Aid Estimates for 2007–08: First Look* (NCES 2009-166). Washington, DC: National Center for Education Statistics, Institute of Education Sciences, U.S. Department of Education, 2009. http://nces.ed.gov/ pubs2009/2009166.pdf.

Wei, Christina Chang, Xiaojie Li, Lutz K. Berkner, and C. Dennis Carroll. *A Decade of Undergraduate Student Aid: 1989–90 to 1999–2000.* Washington, DC: U.S. Department of Education, Institute of Education Sciences, National Center for Education Statistics, 2004.

Weimer, D. L., and A. R. Vining. *Policy Analysis: Concepts and Practice.* 5th ed. Boston, MA: Longman, 2010.

Wellman, J. V. "State policy and community college-baccalaureate transfer." Washington, DC: The Institute for Higher Education Policy, 2002.

Western Interstate Commission for Higher Education. *Knocking at the College Door: Projections of High School Graduates by State and Race/ethnicity, 1992–2022.* Boulder, CO: Western Interstate Commission for Higher Education, 2008. http://www.wiche.edu/knocking.

Wikipedia. "List of Land-grant Universities." http://en.wikipedia.org/wiki/List_of_land-grant_ universities.

Wikipedia. "Sallie Mae." http://en. wikipedia.org/wiki/Sallie_Mae.

Wilkinson, Rupert. *Aiding Students, Buying Students: Financial Aid in America.* Nashville, TN: Vanderbilt University Press, 2005.

Wimberly, George L., and Richard J. Noeth. *College Readiness Begins in Middle School: ACT Policy Report.* Iowa City, IA: ACT, 2005. http://www.act.org/research/policymakers/pdf/ CollegeReadiness.pdf.

Winston, Gordon C., and David J. Zimmerman. *Peer effects in higher education.* Discussion Paper DP-64. Williams Project on the Economics of Higher Education. Williamstown, MA: Williams College, 2003.

Wirt, Frederick, Douglas Mitchell, and Catherine Marshall. "Culture and Education Policy: Analyzing Values in State Policy Systems." *Educational Evaluation and Policy Analysis* 10, no. 4 (1988): 271–284.

Witkowsky, Kathy. "Indiana's 'Eighth University.'" *National CrossTalk*, December 2010, 4–6.

Wolfle, Dael Lee. *The Home of Science: The Role of the University*. New York: McGraw-Hill, 1974.

Wright, Austin. "Education Department Prepares for Switch to 100% Direct Lending." *Chronicle of Higher Education*, July 9, 2009.

Wyatt, Ian D., and Kathryn J. Byun. "Employment Outlook: 2008-2018, The U.S. economy to 2018: from recession to recovery." *Monthly Labor Review* 132, no. 11 (2009): 11–29.

Zachry, E. M., and E. Schneider. *Building foundations for student readiness: A review of rigorous research and promising trends in developmental education*. An NCPR Working Paper. New York: National Center for Postsecondary Research, September 23–24, 2010.

Zarkin, Gary A. "Cobweb Versus Rational Expectations Models: Lessons from the Market for Public School Teachers." *Economics Letters* 13 (1983): 87–95.

Zumeta, William. "Accountability and the Private Sector: State and Federal Perspectives." In *Achieving Accountability in Higher Education: Balancing Public, Academic, and Market Demands*, ed. J. C. Burke, 25–54. San Francisco: Jossey-Bass, 2005.

———. "California." In *National Innovation and the Academic Research Enterprise: Public Policy in Global Perspective*, eds. David D. Dill and Frans Van Vught. Baltimore: Johns Hopkins University Press, 2010.

———. "The Great Recession: Implications for Higher Education." *The NEA 2010 Almanac of Higher Education* (2010).

———. "Meeting the demand for higher education without breaking the bank; a framework for the design of state higher education policies for an era of increased demand." *Journal of Higher Education* 67, no. 4 (July/August 1996): 367–425.

———. "The New Accountability: The potential of performance compacts in higher education." From *National CrossTalk*, Winter 2007. San Jose, CA: National Center for Public Policy and Higher Education. http://www.highereducation.org/crosstalk/ct0107/voices0107-zumeta.shtml.

———. "State Higher Education Financing: Demand Imperatives Meet Structural, Cyclical, and Political Constraints." In *Public Funding of Higher Education: Changing Contexts and New Rationales*, eds. John Edward P. St. John and Michael D. Parsons, 79–107. Baltimore: Johns Hopkins University Press, 2004.

———. "State Policies and Private Higher Education in the USA: Understanding the Variation in Comparative Perspective." Special Issue, *Journal of Comparative Policy Analysis* 13, no. 4 (2011): 425–442.

———. "State policies and private higher education: Policies, correlates and linkages." *Journal of Higher Education* 63, no. 4 (July/August 1992): 363–417.

———. "Utilizing private higher education for public purposes: Policy design challenges facing efforts to help meet higher education access challenges through the private sector." In *The Substance of Public Policy*, ed. S. Nagle, 191–230. Commack, NY: Nova Science, 1999.

———, and Deborah Frankl. *California Community Colleges: Making Them Stronger and More Affordable*. San Jose, CA: National Center for Public Policy and Higher Education, 2007.

———, and Alicia Kinne. "The potential and reality of performance agreements between public higher education and state governments–early evidence." Paper presented at the American Educational Research Association annual conference, San Diego, CA, April 15, 2009.

———, and Alicia Kinne. "Accountability policies in higher education: directions old and new." In *The States and Public Higher Education Policy: Affordability, Access, and Accountability*. 2nd ed., ed. Donald E. Heller, 173–199. Baltimore: Johns Hopkins University Press, 2011.

———, and Robin LaSota. "Recent Patterns in the Growth of Private Higher Education in the United States." In *The Global Growth in Private Higher Education*, eds. Kevin Kinser, Daniel C. Levy, Juan Carlos Silas, Andres Bernasconi, Snejana Slantcheva-Durst, Wycliffe Otieno, Jason E. Lane, Prachayani Praphamontripong, William Zumeta, and Robin LaSota, 91–106. ASHE Report 36, no. 3. San Francisco: Wiley, 2010.

About the Authors

William Zumeta is a professor in the Daniel J. Evans School of Public Affairs and the College of Education at the University of Washington, a former senior fellow at the National Center for Public Policy and Higher Education, and a fellow of the Teachers Insurance and Annuity Association–College Retirement Equities Fund Institute (TIAA-CREF). He has served as associate dean and acting dean of the Evans School. Zumeta received his master's and PhD degrees from the Goldman School of Public Policy at the University of California, Berkeley, and has previously taught at the University of British Columbia, UCLA, and the Claremont Graduate University. He has studied and written on a wide variety of issues in state and federal higher education policy, finance and accountability, and in a number of chapters and books; he has also contributed to such journals as *Policy Sciences, Journal of Policy Analysis and Management, Journal of Comparative Policy Analysis, Economics of Education Review, Journal of Higher Education, Review of Higher Education, Higher Education,* and *Issues in Science and Technology,* among others.

Among his recent publications are "State Policies and Private Higher Education in the U.S.A.: Understanding the Variation in Comparative Perspective," in "Private Higher Education and Public Policy: A Comparative Global View," Daniel Levy and Zumeta, eds., special issue, *Journal of Comparative Policy Analysis* 13, no. 4 (2011); with Alicia Kinne, "Accountability: Directions Old and New," in D. Heller, ed., *The States and Public Higher Education Policy: Affordability, Access, and Accountability,* 2nd ed. (Baltimore: Johns Hopkins University Press, 2011); and "States and Higher Education: Alone in a Stagnant Economy," in *The NEA 2012 Almanac of Higher Education* (Washington, DC: National Education Association). He has held grants from the U.S. Department of Education, National Science Foundation, William and Flora Hewlett Foundation, Lilly Endowment, Pew Charitable Trusts, Sloan Foundation, and the Spencer Foundation, as well as from numerous state agencies and national organizations.

David W. Breneman is a university professor and Newton and Rita Meyers Professor in Economics of Education at the University of Virginia. His books include *Smart Leadership for Higher Education in Difficult Times (2011), Earnings from Learning: The Rise of For-Profit Universities* (2006), *Liberal Arts Colleges:*

Thriving, Surviving, or Endangered (1994), *Finance in Higher Education* (1993), *Academic Labor Markets and Careers* (1988), *Financing Community Colleges: An Economic Perspective* (1981), *Public Policy and Private Higher Education* (1978), and numerous articles, including several on the federal education budget in the Brookings series *Setting National Priorities*. He has served as senior fellow of The Brookings Institution, president of Kalamazoo College, visiting professor at Harvard, dean of the Curry School of Education, and director of the Public Policy Program at Frank Batten School of Leadership and Public Policy at the University of Virginia. He was a member of the Organisation for Economic Co-operation and Development (OECD) country review team for tertiary education in Japan and has served as a trustee of Goucher and Sweet Briar Colleges.

Patrick M. Callan is president of the Higher Education Policy Institute (HEPI), an independent, nonprofit, nonpartisan corporation founded in 1991. The Institute established and sponsored the California Higher Education Policy Center from 1992 to 1997 and the National Center for Public Policy and Higher Education from 1997 through June 30, 2011. Mr. Callan served as president of both organizations. Prior to his association with HEPI, Mr. Callan served as executive officer of state higher education boards and commissions in Montana, Washington, and California, and as vice president of the Education Commission of the States. He has chaired the boards of the State Higher Education Executive Officers Association, the Western Interstate Commission for Higher Education, and the National Center for Higher Education Management Systems. Mr. Callan has served as an advisor to national and regional organizations, state higher education boards and commissions, governors' offices, and state legislative committees. He is the author and coauthor of books, articles, and papers on education policy, educational opportunity, public accountability, financing of higher education, and public policy leadership. As president of the National Center, he oversaw the first report cards on the state-by-state and national performance of American higher education. The five *Measuring Up* report cards, issued biennially since 2000, have helped define national and state policy agendas.

Joni E. Finney is professor of practice at the University of Pennsylvania and vice president of the Higher Education Policy Institute. She previously served as vice president of the National Center for Public Policy and Higher Education. At the University of Pennsylvania, Dr. Finney is director of the Institute for Research and Higher Education, and is completing a five-state study of the relationship of state policy and performance. Dr. Finney directed *Measuring Up*, the nation's report card on higher education, and was principal author for the *Measuring Up* state reports. In addition, Finney has written articles for academic and policy leaders related to higher education finance, governance, and performance. She is coeditor and author of *Public and Private Financing of Higher Education: Shaping Public Policy for the Future* (ACE/Oryx Press, 1997) and *Designing State Higher Education Systems* (ACE/Oryx Press, 1997). She also coauthored *Claiming Common Ground* (The National Center for Public Policy and Higher Education, 2007), which focuses on the policies that link high schools and colleges. In addition, Finney has authored *Good Policy, Good Practice* (The National Center for Public Policy and Higher Education, 2008), a publication that identifies effective educational practices and the public policies that support them. Finney has served on numerous advisory boards and is a founding board member of the National Clearinghouse Research Center.

Index